GOD IS AN OCTOPUS

GOD IS AN OCTOPUS

Loss, Love and a Calling to Nature

BEN GOLDSMITH

BLOOMSBURY WILDLIFE
LONDON · OXFORD · NEW YORK · NEW DELHI · SYDNEY

BLOOMSBURY WILDLIFE
Bloomsbury Publishing Plc
50 Bedford Square, London, WC1B 3DP, UK
29 Earlsfort Terrace, Dublin 2, Ireland

BLOOMSBURY WILDLIFE and the Diana logo are trademarks of Bloomsbury
Publishing Plc

First published in the United Kingdom 2023

A catalogue record for this book is available from the British Library.

Library of Congress Cataloguing-in-Publication data has been applied for.

ISBN: Hardback: 978-1-3994-0835-6; Audio download: 978-1-3994-0832-5;
ePub: 978-1-3994-0834-9; ePDF: 978-1-3994-0833-2

2 4 6 8 10 9 7 5 3 1

Typeset in Deanta Global Publishing Services, Chennai, India
Printed and bound in Great Britain by CPI (Group) UK Ltd, Croydon CR0 4YY

To find out more about our authors and books visit www.bloomsbury.com
and sign up for our newsletters.

For Iris, my brilliant girl

Contents

Prologue

On Monday, 8th July 2019, I lost my fifteen-and-a-half-year-old daughter, Iris, in an accident on our family farm in South Somerset. Iris's death left me reeling and grasping for answers. In the rawness of my grief, I simply could not accept that a girl so sparkling in preparation for her future ultimately did not have one. I threw myself into searching for some ongoing trace of her, exploring ideas that until now had seemed too abstract to mean much to me. Do we have a soul? Could there be truth in the widely held belief that we exist on a continuum beyond death, our souls maybe even returning to the world in a cycle of reincarnation? Is there a God, and are events like Iris's death in some way foretold in a grand and mysterious unseen plan? Mostly I just missed my Iris terribly, struggling to conceive of how I would face the rest of my life in the shadow of this loss. In the depths of despair, I found solace in my family, in the love of my wife, Jemima, and in the natural world, the object of a lifelong fascination. I found myself irresistibly drawn back to nature, which became a vital source of meaning, hope and – in time – joy. This book is the story of a year of soul-searching after being floored by a terrible loss. In an instant, my world turned dark. Yet, unbelievably to me, the seasons kept on turning, and as I immersed myself in the wildness rebounding in the place where it happened, I began to find healing.

I

Gone

And did you get what
you wanted from this life, even so?
I did.
And what did you want?
To call myself beloved, to feel myself
beloved on the earth.

RAYMOND CARVER,
'Late Fragment'

That spring, just three months earlier, some of us had scrambled out of bed at dawn to see a huge humpback whale brought in by the whalers. It was the morning after arriving on the tiny West Indian island of Bequia, a long-planned trip during the Easter of 2019. From the hillside on the way down, we saw the vast form bobbing, the immense flank translucent in the early morning sun. I loved that Iris had chosen to join us at that hour, a teenager now – a grown woman almost, I had noticed at the time. Her fascination with nature; her gentleness with animals of all kinds; the way she bent to catch pigeons at Barnes before freeing them to amuse her baby sister; her reverence for the sea; these things gave me such joy. Islanders thronged the little harbour, jostling to get their piece, the air above them thick and sweet with marijuana smoke. The great carcass was tethered between two jetties, on one of which a handful of jubilant young men sharpened their machetes and adjusted their masks. We wove our way to them, Iris walking behind me, the others single file behind her. Without hesitation, Iris stepped forward and asked their permission before kicking off her shoes and slipping into the water in her shorts and t-shirt. She swam across to the floating giant, the belly high suspended above the water, the great tail submerged at one end and at the other, also the head, mouth agape. Iris laid both her hands on the whale's grey skin, gently mesmerised, and felt her way around its vastness, oblivious to the yakking of onlookers delighted to see a teenage girl in the blood-red water unafraid, tenderly handling the dead monster. 'Awesome; and so sad, Dad,' she said, clambering out and wringing out her auburn hair with her hands.

Now I sat dull-eyed in one of the fold-up wooden chairs scattered about the terrace, still wearing the grass-stained cricket whites and clacking metal-spiked shoes in which I'd left Cannwood that morning. Someone handed me a slice of cold pizza from one of the greasy-looking boxes on the outdoor table, where we'd eaten a hurried breakfast just a few hours earlier. A murmur of activity around me barely registered; the steady arrival of family, hushed snippets of conversation, someone sobbing gently around a corner, the thin, reedy song of a little dunnock lurking in the low branches of a lime tree behind me. I observed from a great distance the unfolding nightmare. My nephew Kasim dutifully entertained Eliza and Arlo, Iris's oblivious toddler half-siblings, with a long-suffering guinea pig named Peanut on the other side of the vegetable garden; a police car doubled back on itself before cruising silently up the lane and out of sight. I pinched the sensitive skin on the underside of my forearm between the nails of my thumb and forefinger. I was here; it was real. Iris was dead.

As a little girl, Iris was like a faery from Celtic mythology, with big blue eyes and long reddish-blonde hair, the product of Irish heritage on her mother's side. There had always been an otherworldliness about her. Shortly after Iris died, my niece, Tyrian, wrote that people 'were instinctually drawn to her. It was impossible not to be. She seemed to be in on some ethereal secret that the rest of us weren't capable of grasping.' Something of a dreamer, happiest lost in play by herself, Iris nonetheless found herself naturally the centre of attention among the children, always the one inventing the fun or the trouble. From her earliest years, she was outlandishly charismatic, with an adult's quick wit and the confidence to use it. She was five when we arrived at Cannwood in Somerset's Brewham Valley. Though school was in west London, she and her two younger brothers, Frankie and Isaac, spent virtually every free day, every weekend, every holiday in Somerset. Cannwood is where they did their adventuring, where they grew up.

The Oakley family at neighbouring Dreamers Farm became our first local friends. Calling after a runaway dog with all three children, we had found our way one autumn afternoon into their unruly yard. Adjacent to Cannwood, the farm is dominated by two large livestock sheds that squat open-fronted, side by side, set apart from a pretty stone farmhouse at the corner of the yard. The scruffy, richly productive vegetable garden to the front of the farmhouse is enclosed by a low chicken-proof fence. We came across the children first, eyeing us from the top of a stack of hay bales inside one of the barns before clambering down rowdily to show us a pair of orphaned lambs they were bottle-rearing. Their father, Simon Oakley, strong and handsome still in his late fifties with three much older children from a previous marriage, and Kate, his formidable second wife, who seemed always to know a great deal about everyone, had moved in a few years earlier. They were raising their four young children on the farm alongside a herd of Jersey cows that they brought in to milk twice daily, some Poll Dorset sheep, a handful of pigs that rootled at the back of the sheds, and an assortment of layer hens.

Simon had built the farmhouse himself, enlisting occasional help from his grown-up sons and various friends, even using stones dug out from a new slurry pit on the farm and cracked using an ancient stone-cracking machine salvaged from the scrap yard at Nunney. It had taken them several years, during which the family had lived in two caravans welded together at the other end of the yard. The oldest of their children, Mikey, softly spoken and shyly capable with machines and animals, became a loved role model to my two boys, Frankie, just eighteen months younger than Iris, and Isaac, two and a half years younger than Frankie. Mikey's younger sister Monica became instant best friends with Iris. Willowy Annabelle came next, and the youngest, a tiny, feisty blonde girl named Claudia, was nicknamed 'Queen' by the others. From that day, a gang of seven children was formed that spent every possible moment together, running feral. We made a rough hard track down through newly planted woods at Cannwood to the yard at Dreamers. Iris, their ringleader, wearing tight-fitting blue jeans, scuffed riding boots and a garish oversized t-shirt, could be relied upon to get the others into some scrape or other. The three boys unfailingly wore army camouflage. The girls each had a pony; Iris's was Ben, who arrived with that name, a capricious Welsh hill pony that tried to kick me every time I went too near him. They spent hours caressing and grooming them, climbing on them, competing over improvised jumps in one of the fields and cantering off together, sometimes not bothering with saddles and bridles. I mostly trusted them and enjoyed how they spent their time out of doors, immersed in nature, often free from adult interference.

More recently, Iris, who was at boarding school, had discovered London. Along with the other girls, she had grown less interested in tearing around the farm, and when she was at Cannwood, she was more interested in teenage affairs in nearby Gillingham or Bruton. Her trips to Somerset became an increasingly rare delight. On what was to be her last visit, she had arrived late on a Sunday evening, a day earlier than I was expecting. She had chosen to spend the first week of her summer holiday working through a list of school tasks in order to enjoy the rest of the holiday unencumbered. Iris loved lists. She had always been a star at school, not without effort. Enormously diligent – more so than any child I've known – that summer, Iris was weekend volunteering in Reading with a charity called City Harvest, gathering unsold food from restaurants and retailers for distribution to the needy. In due course, she had decided, she would become a barrister. Earlier that year, I had taken her out for lunch in London, and I had tentatively broached the subject of drugs. 'You are careful, aren't you, my love, when you're out? A lot of the drugs going around at these parties are dangerous. I worry,' I said. Her reply has haunted me ever since. 'Dad, please don't worry. Let me tell you the difference between me and all the others: There's never a moment when I haven't got one eye on my future.'

It was already past sundown on that Sunday when Kate, Iris's mother, called to tell me that Iris and her friend Raffy were on a train about to roll into Warminster. My first thought was, why Warminster? Did Warminster even have a station? I was sitting in the garden with my nephews Sulaiman and Kasim, my niece Tyrian and their cousin Shershah, who was over from Pakistan for the summer. Excited to see Iris, I nonetheless felt a twinge of irritation that she should show up like this: late at night and unannounced, a day early. Mostly I was annoyed because none of us would be at home the next day, so we wouldn't get to be with her. We were getting up early to travel to Charterhouse to play cricket against a regular opponent, a bunch of friends who travel to England from India each year to play a series of friendly matches. A few years ago, we started calling ourselves the Cannwood Cupcakes. (We had toyed with the Cannwood Cutthroats, but the girls had insisted on cupcakes.)

I booked Iris a taxi in Warminster which, after a time, pulled up alongside us on the lane. Iris hopped out a little grumpily, wearing grey tracksuit bottoms, a shortish yellow t-shirt with 'Brazil' emblazoned across the front in green, white socks and a pair of sliders. Raffy trailed behind her; each girl had a rucksack on her shoulders. Iris went first to Shershah (who had been our secret weapon in several cricket matches that year) and hugged him, and then to me, whispering in my ear with a breathy giggle that, in the semi-darkness, she had thought he was Sulaiman, having never met Shershah before. I noticed she was now taller than Tyrian, putting them back to back and marvelling at how my girl had grown. With that, I pointed the two girls to where they were sleeping, on the ground floor of the former barn that lies perpendicular to our house. Recently Iris had always slept in the barn, staying up late in the high-ceilinged sitting room, far away from the rest of us in the house.

That was the last time I saw her, sloping off down the path in the darkness, in her sliders. They didn't stay up late, I was told later, but nevertheless, I curse myself for not having spent a little time with them before heading off to bed.

I was downstairs the following morning, calling the others to get a move on while I threw some breakfast together. Fried eggs are virtually the only thing I can cook; always the yolk split, the egg cooked on both sides and placed on a piece of buttered toast atop two slices of fresh tomato and two strips of bacon, a cup of tea at the side. Iris, who loved cooking, used to make a point of telling her friends that her dad makes 'an insanely good fry-up'. Sitting at the round table outside the kitchen, we ate hurriedly, in the early morning sun, before setting off together. My wife Jemima was heading back to her restaurant in London; Tyrian was coming with us to watch the match at Charterhouse. Iris, Raffy and our two youngest children, Eliza and Arlo, were left at Cannwood; Iris and her friend sleeping soundly in the barn room; and the little ones under the watchful eye of a lovely Persian-German girl named Shari, who had spent that summer living with us, helping out with the children.

Piling into two cars with cricket bags stacked high in the back windows, we swung by Kate's cottage at nearby Stourton to collect Frankie and Isaac, arriving at Gillingham Station just as our train rolled in. Breathless in our seats on the train, I took a selfie with my two nephews and my two sons, sending it to both my sister (also called Jemima) and to my first wife, Kate, captioned 'The best of days.' After a while, Kate replied with a heart; and shortly afterwards with the words, 'Do you know what day it is today?' 'No,' I replied. '8 July, not only the anniversary of my father's death but also the birthday of BOTH my brother and my sister's oldest child. It's too much; I can't get over it.' Caught up changing trains at Basingstoke, I never acknowledged her message.

After arriving a little late in three taxis that snaked in convoy along the extravagant driveway of the famous public school, the match kicked off almost immediately. The Charterhouse pitch was mown with verdant green stripes that stretched away from the grand main school building. We chose to field first and were pleased with how things went. We kept them to under 250 runs, and I was privately relieved to have held onto a catch at square leg. Mostly we lavished praise on 11-year-old Isaac for having taken his first wicket in one of these games. Beaming, he had hummed quietly to himself while scoffing a bowl of pasta at our table during the short mid-innings lunch. The cricket pavilion and one whole wing of the school were under scaffolding that summer, so lunch was arranged in a makeshift tent laid on by the Indian friends a little back from the boundary rope. Our opening batsmen glugged down some lukewarm coffee before striding out to the crease. One of the two fell quickly. It was hot. Restless, Frankie and I decided to walk the boundary length in the sunshine.

Heading anticlockwise, we took a brief detour to try opening the gargantuan, locked wooden door of the school church overlooking the field before rejoining the boundary rope. A Canadian photographer named Robert Leslie, hired each year by the friend group from India, was snapping the game with a large lens from the school steps. We paused by his side to look down on the game. Their teenage fast bowler was even faster this year. Robert told us his wife was expecting a baby girl any day now. He wondered if I had any last-minute parenting advice. I don't remember my reply, but mulling Robert's impending first-time parenthood in the heat of that July afternoon was a happy moment. It was to be the last before the sky fell.

Frankie and I made our way to the furthest point from the pavilion, where we stopped to sit cross-legged on the grass behind the boundary rope.

It was Frankie who first spotted something was up. Following the route we had taken moments earlier, Kate's boyfriend Paul was running around the boundary rope. Ashen, breathless, he handed me his phone.

'It's Kate. Iris has had an accident on the Mule,' he said.

I took the phone.

'Ben, Iris has had an accident on the Mule.' Kate said.

My first reaction was one of anger. 'Oh God, what's she done now?' I asked.

Quiet, desperate, Kate replied: 'Ben. She's not breathing. Ben, oh God, Ben.'

The Mule is a heavy, slow and really quite dull utility vehicle. Three can sit in the front, three behind, and it has a truck-bed at the back. So much of our family life has taken place in that vehicle, and it was used continually by everyone on the farm: to round up sheep and cattle, to bring firewood up from the woods, or to transport everyone to a good place for a picnic. As it was slow, steady and more comfortable than a quad bike, I used the Mule to show my older neighbours, or those with young children, around our place. It wasn't made for speeding, for racing, as you might with a quad bike, which is undoubtedly a risky vehicle. I just never thought of the Mule as being dangerous.

On the contrary, the Mule was the safe option. The children had been allowed to drive it from the age of eight or nine, initially under supervision from an adult until – reaching their teens and having passed a pretend driving test – one by one, they were trusted to drive it on their own. I later learned that Iris and one of her school friends got the Mule stuck in a ditch the previous winter. Simon Oakley towed it out with his tractor. Later I wished I had known about that, but even if I had, I doubt things would have turned out differently.

It took a moment for me to take Kate's words on board. My heart dropped, racing, my body cold with adrenalin. Kate was in her car, alone, having turned around to tear back to Cannwood from London. Earlier that morning, she had passed by to have breakfast with Iris and Raffy before heading to London for work. The three of them had sat in the sunshine with mugs of tea and played with little Eliza and Arlo. There had always been a unique, intense bond between Eliza and Iris, her big sister. Seeing them together gave me such happiness. The first thing Iris had told Kate that fateful morning was that she had seen a ghost in her room the previous night. Iris had never been that kind of a fantasist, and I don't recall her, or any of my children, ever having claimed to have seen a ghost. She had never suffered night terrors. She was, at heart, a rational child and made her own magic.

'Mum, I'm telling you there was a ghost in my room, a girl, my kind of age, just standing there at the end of my bed. I even woke Raffy up to tell her, didn't I, Raffy?'

'Yes, she woke me up to tell me there was a ghost in the room.' Raffy had chimed in obligingly.

Kate had left for London at midday, and the girls went to lie in the sun at the back of the house, leaving the little ones with Shari by the kitchen door.

By now, Jemima had made it to the shiny new kitchen at her restaurant in London. Iris and Raffy were called inside for lunch with Shari and the little ones. They each had a bowl of German-style gnocchi before returning to the garden to knock about on the tennis court. Tennis had always been a source of friction between me and Iris. 'It's the one game you'll actually want to play as an adult,' I used to insist. Still, no amount of pleading, cajoling or bullying could persuade her to join her brothers and cousins in tennis lessons on family holidays. Iris was defiant. During that last year at boarding school, however, she had taken up the sport; she loved it and played almost daily for half a year without telling me. It was going to be a surprise, she had told Kate. 'Dad has no idea; I'm really quite good!' Wandering dumbly through the garden the day after she died, I found cans of brand-new tennis balls, two racquets and an empty bottle of water on its side on the tennis court.

At three o'clock, Iris announced that she and Raffy should head off to collect Monica Oakley, who would soon be back from school. She had been excited to have these two friends together from different corners of her life. Unusually for a weekday afternoon, the Mule was sitting there unused, so they hopped in and, with a little time to kill, zoomed off in the opposite direction down the lane. Evidently they thought they would be back very soon because they didn't bother wearing shoes, which they left by a little speaker on the grass. At some point the two girls looped back on themselves, perhaps having driven in a circle down through the big wood, and made their way back up the lane, past the house, and out into the field adjoining Dreamers Farm. Had Iris simply taken the direct route, following the hard track that crosses the field diagonally, she would have collected Monica at the bottom, turned around, driven back, and the three of them would have spent a happy afternoon in the garden until the boys and I arrived home having won our cricket match. I've replayed the scene over and over in my mind. We would have had dinner together that evening on the round table outside the kitchen. I would have made sure to sit next to Iris, having not seen her for a while. How different that day, and our lives, might have been.

Instead, Iris veered left off the track onto the newly cut grass, snaking the Mule left and then right as fast as it would go, doing her best to frighten her friend Raffy. I can picture it clearly, Iris at the wheel, peals of laughter, failing to grasp the actual risk in what she was doing. Veering right out of a left-hand turn, back towards the track, on ground as dry and hard as I can remember it being, the Mule lost balance. Since it was American-made, Iris was driving on the left-hand side. As it tipped over, in slow motion, as Raffy told us later, Iris fell out. I don't know why she didn't just hold tight to the steering wheel; whether she saw the ground coming up towards her and just put her foot out to meet it, as you might on a bicycle; or whether the force of the turn just threw her from the vehicle.

In any case, it had still seemed like fun. According to Raffy, 'It just didn't feel very bad. I think I was laughing, climbing out the other side, until I saw that Iris was pinned by her neck.' When Raffy and I talked it through several weeks later, somehow, this detail had sent me into a spiral of raging grief.

Iris was trapped lying face down, her feet out from the vehicle, the edge of the heavy metal roof lying with perfect precision across the side of her neck. We learned much later that her left thigh and her right collarbone were both broken. 'Please help me, Raffy,' she had whispered. By now, Raffy was on her hands and knees, trying to work out how to free her. 'Until then, I had never seen her crying.' she told me. 'What do I do? What do I do?' Raffy had pleaded. She was able to pull Iris's arms out from under the vehicle and made a vain attempt to lift the whole thing up, but it was far too heavy. When her panicked calls to the house and to me went unanswered, she dialled the emergency services, who dispatched a helicopter and an ambulance by road. Realising that Iris was slipping away, Raffy began to scream as loud as she could. Hearing her cries, Nick Marsh, the Cannwood gardener, who was 200m or so away, leapt onto a quad bike. Thinking at first that there had been an accident in the cowshed, he stopped halfway, turned off the engine, and then sped on in the direction of the screams.

'I tried to lift it up; it was too heavy, I couldn't lift it,' Nick had sobbed in my arms later that day. He arrived on his quad to find Iris trapped and unconscious, possibly by now dead, and Raffy standing by her in a state of hysteria. The two of them were unable to lift the machine, so Nick called for help from Hayley Lippiatt, who ran a small horse livery out of the yard, before the emergency services rang back for more precise directions. Hayley arrived moments later, running with Shari and a neighbour, and the group heaved the Mule high enough to pull Iris out before dropping it back down. When

I arrived at the scene an hour or so later, the vehicle was still on its side; its monstrous wheels pointed back up towards me in the afternoon sun. Hayley had followed the instructions from a lady in the emergency call centre, pumping Iris's chest and breathing into her lungs, which she continued until the first ambulance crew arrived by helicopter. By then, according to Kate Oakley, Iris was certainly dead. 'She was the wrong colour,' she had said later.

The emergency services continued to arrive, one vehicle after the next, until at one stage, there may have been 30 people there, all desperately trying to save my Iris's life. They never stood a chance. Several months later, in a drab meeting room at the back of Yeovil Hospital, the three paramedics most closely involved explained to me that the chances of saving someone with the blood flow to their brain restricted in that way for any more than a minute are infinitesimal. I took some comfort from that; in all likelihood, Iris fizzed out pretty quickly without too much suffering. The story could have been even worse.

In the days that followed, I obsessed over the exact time of Iris's death. The girls left the garden at 3.00 p.m. The accident must have happened at about 3.15 p.m. Nick was on the scene at 3.20 p.m. The others arrived at 3.28 p.m. The air ambulance landed at 3.40 p.m. I got the call, sitting on the boundary at Charterhouse, at 3.55 p.m. Iris was declared dead at 4.30 p.m., but she had been dead long before that, most likely before Nick had even arrived on the scene. What had I been doing at 3.15 p.m.? Pacing in front of the tent, coffee in hand, perhaps? Or did Frankie and I walk for longer than it seemed, and did Iris die as I grappled with the church door? Or during my conversation with Robert Leslie? I've tried to recall whether I felt anything, anything at all. But no, the world I knew broke with Kate's call.

With Kate's words, I dropped to my knees, overcome by a great dread that engulfed me. How could this be happening? Please, God, don't let her die. They'll resuscitate her; of course, they will. Please, God. She can't die. I caught sight of Frankie's panic-stricken face and realised that I must get myself out of sight. 'Iris has had an accident on the Mule. Everything is going to be okay. Go with Paul.' I told him, doing my best to keep as even a voice as I could manage. Then I set off running around the boundary of the cricket field, my heart pounding in my ears, stopping to grab my own phone from its charger in a little outhouse before dashing behind the construction site screen and tumbling into the door of a builders' mess room. Inside were two workmen, seated, having a break. I sank to the floor and appealed to them, sobbing that my daughter had been in an accident and, please, God, let her be alright. They were appalled, rooted to the spot, before one jumped up, grabbed a small bottle of flavoured water and knelt by me, urging me to have a sip. The other went out to find help, returning moments later with Ben Elliot, who urged me to get a grip of myself. 'Your boys are outside. You've got to hold it together, just thirty seconds to get to my car,' he said. The match was called off.

Bundling me into the front seat of his car, Ben told Paul to follow with the boys. Kate called again, this time on my phone. She had spoken to Kate Oakley; an air ambulance team was working on Iris in the field. Which field? We should head for Yeovil Hospital. There was hope. I begged God for mercy, to save my little girl, writhing in my seat, my forehead pressed against the coldness of the car window, pleading, begging.

Ben drove in silence, jaw set, two hands gripping the wheel.

Nobody called.

The minutes passed.

I began to call people at Cannwood, one after the other; none picked up. I called and called. Perhaps they've revived her, I thought, and they're all busy loading her into the ambulance – a fragment of hope. Deep down, however, I think I already knew. Iris's mother, Kate, called me again. Calm, quiet, the gentle hum of her car on the motorway.

'You know why they're not answering our calls, don't you? It's because she's dead, and none of them wants to tell us on the phone.'

'Don't say it, please don't say it, Kate,' I begged.

I began calling again, and finally, Kate Oakley answered. 'I think you had better come here to Cannwood,' was what she said.

'Is she dead, Kate? You need to tell me. Please tell me.'

'They haven't *pronounced* her dead,' she replied, and it was then that I knew hope was extinguished. I hitched up my legs into a foetal position, head buried in my elbow, and sobbed quietly, muttering, 'How can this be happening,' over and over. I was dimly aware of Ben crying beside me as he drove, speaking to my brother. 'It doesn't sound good; you had better come,' he told Zac, and the same to my mother and my sister. My wife Jemima called from the train, having raced out of the kitchen to the station on hearing news of the accident from Shari. She had also spoken to Kate Oakley, who had passed the phone to the policeman at the scene. 'I'm so sorry, my love; it's so, so bad; Iris has died,' Jemima told me.

Ours was the first car to pull into the lane at Cannwood; by this time Kate was right behind us, the boys and Paul not far behind her. Jemima was to arrive half an hour later. A gaggle of people had congregated to the right of the lane, wide-eyed and tearful. To the left, at the opening to the field leading down to Dreamers Farm, were two paramedics and a policeman standing between us, and an ambulance parked a little way down on the grass. The side door of the ambulance lay open.

'Are you Benjamin Goldsmith?' the policeman asked. 'Yes,' I replied, seeing him at the end of a long tunnel.

'And Kate Rothschild?'

'Yes.'

I reached for Kate's hand.

'Do you know what has happened here today?' he asked. I replied that I did, even though I didn't, not really. All I knew was that my greatest fear, the fear that grips all parents, had been realised here at Cannwood, in a field that lay quiet but for the birdsong, beneath the dazzling sunshine of a July afternoon.

'I'm sorry to tell you that your daughter Iris has died in an accident here today. The paramedics tried very hard to save her.' Stepping forward, a young paramedic in green overalls asked if we were ready to see our daughter. 'I must warn you, Iris is in a body bag,' the kindness in his voice no match for the stark reality of these words. He led us to the single step up into the ambulance. My ears rang. There was my beautiful girl lying on her back on a metal trolley, partially zipped into a black body bag, her hands visible at her side. I remember noticing the beauty of her profile, aquiline now with the transition away from childhood, the only sign of injury a few flecks of blood beneath the nostrils. I noticed her hair, which she had dyed blonde since beginning at boarding school. I had told her it was a shame, given how blessed she was to have such a uniquely beautiful hair colour – a colour that Jemima's sister Quentin had once said she wished she could bottle and market for sale.

'Teenage boys aren't sophisticated, Dad; they like blondes! I won't be blonde forever, I promise,' she had explained.

Laid out in the ambulance, it seemed to me that her hair had somehow returned to its natural colour. Kate stumbled, so I held her around the waist with one arm as she began to plead with the paramedics, 'Please, try again. There must be something more you can try. They bring people back all the time. Oh please, please God, save her.'

The policeman stepped into the ambulance and tapped me on the shoulder to let me know that the two boys had arrived and were dashing across the lane towards the ambulance. I leapt past him and out of the ambulance towards them, knowing my duty at that moment, and heard the paramedic behind me sliding the ambulance door shut. I held them both tight. Kate joined us, sobbing.

'Iris is dead,' I said simply. Frankie let out the noise of an animal. We held each other tight. How could this be happening? How could such a thing have happened?

At some point, I walked alone down the lane towards the house. My eyes turned upwards to where the arms of the trees meet, forming a tunnel that shades the length of the lane. Narrow shafts of sunlight shone through the gaps onto the uneven surface beneath. By July, the lane was overgrown on both sides with a tangle of wildflowers, many of which had now spent and turned to seed. The delicate flowers of spring were a distant memory, the lesser celandine, dog violet and bluebells long since smothered by the summer vigour of the hogweed, hemlock water-dropwort and nettles that take their place each year. I wondered how things could look exactly as I'd left them, the sounds and the smells all around me when my whole world was broken.

Waiting for me at the other end of the lane by the house was the policeman's car, its engine still running. Calm, unflustered, matter of fact, the officer guided me into the front passenger seat, closing the door behind me. A few yards away, a handful of friends and family members, some wearing cricket whites, were gathered in silence at the round table. They looked in my direction, dumbstruck. Between them and me, an assortment of clay plant pots divided the hard surface in front of the kitchen from a small square of lawn running down to the lane, shaded by an unusually large and straight holly, which at times, we've debated felling to allow in more evening light. I cried silently, wanting this stranger to hold me, to tell me that there was a way out of this. But his job was to prepare a statement, not to offer comfort. As he asked me one simple question after another, I remember thinking that the process of recording an earth-shattering event of this kind is strangely basic. Policemen deal with these things all the time.

Kate left with her mother to see Iris in the morgue beneath the hospital. I couldn't bear to accompany her. I was too afraid, but I said I needed to stay with the boys. In the days that followed, Kate went again and again. I did not go. Between visits, Kate had told me quietly that she felt like she could still hear Iris's voice, as she sat there next to the lifeless body. Amid the delirium of grief, she heard Iris tell her she was scared, asking her not to go.

'Come with me, Iris.'

'I don't know how. Please, Mummy, stay here with me.'

2

Grief

i carry your heart with me(i carry it in
my heart)i am never without it(anywhere
i go you go,my dear;and whatever is done
by only me is your doing,my darling)
i fear
no fate(for you are my fate,my sweet)i want
no world(for beautiful you are my world,my true)
and it's you are whatever a moon has always meant
and whatever a sun will always sing is you

here is the deepest secret nobody knows
(here is the root of the root and the bud of the bud
and the sky of the sky of a tree called life;which grows
higher than soul can hope or mind can hide)
and this is the wonder that's keeping the stars apart

i carry your heart(i carry it in my heart)

E. E. CUMMINGS,
[i carry your heart with me(i carry it in]

I find it hard to remember the days following the accident with
any clarity, one merging into another in a continuous loop.

I made a conscious effort not to drink too much; a single beer before lunch and one large whiskey with ice at half past six. Any more produced the opposite of the desired effect. My doctor prescribed Xanax. Unused to any kind of sleeping pills, I took half a tablet each night, which seemed enough to guarantee a continuous night's sleep. The pills made me groggy the following morning and left a slight metallic taste in my mouth.

I've always responded to intense stress and sadness with a strong desire to sleep. I've been in domestic arguments in which she presumed I was lying silent in the dark, remorseful for the things I had just said, or reloading for the next salvo, when in fact I was asleep. I'm lucky in this way, so after a while, I decided not to take the medication and found, with relief, that I quickly dozed off and did not wake in the night.

Each morning brought fresh agony. For a fraction of a second after waking, I was conscious only of blinding fear and, after a momentary searching, alighted on the source with a sickening realisation that hit me in the guts. A crushing dread followed me night and day, permeating my dreams, my mind and every cell of my body. Jemima took to bringing me a cup of tea, placing it silently on the little wooden table by the bed and sitting back on the bed beside me, a hand resting on my head. Hearing the little ones stirring and the patter of their feet as they scampered from their room into ours, I often rolled onto my front, pulling up my knees and holding myself round the belly as they clambered joyfully up onto the bed, outwardly oblivious to the storm of grief raging beneath the wide, white duvet that covered me. 'Why's Daddy hiding? Daddy. Get. Up.' Rolling back and manufacturing a smile, I would grab one or both and hold them tight to kiss them good morning. 'Do you want your Iris back?' Eliza took to asking me, upbeat, looking me straight in the eye, dabbing a hand on my chin or cheek and trying to compute why my face was wet.

I had taken to muttering over and over in a whisper to myself, 'I want my Iris back,' while making a coffee, while walking up the stairs, while sitting alone, cross-legged, head in my hands on the grass at the back of the house. Even though Eliza's grasp of where exactly Iris had gone was foggy, she had heard me say this to myself enough times that she wanted in. We both wanted our Iris back.

There were times when, in despair, I allowed my mind to wander to a darker place, to imagine what it might feel like to hang myself by the neck, allowing my eyes to look upwards for a place where the rope might be attached, to rest there. I tried to imagine the feeling of the weight of my body pulling me downwards, closing off my airways, the darkness of sleep enveloping me. There was never a danger of me doing it, but the fantasy in those moments was darkly comforting. A side door existed, even if I knew I'd never use it. I wanted to threaten God, if He was listening. I remembered it being said that God gives us no more than we can bear. Well, maybe He had gone too far, meting out this injustice. Maybe I might just throw in the towel.

Cannwood was filled with family: my brother Zac and my sister Jemima, and her children, Tyrian, Sulaiman and Kasim, who cancelled their summer plans in order to stay indefinitely. They kept Frankie and Isaac occupied unendingly. Some slept on sofas. Kate, her sister and her mother slept at the cottage nearby but spent most of each day at Cannwood, sitting, drinking tea, drifting, crying. One or other of my oldest and closest friends was always with us too. They must have put together some sort of rota because, for weeks, I was never alone. My Jemima was by my side constantly. I clung to her like a beautiful railing which kept me from falling; and a warm, kind, soft blanket in which I came to hide, crying and pleading. We ate together, all of us always, lunch at a series of fold-up plastic tables placed end to end and covered with three white tablecloths outside the kitchen. Mostly I sat beside Jemima; Kate cosseted across the table with her two boys, her mother and Paul, no stranger to trauma himself. As a teenager, Paul had lost his parents in the Indian Ocean tsunami of 2004. They had been travelling in Sri Lanka when the disaster struck. I was especially glad for the presence now of his steady kindness and earthy wisdom in Kate's life. The others did their best to conjure a normality of sorts. We began referring to our commune as the *grief kibbutz*.

Life took on a strange hue, like being on a ship traversing a prolonged and dense fog, the sun's great disc representing the outside world, just perceptible through the gloom. We played garden cricket endlessly, ostensibly to keep the younger boys occupied, but it helped us to pass the time. I did my best to be upbeat, pushing back continual waves of anxiety. After writer Joan Didion lost her only daughter, she wrote that grief, it turns out, feels very much like fear. C. S. Lewis wrote of a sense of endless waiting following the early death of his wife. I felt constantly afraid, waiting for something that never arrived, tight-chested, lumpen-throated. Like a barrel filling inexorably with rainwater beneath a storm gutter, I felt the emotion build and build inside me until it had to overflow. At such times I slunk off, often at a trot, hiding around corners and in bathrooms and crying until my chest ached and the tears ran dry. There were times when the crying was so intense, so uncontrollable, that I struggled for air and pins and needles ran through my lips and my hands. At the subsiding of each storm came a transient relief, and the barrel would begin to fill once more. I dreaded the funeral.

The smallest events took on a whole new significance: going out to the chicken run alone to collect eggs for breakfast, making and drinking another cup of tea, an hourly cigarette smoked alone at the back of the house on a bench overlooking the bird feeders. They didn't need feeding at this time of year, I noticed; the feeders were deserted, the birds busy elsewhere in the field margins and hedgerows fattening themselves for the winter ahead. I swam in the pond often. I walked with Jemima; our shared silence interspersed with my unanswerable babbled questions as to how such a thing could possibly have happened; what we were going to do. We walked a regular loop down the lane, turning left into the big wood and back on ourselves along a broad, sun-dappled, flowery ride, known to us as the cathedral for the grand oaks towering on either side.

I wondered if the feeling of waiting was for a chance to travel back and fix things, as if somehow this didn't *have* to be; if only we could just think of a way to unpick it. I lost myself in a maze of what-ifs, agonising over every detail of the events of that day, tortured by looping uncertainties, my mind coursing hot and red like the revved engine of a car raised off the ground in a mechanics' yard. What if Iris had arrived as planned that Monday evening instead of a day early? What if the Mule hadn't been free that afternoon? It was always being used by someone – why not then? What if someone, anyone, had been walking or working near that field when the accident happened? They could have lifted the machine off her in time. What if the long grass hadn't been cut for the hay the previous week? Iris would have had to stay on the hard track rather than veering out across the field as she did. What if I had been there?

Most of all, I went over and over in my mind whether I should have allowed the children to drive any of the farm vehicles in the first place. My generation had grown up with tremendous freedom. Kate had been raised with her brother and sister on a large arable farm in Suffolk, and Zac and I had spent whole days on two-wheeled scrambler bikes, exploring the thickly wooded common that lies on both sides of our family home in Richmond. I had learned to drive a car in my early teens, a battered open-top jeep on our family farm in southern Spain, which I rattled along dirt roads without adult supervision by the time I was 14 or 15. Ultimately, I could not convince myself of any conceivable alternate world where my children were barred from experiencing these freedoms. I might have banned Iris from driving the quad bikes for a while if I had known that she was behaving irresponsibly, but not by the age of 15. Iris had grown out of all of that, I presumed. She was on the cusp of adulthood, and even if I had laid down that particular law, she would simply have driven the sleepy old Mule instead.

I remembered a book I'd studied at school, *Chronicle of a Death Foretold*, by Colombian writer Gabriel Garcia Marquez. In it, a young man is seemingly destined to die, his murder foretold by the circumstantial missing of one chance after the next to save him. Perhaps events simply do unravel by design. I found that notion distantly comforting. My old friend George Frost, who had lost his older brother Miles – also one of my closest friends, to a sudden heart attack while out running several years earlier – arrived soon after the accident, flamboyant with presents for the children. George had told me bluntly that the greatest curse of the thing, which is that there is nothing to be done to change what happened, would, in time, become a blessing. Powerlessness eventually bestows on exhausted, grieving minds a peace of sorts. I just needed to wait. In time my suffering would wane. I had lost touch with time as the days rolled by; aware only of the widening gulf since Iris had last been alive, breathing the same air as me; and the unfathomably vast expanse ahead in which, not yet 40, I would grow old in the pain of remembering the vibrantly brilliant teenage daughter we once had, denied her chance to take on the world.

One morning a robin found its way into the high-ceilinged sitting room of the barn, the room where Iris had spent her last evening with her cousins and Raffy. The robin had become trapped, darting back and forth between the large windows on two sides of the room. Another day a house martin fledgling flapped frantically against the window of a guest bedroom on the top floor. A little wren was discovered sitting on top of the curtain rail in the children's bedroom. We called on Frankie each time to catch them softly, competently, in his hands, or with a tea towel, before letting them out of a window. Like Iris, Frankie had a kind way with animals from a young age, sharing Iris's fascination with nature but with a fiercer intensity that drew him outside from morning until night. When Frankie was about seven, one of my friends nicknamed him the 'spawn warden' for his obsessive scouring of ditches and puddles each February for otherwise-doomed frogspawn. Using his hands, he would carefully spoon it up from the icy water in gelatinous clumps and place it in a bucket on the back of his little quad bike. Then he'd transfer his precious cargo to one of the new ponds along the stream where there'd be enough water for the eggs to have a chance to hatch into tadpoles. He was determined not to leave a single egg behind, and when the ponds later teemed with tadpoles, he would visit them several times a day, mostly just to gaze at them, wondering how many would reach adulthood and what else we could do to improve their lot.

In all the years we had lived at Cannwood, I don't recall any bird ever having become trapped in the house before. Some of the others suggested the birds were a sign from Iris, along with an unusually convivial town pigeon, which rested on the barn roof and waddled across the lawn to beg for titbits. Implausible as it was, this idea was strangely consoling. In any case, Iris was everywhere: in framed photographs; in novels she'd annotated in her familiar handwriting; in childhood drawings; a handmade book she had written and illustrated herself called *Guinea Pigs and Their Care*. There were coats and hats she'd worn, shoes and boots, and her pony in the field outside. Iris was simply woven into the fabric of Cannwood.

The funeral was organised by my brother and sister and by Kate's sister Alice. I didn't have the strength to be involved except to ask that they include a soaring 'Ave Maria'. I chose to read the poem 'I carry your heart with me', by e. e. cummings, sent to me by someone or other in the immediate aftermath. The evening before the service, Jemima drove us both to London. As we turned out of Cannwood lane for the first time since the accident, I began to cry uncontrollably, so much so that after a time, Jemima pulled over and stopped in a lay-by, pulling me towards her and holding my head to her belly. Like a three-year-old, utterly depleted, I fell asleep against the car door. We had decided to stay with my mother in Richmond at our family home, Ormeley Lodge, a red-brick Queen Anne house, majestic at the end of a row of terraced cottages set back amid the woods of Ham Common. After our divorce, Kate and the three children had moved here into one of the cottages, named Bramlings, which adjoins my mother's house. They lived there for five years, during which time Iris had formed a close bond with my mother, making her way most days across the garden and in through the back door to do her homework at my mother's dressing table or to climb into bed with her and watch evening television. They adored each other.

Turning off the road onto the gravel in front of the house, we thought we would go for a walk before going inside to see my mother, so I might clear my head after sleeping and regain some composure. We parked up, climbed out of the car and made our way into the woods where I'd spent so much of my childhood. These hundred or so acres had once been communal playing fields, grazed sporadically by sheep and eventually abandoned between the wars. During that period, they'd grown into a riotous woodland dominated by oak, hazel and holly and carpeted each spring with bluebells. As children, Zac and I had spent our days in these woods, looking for birds' nests, tearing about on two little scrambler bikes my uncle had given us after his own sons had outgrown them. We knew every path and clearing, even naming the ones we used most often: 'wood pigeon alley', 'woodpecker lane', 'main road'.

One summer, Zac had returned from boarding school with the idea of making our very own Molotov cocktail, using a glass milk bottle half filled with petrol, cotton wool stuffed into the neck. We lit and hurled it into the middle of a clearing, where the fire immediately began to spread in all directions, quickly igniting tussocks of brown grass and fallen leaves tinder-dry from months of sunny weather. Ordered to get help, I dashed through the undergrowth to the road, and by miraculous luck, a motorbike driven by a scout leader and his teenage son had pulled over. The man leapt into action, rushing to where the fire was now getting out of control. We found Zac frantically thrashing at the flames with a stick. The man calmly extinguished the inferno using a leafy branch, issuing instructions to the two of us as he worked before making us promise to join the Scouts, an undertaking I'm afraid to say we didn't honour. As a child, I had fantasised about bumping into a wild boar or a lynx in these woods. They were especially beautiful on this day, though different; the paths and clearings we had known were long overgrown, replaced by new ones carved out by a small army of dedicated conservation volunteers that now manages the wood.

My mother was waiting for us, hovering in the kitchen dining room. Tea was laid out on an oak table covered by a flowery tablecloth, exactly as I had known it throughout my childhood. She held me tightly, crying silently. I had grown up here under the shadow of the sudden disappearance of my older brother Rupert, who had been swept away in the ocean off Togo, West Africa, when he was 31. My mother's oldest child, born when she was just 21, Rupert had shone, just like Iris. Beautiful, charismatic, popular and academically gifted, he had led a blessed life. Rupert had been fluent in Russian and had spent several years working at the *International Herald Tribune* behind the Iron Curtain in St Petersburg before heading to West Africa to seek his fortune. One day they had simply found his watch, shirt and shoes on a beach at Lomé. No other trace of him was ever found. Devastated, my mother had managed to muster the strength to raise the rest of us, single-handedly save for our nanny Mimi, a second mother to me. 'I can't make you believe me now, but you will feel better. Chinks of light will start to come back into your life. It gets easier; it just does,' she told me. I didn't want to hear it. I couldn't imagine feeling joy again after this appalling injustice, and why should there be? Why should I be entitled to live and laugh after Iris had been deprived of everything?

We slept in the guest room, which had been my sister Jemima's bedroom when we were children. The room was bathed in shafts of evening sunlight, which poured in through two sash windows overlooking the garden. Things were as she had left them, her teenage pony books lined up neatly still in the little bookshelf above a chest of drawers. I had always marvelled at the oddity of a basin inside her actual bedroom, complete with hot and cold taps. My uncle Alastair had succumbed to pancreatic cancer in this room several years previously, and I hadn't slept in it since. That evening my mother lay on the bed with us in her pink dressing gown while we watched some banality or other on television. Having her with us was comforting.

The day of the funeral was surreal in its awfulness. I drifted between registering in disbelief the reality of what was happening to us and a state of disconnection. I wondered if, really, I was just observing the suffering of another family in a novel or a film, perhaps. I had opted to visit Iris at the funeral home, and I would take the boys with me. Jemima and I drove to collect Frankie and Isaac from Kate's home and across Barnes Bridge, making for Notting Hill. Familiar shops and buildings sailed by unchanged, exactly as they had been during countless school runs, people milling about, oblivious to our catastrophe. I wanted to wind down the window and yell out to them. We pulled up outside J. H. Kenyon funeral directors on Westbourne Grove. Jemima turned off the engine, and we all sat silently for a while. Jemima and I had lived round the corner from here, on St Luke's Mews, for several blissful years after meeting not long after my separation from Kate. We had referred to ourselves as *the rebounders*, Jemima similarly having emerged that summer from a long-standing love affair. The children came each week to stay with us here in camp beds, always on a Tuesday. We spent weekends at Cannwood.

Opposite J. H. Kenyon is a Sainsbury's Local. A recollection flashed through my mind of popping in with Iris to pick up something or other – just yesterday, it seemed. I saw the five of us having breakfast at one or other of the little cafés on this street before heading to school, Iris, in her uniform, skipping to the car ahead of the others. I remembered telling the three children in a hushed tone on one Tuesday afternoon that a little Italian restaurant close by was famous for making the 'best spaghetti Bolognese in the world'. Their mouths watered, and to my great satisfaction, when it had arrived on their plates, they had wolfed down every last shred. Now here we were, greeted at the door of the funeral home by a kind but sombre undertaker who was to take us inside to see Iris for the very last time. He led us down a set of dimly lit stairs and along a corridor to a strangely illuminated little room, at the centre of which stood the wicker coffin all covered in flowers.

We stood at her side, and I gazed at her face, which bore a stony expression. I was calm. The sight of her body – my firstborn child, my beloved daughter – did not wound me in the way I had imagined it would. That room was peaceful. I had the strong sense that this was not Iris, that she wasn't here any longer. Nobody spoke. I was jolted by Jemima creeping out of the room, offering a muffled apology, and I looked sideways and saw Isaac looking at his big sister, aghast through gaps in his fingers. So I led them out, turning back momentarily alone to lay my hand on Iris's icy cold forehead and to mutter into the silence, 'Goodbye, my angel'. Jemima, ashen, bought us Coca-Colas while the funeral director gave me a paper to sign before handing me a small bag containing the ring, earrings and hairband Iris had been wearing when she died, as well as a lock of her hair in a tiny draw-string purse.

We drove back in silence. Members of Kate's family and mine were gathering at the house in Barnes to wait for the hearse to arrive. We drifted through the door; I hugged Kate and then my mother. A large pink book lay on the kitchen table, each page a collage of photographs and messages from Iris's friends and teachers at school. I didn't have the strength to open it. Kate had sent me some snippets when it had first arrived from Carlota, Iris's best friend at her boarding school, Wycombe Abbey, and reading those had been painful beyond description, so I had resolved to save the book for later. From one of the snippets Kate sent, I had learnt that Iris had been appointed 'house mother' to a younger girl who was being picked on by a girl from another boarding house. When Iris discovered this, she had frogmarched the culprit over to apologise in person. Another girl will always remember Iris comforting her when she was homesick. Iris had sat with her in her room and made her laugh. 'By being so happy herself, Iris made all the other girls happy,' another girl had written. All her life Iris had been there for the younger ones and the weaker ones, using her own popularity to lift them up, just as she was always there for her own friends, who meant so much to her.

Kate suggested I go and see 'Iris's magic tree', her favourite place in the woods behind the house. So I slipped out of a black gate in the wooden fence enclosing the garden at the edge of Barnes Common. A row of squat London plane trees runs parallel to the other side of the fence. In recent years, the people who managed Barnes Common had begun to dispense with the previous generation's unhealthy obsession with tidiness, and thorny scrub has been allowed to proliferate beneath and between the giant trees, a haven for songbirds of various kinds. In my shiny black shoes, so inappropriate for this semi-wild place, I picked my way along one of several narrow footpaths that thread the undergrowth, converging at an especially elegant plane tree that is much bigger than the others. This tree had been Iris's hangout. Too young for pubs and bars, she and the other teenagers spent hours here, Iris generally in her pink tracksuit bottoms, black bomber jacket, beanie and sliders, a little stereo thumping. In the hours after news of the accident had reached her gang, they had gathered under the branches here in their droves, boys and girls, disbelieving that such a thing could have happened. Between her death and her funeral, they stayed at this spot, remaining late into the night. The tree began to look like a Hindu temple during a festival, decorated well above head height with flowers, flickering candles, photos and drawings of Iris, glittering tinsel, cards and notes. Kate had spent hours helping the teenagers and has continued to do so, the decorations changing with the seasons through the year. I recognised several of her friends beneath the tree and hugged them wordlessly, trying to contain my tears behind a rictus smile. Like the black-clad family members milling about in Kate's kitchen, the teenagers gathered to make their way across the common for the service.

I was unsteady on my feet, trembling as we climbed into the Kenyon limousine behind the hearse; Kate, Paul, Jemima, the two boys and me. Approaching the church, St Mary's, on Barnes Common, it occurred to me that I had explored the churchyard with Iris just six months earlier. We had met for tea in a café on the high street before going for a walk in the winter darkness, detouring into the churchyard to read some of the headstones. I remember Iris telling me that she had a fascination with churchyards, 'mysterious and beautiful places', she had said. I told her that churchyards are often havens for wildlife.

The church was full to the rafters; perhaps five hundred people gathered, some outside where a screen had been erected. Iris's friends were directed to the front, the adults further back. Six of us would carry the coffin into the church, including Frankie, scarcely a teenager himself but tall for his age, sinewy and strong, and insistent on walking alongside me at the front despite reservations from some of the others. Iris's cousins Sulaiman and Kasim were in the middle, and at the back were her two uncles: my brother Zac and Kate's brother James. Kate and young Isaac walked behind them. We carried the coffin at waist height rather than on our shoulders to accommodate Frankie.

The funeral service was piercingly beautiful. As we carried the coffin back out, I was unable to see where I was going through a mask of tears, no free hand to wipe them, and I stumbled repeatedly. As we heaved the coffin into the hearse, a great river of mourners streamed out of the church doors in our wake. In a trance, Kate and I climbed into a funereal limousine, dimly aware of Kate's mother, Anita, calling for a doctor. Her husband, Kate's stepfather James Wigan, had collapsed onto the pavement. Out of the back window, we saw the crowd surging forward before parting to allow a doctor through, discovering later that James had merely fainted. Numb with shock, Kate and I held each other as the coffin was conveyed into the flames at Mortlake crematorium to the words of Psalm 23, read by her school chaplain, *Yea, though I walk through the valley of the shadow of death, I will fear no evil: for thou art with me; thy rod and thy staff they comfort me. Thou preparest a table before me in the presence of mine enemies: thou anointest my head with oil; my cup runneth over.* Later that chaplain wrote to us, to tell us of her sorrow on our behalf and that Iris had visited her several times in her last term at school to ask questions of faith, and spirituality, and death.

At some nearby playing fields, a reception was laid on beneath a white tent before which were strewn outdoor tables and chairs. We arrived frightened, climbing out of the limousine, and the gathered mourners did their best not to notice our arrival too obviously. They didn't know what expression to wear, nor what to say when we reached them. Gangs of teenagers milled around the periphery. Tentatively at first, the crowd absorbed us, and soon I found myself passed from one set of arms to another, squeezed tightly, kisses to my face and neck, tears running down to soak my clothes. I gave in to this loving morass, powerless; flotsam in some great human whirlpool. Jemima hovered close by, watching. I whispered to her to make sure Kate was alright. As I reached the far corner of the arrangement, where a group of Kate's oldest girlfriends had congregated around her at one of the tables, a young boy approached me shyly. He was perhaps 14, his mousy hair parted at the centre in two curtains on either side of his freckled, anguished face. He introduced himself as Tom. He was deeply sorry for our loss.

'Iris was the most amazing person I've ever met. She was so kind. She looked out for me at parties,' he said. The boy began to sob. 'I saw Iris at a party on the Saturday night just before she died. We talked for ages, nearly the whole night.' I noticed the colour fading from his lips and face as he smeared away tears using the sleeve of his shirt.

'Iris wanted to talk about death. She asked me where I think we go when we die. She seemed so sure about what happens.'

'What did she think happens?' I asked him. Just then, I noticed a middle-aged lady, face streaming with tears, striding towards us.

'She said we have a choice...' Tom began, at which point the lady stepped between us and hugged me tightly. 'I'm so very sorry; my son Tom loved Iris very much. I can't even begin to imagine,' she said before whisking him away.

With that, the crowd enveloped me again; a cousin, an old school friend not seen in years, my work colleagues in a polite huddle nearby, separate from the group, and I lost sight of Tom. I never found out what Iris believed happened after death.

Before I knew it, I was in the front passenger seat of the car, being driven back towards Somerset by Jemima, all four windows down, a freshly lit cigarette in my left hand. Overlaying the ever-present knot in my chest and belly, a strange and fleeting sense of euphoria came over me. Perhaps this was relief that the funeral was over. Or maybe what was lifting me in the stunning aftermath of that awful day was the magnetic idea that Iris somehow might have intuited she was going to die soon, that perhaps we are all participants in some kind of a grander plan, beyond our comprehension, but of which Iris may have developed an inkling. Perhaps our free will in this life really is far more limited than we believe it to be. Maybe we are no more than driftwood bobbing on some great ocean, doing our best but incapable of fathoming the meaning of it all. Maybe death isn't what we think it is.

3

Pond

When despair for the world grows in me
and I wake in the night at the least sound
in fear of what my life and my children's lives may be,
I go and lie down where the wood drake
rests in his beauty on the water, and the great heron feeds.
I come into the peace of wild things
who do not tax their lives with forethought
of grief. I come into the presence of still water.
And I feel above me the day-blind stars
waiting with their light. For a time
I rest in the grace of the world, and am free.

WENDELL BERRY,
The Peace of Wild Things

It was early evening by the time we pulled back into the lane at Cannwood. Climbing stiffly out of the car, I took off my jacket, shoes and socks by the outdoor table, turned and walked alone through the vegetable garden and down through the long grass to the pond. Beneath my feet, the grass was warm as I made my way along a freshly mown path. Alone on the wooden pontoon that had been completed just weeks earlier, I stripped naked and dived into the cool water, swimming down and down and staying under for as long as I could. Coming back up for air, eyes open, I noticed that the water of the new pond still bore a yellowish tinge and a faint taste of clay. I went back down as far as I could, into the coldness of the deep before curling into a ball and allowing my body to drift up slowly once again. There was refuge in the murky silence of the pond. Breaking the surface, I drew a deep breath of air and rolled over to float on my back, around to the other side of a willowy island at the centre of the pond. It felt good to swim in the gently rippling water of this small wild place, bathed in birdsong and the late afternoon sun. I gazed up at a young oak standing taller than the willows on the island, the richly green vigour of its crown set against the brilliance of the blue sky above. I wondered if the events of that day had really happened or if I had imagined them. With a flash of delirium, I understood that they had. I lost my balance in the water.

Aching with grief, I bobbed for a while, wondering what to do next. I was dimly aware somewhere of a sense of relief. It dawned on me that I was alive still to the beauty of nature, here, now, on this of all days. I had doubted whether anything would matter now, whether my world was forever drained of warmth and colour. I had wondered if we could stay at Cannwood after what had happened here. Now, immersed in the pond looking up, a frog's-eye view, I felt an unmistakeable connection to the nature that hummed benevolently all around me. I felt nature enveloping me, reassuring me, beneath a sun that shone hot even as it approached the conclusion of its long, daily descent westwards over Dreamers Farm. A warm breeze whispered across the water. I knew I would stay here; that my survival might even depend upon me staying here.

A stream enters the big pond at one end. After it rains, water flows over a small concrete dam at the other, continuing down a channel along the valley bottom to another pond, smaller and wilder than this one. We had made that one first. An enormous digger had arrived one winter, and a local contractor, my friend Dave Marshall, had operated it for several days in tandem with a dumper truck driven by Simon Oakley's adult son Ben. The dumper had made its way back and forth, grinding, slipping and sliding between the expanding hole in the ground and a growing arc-shaped mound of clay on which we planned eventually to have picnics overlooking the pond. I have always loved ponds. We've lost so many in Britain, mostly filled in to free up an extra acre or two of farmable land, in a quest for tidiness, or sometimes in the pursuit of safety. Nature rebounds astonishingly quickly wherever a new pond appears. As children, Zac and I had tried to create a tiny pond in a corner of the garden at Ormeley. We discovered that the sandy soil was too porous, so we reluctantly resorted to lining the hole with a thick plastic sheet. At first, the little fish and water bugs that we carefully transferred from one of Richmond Park's big ponds seemed to thrive, but before long our pond was overtaken by an algal bloom so vigorous that even a small electric oxygenation machine was unable to keep it at bay. Great mounds of leaves accumulating that autumn, beneath the copper beech that towered over the corner of the garden, signalled the death knell for that particular project.

As the first new pond at Cannwood was built, I sat for hours on a tree stump, transfixed by Dave's skill on top of the enormous digger. It seemed to me like an extension of his own body as he scraped and carved away great mounds of the blue-grey clay. We gave plenty of space to an old oak in the middle of the pond, a gnarly specimen with dead boughs that give it the appearance of a Japanese bonsai sitting there on its island of clay. Now the banks are cloaked with young willow and alder, and a thick fringe of reeds and rushes advances outwards each year across the water. When that first pond was newly dug, we swam here often, until it became overgrown, by which time a larger pond had been dug out further upstream. Now, left entirely to nature, this first pond was festooned with floating pondweed, a haven for amphibians, which congregate in huge numbers each February among the withered bullrushes, filling the icy water with their spawn, that of the frogs in clumps, while the toads wove long black strings along the bank. At times we glimpse kingfishers. Cartoonishly blue, a pair have taken to nesting on the island, hunting the minnows and sticklebacks that give the game away with a brief flash of silver beneath the water. A heron comes to spend time here too, creeping silently through the rushes or standing statue-like at the water's edge. There'll be beavers before long. They're in the area.

We made sure to make the second pond much deeper than the first to ensure swimmable open water. Iris swam there just once, during her summer half term, Monica Oakley had told me later, before the pontoon had been built. They had hauled my mother-in-law's Canadian heirloom canoe all the way from the house, using it as a platform from which to leap in and climb out of the water. Swimming alone afterwards, I tried to imagine the scene, sometimes finding myself straining to catch on the wind an echo of their laughter, the seven of them together for the very last time. Iris loved wild swimming and, like me, never much liked chlorinated swimming pools, especially clammy indoor ones, pee-warm and pee-infused, echoing with the shrieking of children. Swimming pools always feel colder than natural water, even when they're not, Iris had once pointed out, presciently.

She and I had both spent our school years dreaming up excuses for skipping weekly swimming classes and the annual gala. The Harrodian school never knew a child more prone to ear infections than Iris. In my case, I think I was traumatised after finding myself in the swimming team for the interschool gala at the age of 10 after almost everyone else had gone down with a bug. Having spent so little time in swimming classes, but plenty splashing around in ponds and the sea, I had agreed to compete, under the illusion that I was, in fact, rather a strong swimmer. Arriving at the Brentford Leisure Centre that evening, I had felt calmly confident, so much so that earlier I had encouraged everyone at home to come and watch. I emerged from the humid dressing room in a pair of baggy swimming shorts and realised with a jolt, as the spectators craned from the seating above, that I had oversold my ability. I was the only participant without skin-tight swimming shorts, a rubber hat and goggles. I finished a floundering last and had burned with shame for days.

In the days after the funeral, swimming in the pond became a ritual. It was the only tonic that offered temporary relief. Sometimes I swam half a dozen times a day. Plunging into the pond seemed to cleanse away my anxiety for a time, and I emerged feeling reborn. Perhaps this is why initiates to certain religions are baptised; the water has transformative qualities. The weather made no difference to me; I was as happy to swim in the rain as in the sun, enjoying the subtle differences each time. Often, I sat for a while on the bank beside the pontoon before diving in, observing the goings on around me. If you sit quietly anywhere, it doesn't take long for wildlife to become comfortable enough in your presence to resume their usual bustle around you. I noticed that the shallower water abounds with life. Small predators patrol the fronds beneath the water, sticklebacks, bitey water boatmen, pond skaters and the fearsome larvae of dragonflies and damselflies, creeping, darting, hunting in their underwater jungle. Effortlessly cruising above the water, dragonflies of different colours, shapes and sizes with epic names; broad-bodied chasers, southern hawkers, emperors, and bright red, emerald and blue damselflies. At times a pair join to mate in mid-flight, then turn themselves into a single, long, unwieldy creature, delicately hovering to dab eggs from the tip of a tail onto the surface of the water. Peacefully observing the intricacies of life around the pond, I forgot myself, losing touch with the sadness, lessening the grip of fear that otherwise constricted my breathing. In those moments of distraction, while small gangs of swallows took turns skimming the pond's surface to drink, my senses were consumed by the colours and the sounds, the scents on the breeze, innumerable interactions unfolding before my eyes, patterns revealing themselves; a magic all around me.

I had never considered that there might be anything amiss with the stream that threads the two ponds, running dead straight along the bottom of the valley at Cannwood. Even though we could see it marked clearly on the map at the beginning of the River Frome, we thought of it as a drainage ditch, conveniently funnelling water into one pond after the next following rainfall. In fact, this is the very headwater of the River Frome, *Fromehead*, drawing occasional river pilgrims who, having walked the entire length of the river, sit triumphant on the grass at the end to unpeel a clingfilmed sandwich and pour themselves a cup of tea from a thermos flask. Dave Marshall had cleared the ditch out for us one winter with a small digger, neatly arranging the excavated clay in an elongated bund that ran along the entire length of the valley so that rainwater would flow unimpeded from the fields. Then one year, I met a naturalist named Chris Couldrey, who suggested that we rewild the stream. Softly spoken and tousle-haired in brown denim dungarees, Chris was apt not only to come up with ideas for creating new habitats at Cannwood and elsewhere locally but also carried out the work himself, often working with a majestically bearded and warm-hearted local forester named Garry Mitchell. Chris and Garry had recently completed a series of newt ponds in the fields across Cannwood. These were deliberately placed away from the fish and other predators of the watercourse, no more than a metre deep, and magnetically appealing not only to newts but to ducks and wading birds, woodcock and snipe that exploded from the pond edges at the sound of approaching footsteps.

A few days after the funeral I saw Chris for the first time since the accident. I was sitting alone in the sunshine at the edge of the big pond mid-morning. Without a hint of awkwardness, Chris walked across the meadow and sat next to me on the grass. 'This pond is bedding in well, isn't it?' he said, choosing not to acknowledge in words the catastrophe that had engulfed my world just three weeks earlier but registering his sympathy in his eyes and the gentle tone of his voice. 'Have you seen the newt ponds? They're really coming to life as well.'

'Are you busy? Shall we go and have a look at them?' I asked, rising to my feet, surprising myself with my eagerness. Grief had been energy-sapping; I felt perennially exhausted, finding it difficult to do anything much. Even answering a message had become a tall order. Outside of the funeral and the grief kibbutz, I hadn't seen people. I couldn't face it.

Each of the newt ponds had the appearance of a small crater blasted into the blue-brown clay that lay beneath the green. It was as if a cluster of small meteors had thumped into Cannwood. The ponds were filled quickly by April's spring showers, and the water, loaded still with a yellowish sediment, was beginning to settle. It hadn't taken long for the seeds of pond plants to find their way to the banks, transported in the plumage of ducks; seedlings of brooklime, figwort, rushes, and, poignantly, yellow flag iris jostled amid submerged grasses around the water's edge. Beside one, we stopped to squat and peer into the shallows. A fat green frog made a plop as it leapt into the water before us and swam breaststroke to lie submerged, flat against the clay near the middle of the pond. A steady inflow of animals busy colonising the pond and its surrounds filled the atmosphere with a soft humming.

We made our way in a loop from one of the newt ponds to the next and on to the top of the stream. 'We should rewiggle it,' Chris said. 'Right now, it's just a straight ditch, dry for most of the year, and no good for wildlife. We should restore its natural bends. It's really easy to do with a digger.' I was sold instantly.

Drawing inspiration from Stage Zero, a method for restoring entire river systems that is taking off across America, and now here in the British Isles and Europe too, we planned to fill in the entire length of the ditch, and create in its place a broad and shallow, naturally meandering stream. A river system, Chris explained, is a bit like a lung. A huge network of small brooks and streams are its bronchioles, feeding the tributaries, which in turn flow down into the main channel of the river. The state of these little streams determines the health of the whole river system. Modifying them into artificially straight, deeply incised drainage ditches triggers a flashing of water through the system every time it rains, often leading to catastrophic flooding downstream. This type of engineering of streams across the landscape similarly gives rise to drought. Early summer hosepipe bans after it has rained all winter trigger howls of dismay but are the price we pay for doing away with the gently meandering streams that once threaded our valleys, giving the landscape the ability to absorb and hold back water for gradual release throughout the year.

I thought about the project all the time, even a little obsessively. It was late August when the work began; the first hints of autumn carried on the breeze. Chris used a digger to drag down the soil and clay from both sides, filling the whole ditch that ran the length of three fields and digging in its place a shallow channel that snaked back and forth between a series of big oaks along the hedge line. Garry worked with a chainsaw to clear a path for the digger. We made the stream shallow enough to allow the water to flood outwards, creating semi-permanent pools on either side. Deeper pools studded the length of the rewiggled watercourse, permanent water that would offer summer refuge to wild aquatic creatures. In my imagination, a succulent ribbon wetland would soon run along the length of the valley bottom, noisy with the chirruping of insects, amphibians and birds.

The babbling, meandering streams and rivers that once threaded every valley and floodplain in Britain have almost all been engineered away. In urban areas, many streams have been buried altogether, relegated to underground sewers. The result has been the annihilation of our water meadows and their strange, uniquely fragrant wildflowers and grasses, whose names recall a bucolic past: sweet vernal-grass, marsh marigold, ragged-robin, marsh bedstraw, bugle, water forget-me-not, cocksfoot, meadow foxtail, crested dog's-tail. Such wildflowers and grasses were once interwoven with more vigorous wetland sedges and rushes in an exquisite tapestry that stretched along the bottom of valleys the length and breadth of Britain. These wetlands were not only home to a cacophony of frogs, newts, toads, dragonflies, butterflies and myriad other insects, waterbirds, songbirds, otters and wildlife of all kinds, but they also provided nature with vital corridors through the landscape, staving off the genetic isolation that now threatens so many species confined to increasingly fragmented islands of wildness.

Once the work was done, I walked up and down the dry, snaking bed of the new stream several times each day. I caught myself gazing down at it from a bathroom window. There was no rain, and the earth and clay were soon baked hard, but in my imagination, this was already a paradise. We knelt to plant plugs of tussock sedge along the banks using a small hand trowel, as well as common reeds and some raspberry plant stems cut near the base, for the fun of it. We carefully placed several boughs across the shallow channel to slow the flow of water and create small flooded areas. The scrub that had been cut away from the hedgerow was stacked in three large mounds alongside the stream to create habitat for insects, birds and other wildlife. Then, at the start of September, with everything set, it rained for the first time. A light mist fell as I walked the dogs in the fading of the light, turning to drizzle, and then a metallic scent in the air and the distant rumble of approaching thunder heralded a deluge that later thrummed on the roof and the windows as I fell asleep next to Jemima. Early the following morning, I awoke to the rising sun streaming through a gap in the curtains and made my way directly down to find the stream in full flow, the water galloping around the bends, eddying over obstacles, filling the deeper pools, spreading outwards as it advanced towards the big pond. Was I allowed to feel happy? Cautiously, I greeted an unfamiliar sense of joy that coyly hovered, tentatively awaiting permission to wash over me as I plodded through the shallow water, checking the young plants were not being washed away.

The new stream, and thoughts of restoration, became an essential escape from the endless anxiety that otherwise gripped me. I wondered why what we had done here wasn't being done everywhere. I longed for every single river system in Britain to be restored to life in this way. It would be so easy to do. Rewiggling the little streams and tributaries that make up our rivers would take a tiny fraction of our agricultural land out of production. In any case, the valley bottoms are typically awkward to farm. A small payment per acre to farmers in return for setting aside 20 or so metres on either side of their newly rewiggled watercourses would be repaid many times over in terms of reduced flooding and drought, soil protected from erosion, cleaner water, carbon sucked out of the atmosphere, nature reconnected and resuscitated, and the spirit of a nation inspired. Ecologist John Lawton famously declared that to save Britain's nature, we must think 'bigger, better and more joined up'. Well, this, it occurred to me, is how we join it up. Playing my part in making this happen, spreading the word, hustling and haranguing, may be how I begin to piece myself back together.

4

Autumn

To every thing there is a season, and a time to every purpose
under the heaven:
A time to be born, and a time to die; a time to plant, and
a time to pluck up that which is planted;
A time to kill, and a time to heal; a time to break down,
and a time to build up;
A time to weep, and a time to laugh; a time to mourn, and
a time to dance;
ECCLESIASTES 3:1–4

Each day that summer seemed an endurance test. The hours ticked by slowly. Meanwhile, the weeks flew past, and soon autumn began to make its presence felt, barely perceptible at first, a slight chill in the evening air, gusts of wind that sent the first set of expired, tattered leaves fluttering from the trees, collecting in small mounds on the ground. A ripeness became apparent all around. The branches of the apple, pear and plum trees hung low with fruit, and hedges began to glisten with blackberries. We gathered chestnuts to roast using a heavy wrought-iron pan on an open fire in front of the house; Jemima cooked endlessly, building up a large store of jams, preserves, chutneys, pies and cakes.

Iris was an autumn person, 'an *autumnal* creature,' my mother used to say, never forgetting to add that Iris's colours, so individual to her, were the colours of autumn: rosy cheeks and beautiful auburn hair. Walking up the lane on a past blustery autumn day, I remember mulling with Iris how the wind seems to become visible to us in the autumn, a sinewy, shape-shifting form traced by the plumes of falling leaves, making a strange dance, twisting and circling, playing grandmother's footsteps with itself, slow then fast, at times disappearing altogether before beginning again. Iris was constantly dancing, even when there was no music. I don't remember her ever just walking anywhere. I can picture her movements so clearly: in my mind's eye, it's autumn and Iris is skipping to school along a pavement heaped high with leaves; or she's doing gymnastics beneath the horse chestnut halfway down the front garden at Cannwood. They were always gathering things, Iris and the Dreamers girls: flowers, acorns, chestnuts, conkers, buckets of fallen apples for the Tamworth pigs in the woods. In autumn, she shone, this being not least the start of the school year. I think she relished getting back to work, back to being busy, a bright star bursting with creative energy. Now, as we rolled inexorably into autumn, I dreaded leaving her behind in the summer that was now slipping away. She ought to have been here.

The gathering of gangs of house martins and swallows that tittered as they prepared to make their long journey south brought fresh pangs of grief. Their return to Cannwood each spring has always been such a joyful moment. In recent years, we took to welcoming them back by digging out a large square of turf and watering the clay-rich mud underneath to provide an easy source of cement for nest building. The swallows build theirs each year in the joinery of the stable ceilings, cartwheeling in and out of the windows all day. Meanwhile, true to their name, the house martins choose to build theirs in a tight row under the eaves, along the length of the front of the house just outside the bedroom windows on the top floor. Their endless chatter makes it impossible for anyone sleeping in those rooms to get up late. The sky above Cannwood is filled with the wheeling and twittering of these mesmerising summer visitors until come September or October, finally, they up-sticks and leave, having raised two or even three nestfuls of young. This year I didn't want them to go.

There is a kind of music in the way innumerable tiny birds cross continents and oceans, a back and forth rhythm, following a route taken by their kind for millennia. These vast journeys, from the skies of West Africa back to the very spot where they were born, are a feat of unimaginable endurance and extraordinary precision. Seasonal migrations provide the rhythm by which we experience the passing of the seasons. We are so lucky to live alongside them for part of our year, in quite good numbers in Somerset still. It's not just swallows and martins that raise their young in the British Isles before heading south for winter. Warblers of various kinds; spotted and pied flycatchers; wheatears; whinchats; redstarts; nightingales; yellow wagtails; tree pipits; cuckoos – whose vanishing call heralds the arrival of each spring – swifts; mysterious nightjars, which haunt village streetlamps by night hunting for moths; turtle doves; dragonfly-hunting hobbies; fish-hunting ospreys; terns and shearwaters; all of these come and go with the seasons. In turn, visitors from the north take their place, themselves fleeing winters harsher than our own. Birds that arrive in the British Isles for winter include fieldfares and redwings, which gather in large and noisy mixed flocks, hopping from one frosty patch of scrub to the next; bramblings; Bewick's and whooper swans;

as well as all manner of ducks, geese and wading birds. Then there are certain species that we swap like for like each year, such as blackcaps. The males of these dapper greyish warblers have the blackcaps that give them their name; females have chestnut caps. The blackcap's delightful fluting song has earned it the nickname 'northern nightingale'. Blackcaps from eastern Europe are increasingly spending their winters here before heading back eastwards in the spring, only to be replaced by British-born blackcaps returning from their southern European and African wintering grounds.

Almost nowhere is the terrible depletion of nature more apparent than in the decline of migratory birds. Wantonly, we make their great journeys impossible, and the losses have been catastrophic. Since 1980, the year I was born, we have lost two-thirds of the cuckoos that once spent their summer here, largely because of the deterioration of nature along their migration route between here and their wintering grounds in sub-Saharan Africa. The turtle dove – our only migrating species of dove and a symbol of love through the ages for its monogamous tenderness – has declined by more than 90 per cent during the same period. Facing a range of threats along its flyway, including the loss of critical habitats and merciless hunting, the gentle turtle dove looks likely to be the first of our migratory birds to disappear completely. In modern times most of us have never even heard the melancholic nightly song of the nightingale, once the sound of the British night in summer, inspiring poets for centuries. Nightingale numbers are in freefall, as their winter homes amid the great mosaic of forests and wetlands across the African humid zone of Sierra Leone, Senegal, the Gambia and Burkina Faso are razed and drained for agriculture.

Smack in the middle of the immense East Atlantic Flyway, one of the world's nine major flyway systems, the British

Isles are of global importance for migratory birds. Our own remaining wetlands, already so dramatically reduced in size during the last century, are particularly vital, along with our long coastline, islands, cliffs and the great river estuaries, all of which provide millions of breeding seabirds with a place to stop, feed and rest, before continuing their journey north or south. Bewilderingly, there's no concerted effort by the UK government or any other public institution to protect and restore this or any of the other great flyways. A single seemingly small act of environmental vandalism, such as the draining or pollution of a wetland stepping stone along the way, can decimate a whole species.

If you've ever been fleetingly conscious of a dark, arrow-shaped predatory form flitting by at the very periphery of your arc of vision, most likely it was a hobby, the smallest of our hawks, lightning fast, a specialist at chasing down dragonflies. Hobbies are massacred in vast numbers, for sport, as they pass through the Mediterranean, along with tens of millions of other migratory birds, in one of the most flagrant acts of ecocide in the western world. Up to four million turtle doves are slaughtered on their migration each year. Storks, thrushes, songbirds of all kinds and even robins are blasted from the sky, mostly just for the amusement of it. Malta, Cyprus, Lebanon and the southern areas of Spain and France are particularly notorious for the illegal killing of migratory birds.

Killing creatures to eat them is perhaps more justifiable than killing them for fun, and in some parts of the Mediterranean tiny migrating songbirds are eaten whole, in what seems to me a particularly repellent and now illegal culinary delicacy known as 'Ortolan'. There is a type of bunting named an ortolan, but in fact, songbirds of all kinds end up in this dish during the migration season. The pitiful calls of a solitary caged bird are used to lure others into bushes whose branches are lined with glue.

Stuck fast, the entrapped birds wriggle and writhe to escape before succumbing to exhaustion and dehydration. Those trapped alive using mist nets are kept in darkness for weeks, or blinded, stuffed with grains and grapes, so they become fat, this being the key ingredient to the decadence of this dish when cooked. The birds are then cast live into a vat of Armagnac brandy, which both drowns and marinades them before they are roasted. Ortolan is meant to be eaten feet-first and whole, except for the beak, with a napkin placed over your head – to savour the aromas, or as the tradition goes, to hide your shame from God. Restaurant critic Anthony Bourdain described his own ortolan experience in his 2010 book *Medium Raw*.

> *I bring my molars down and through my bird's rib cage with a wet crunch and am rewarded with a scalding hot rush of burning fat and guts down my throat. Rarely have pain and delight combined so well. I'm giddily uncomfortable, breathing in short, controlled gasps as I continue slowly – ever so slowly – to chew. With every bite, as the thin bones and layers of fat, meat, skin, and organs compact in on themselves, there are sublime dribbles of varied and wondrous ancient flavors: figs, Armagnac, dark flesh slightly infused with the salty taste of my own blood as my mouth is pricked by the sharp bones. As I swallow, I draw in the head and beak, which, until now, have been hanging from my lips, and blithely crush the skull.*

The slaughter of most migrating birds, at least, is not a British occurrence, and the autumn heralds the arrival at Cannwood of a whole new avian cast, many of which are varied thrushes from Scandinavia, who spend their time flitting in mixed flocks between the open ground and the higher branches of the old oaks on the periphery. As the start of a new school term loomed, I turned repeatedly to daydreaming of nature, aching listlessly over the damage we do and over what it would take to put things right. Often, I walked with only my younger children, little Eliza and Arlo, in their boots down to the wood and followed at a small distance as they tumbled ahead along paths used regularly by badgers, deer or boar, climbing, falling, running back to show me an empty swirling snail shell or the cup of one of last year's acorns. Periodically we gathered to clamber over fallen boughs, looking for toads, fat slugs, woodlice and those fast-moving, lithe black beetles known as devil's coach horses. I was theatrical in my enthusiasm for whatever we found and made a point of urging the children to catch up and gently hold the little creatures for a few moments before placing them back on the ground. Mostly I dawdled as they played, turning over the coals of my intensifying conviction that the overriding purpose of our time is to work out how to re-integrate ourselves frictionlessly back into the miracle of nature, before we destroy everything completely.

Protecting and nurturing our migratory birds, bringing them back from the brink and restoring them to their former abundance would be symbolic of a new era of restoration. A concerted effort would be required, initiated by the United Kingdom, to protect and restore our own great flyway. We would need an East Atlantic Flyway Treaty, brought about through a diplomatic effort made with our neighbours, combined with money from our international development budget, to heal and protect key habitats and eliminate illegal hunting in countries along the full length of the flyway. We would support and coordinate with the heroic little organisations already working at the grassroots across the Mediterranean and in Africa, often in difficult and dangerous circumstances, to expose and combat the hunting of migratory birds. Most importantly, we would set about weaving back together our own desperately depleted landscapes so that migrating birds have what they need to thrive and breed successfully when they're here. Our goal would be to demonstrate to the rest of the world how a major migratory bird flyway can be returned to health and rich abundance. Life in Britain without the comings and goings of our migratory birds, so central to our own psychic wellbeing, is simply unimaginable.

As Cannwood has grown wilder and messier in recent years, the swallows and house martins here at least appear to have been growing in number. To birds, hedgerows are merely organised lines of thorny scrub, an essential habitat for many species, providing wildlife with shelter, nesting sites and food in the form of berries, nuts and insects. Since arriving here ourselves, we have allowed our hedges to grow fat and bushy, forming great buttresses of pink and white blossom in the early spring and heaving with berries each autumn; the vivid red fruit of hawthorn, holly and dog rose, the pink of spindle, black-blue sloes in an abundance that makes the branches sag, medlars and varied wild plums, crab apples, pears, and of course blackberries, all garlanded with countless tiny spiders' webs that glimmer with the morning dew. We leave wide margins of unruly, uncut herbage around field margins, along the lanes and in other nooks and corners, creating more winter cover and food.

There is a control fetish in the way that much of our countryside is managed. Across Britain, an obsession with order has been a disaster, not just for migratory birds but for the entire living world. You see it in suburban gardens, each one a small warzone in which a chemical and mechanical arsenal is used to keep real nature out, maintaining in its place a pretend, sterile version of our own making, perfectly manicured lawn, trimmed shrubs and regimented beds of garish, imported flowers. Nine out of ten British households have a garden. Together, these add up to an area larger than all the Wildlife Trusts' reserves combined. Tidiness reigns supreme in most of these, and, in a minority, there are no plants at all, just hard paving, decking or ecologically ruinous plastic turf.

Road verges, often the last refuge for the wildflowers that once carpeted Britain before the advent of chemically 'improved' pasture, and the butterflies and other invertebrates that depend on them, are regularly strimmed, sprayed and mown to within an inch of their lives – at great expense. Scrub, essential for wildlife but much maligned, is cleared away wherever it is found; in parks, alongside rivers and railways. Dead trees, so important for insects and the woodpeckers that prey on them, richer benefactors even in death than they were in life, are felled and tidied away as a matter of course.

Perhaps our desire for control is understandable in small spaces, but on farms and estates, where the land is so often dominated by unnecessary fences and where fallen trees are typically treated as an excrescence, it is harder to accept. Most landowners unthinkingly hack back their hedgerows once yearly, leaving puny, patchy, fruitless lines that are of no use to wildlife. How easy just to cut them less harshly and less frequently, and why not do it later, after the berries have seen hungry wildlife through the winter? Allowing nature a little leeway to grow unkempt costs us nothing and, in many cases, actually saves us money. But mostly, these decisions are not financially driven: they result from an unbending insistence on *order* that pervades the British consciousness.

But change is in the air, undoubtedly. During the first pandemic lockdown in the spring of 2020, something may have changed. As the weeks of confinement rolled on, people everywhere seemed to be refashioning a new, more intimate relationship with nature. For a while, the pace of life slowed for nearly everyone. The pandemic, in all its awfulness, and the panicked, draconian response of governments to it, provided an opportunity for people to explore nature local to them and to reflect on the beauty of the world. The disappearance of traffic provided a glimpse of how clear the air can be if we choose it, how riotous the birdsong, how rich with wildflowers the road verges become when left unmown. A new upwelling of love for nature is being felt across our society, alongside a growing understanding that one of the keys to restoring it is to learn how let go, to grant other species greater autonomy in the functioning of ecosystems, and to embrace unruliness, just a little, here and there. And given the chance, nature rebounds astonishingly quickly. Many councils up and down the United Kingdom have put a stop to the mowing of road-verge wildflower meadows. The rail network is becoming a haven for butterflies. Isabella Tree's seminal book *Wilding*, which tells the story of an industrial farm returned to nature in all its dishevelled, self-willed glory, topped the bestseller list for months. Land agents and farm advisors were inundated with requests for guidance on how to begin the process of restoring nature. As a nation, it has begun to feel as if we have been reawakened, amid the unfurling of a spring that year which seemed especially vibrant, to the vitality of diverse, healthy, abundant nature in our lives.

In the September after Iris died, when I arrived to take Frankie to his boarding school, her things for school were packed neatly in several large storage bags beside a washing machine. She had prepared everything at the start of the summer holiday to save herself the trouble later. Kate hadn't touched them since. It rained a little as we took the motorway west towards Eton, the back of the car piled high with Frankie's bags. Thirteen-year-old Frankie sat in the front, brave beside his mother; I sat behind him in the back. We did our best to be upbeat, the three of us, but for Kate and me, the recollection of Iris's first day at Wycombe Abbey two years earlier hung heavy. It didn't feel so long since it had been me making this journey for the first time with my mother. With a fixed smile concealing gritted teeth, I went about that familiar place alongside Kate, unloading bags, pinning up photographs and posters, meeting the housemaster and the dame, who would be responsible for the pastoral care of the boys in the house, and finally making our way into the historic chapel for the grand welcome service.

I was sick with nostalgia and grief as we headed slowly up the stone steps among a sea of new boys and their parents. Iris would have been so proud of her younger brother starting out here. As we took our seats in one of the old oak pews, a handful of her friends made a point of coming by to whisper 'Hi' to Frankie, older boys who would look out for him in the coming weeks. I cried unnoticed behind the palm of my hand, head stooped, as we sang the hymn *I Vow to Thee My Country*. We sat, and the Eton headmaster rose to address us. I felt as if I were floating above the congregation as he concluded softly with words borrowed from the poem 'On Children' by the great Kahlil Gibran, words that seemed in that moment directed only at me:

> *Your children are not your children. They are the sons and daughters of Life's longing for itself. They come through you but not from you, and though they are with you yet they belong not to you ... For their souls dwell in the house of tomorrow, which you cannot visit, not even in your dreams ... you are the bows from which your children as living arrows are sent forth. The archer sees the mark upon the path of the infinite, and He bends you with His might.*

I leaned over and said to Kate in a whisper: 'We did our best, Kate.'

5

Medium

In sorrow we must go, but not in despair. Behold! We are not bound forever to the circles of the world, and beyond them is more than memory.

J. R. R. TOLKIEN

It occurred to me very early on that the best people for me to call on were other parents I knew who had lost a child. I wanted to spend time in the presence of people who really understood; I wanted to know what to do, how to cope with this. When I got through to these people on the phone, I didn't need to say much – they knew, and mostly I sobbed wordlessly down the phone. One afternoon I rang the mother of an old school friend, James Hooper, whose funny, kind, lanky older brother Edward had died with two friends in an appalling car crash at the age of 19, the first death among our young circle. James had asked me to travel down to Wales to be with him in the days before Edward's funeral. I remember starkly the courage of his mother, whose words down the phone to me in the aftermath of Iris's accident reverberated comfortingly for days: 'A short life has no less validity than a long one.' Thinking back to when Edward Hooper died, I remembered the hushed voices of visitors around the family and how his belongings were strewn about the house as if he had just popped out for a short while. Now I understood that I was part of an invisible club made up of parents unlucky enough to lose one or more of their children, a much rarer event now than it had once been. I made a little list of those I knew, an indistinct plan forming in my mind to see each of them, but mostly I made the list to underscore to myself that we were not alone in having suffered this unfathomable, unacceptable injustice. There were others, others that I knew, in some cases that I'd known all my life.

At the top of my list was my own mother, Annabel, who had lost her oldest son Rupert when I was seven. Second on my list was Kathleen O'Hara, author of a book entitled *A Grief Like No Other: Surviving the Violent Death of Someone You Love*, her son having been brutally murdered on the cusp of adulthood 20 years previously. Kathleen had chosen afterwards to devote her life to helping other parents survive the only thing I had ever imagined I myself could not overcome. My friend George Frost had arranged for me to see her at Cannwood. Appearing, Mary Poppins-like, just days after Iris had died, Kathleen continued to counsel me, Kate and the boys throughout the whole of that first year, at first weekly and then less regularly. Sitting with this remarkable lady who had survived the unimaginable, her head held high, her dark hair immaculate, kindness, understanding and gentle good humour radiating from her face, gave us some kind of a foothold. I longed for her visits to Cannwood. In one of our conversations, two mugs of tea steaming between us in the quiet of the big barn sitting room, Kathleen asked me if I had dreamed of Iris since she died. I said I hadn't. Indeed, I hadn't even thought about my dreams; until one night, I dreamed of Iris.

Asleep in my bed, I dreamed I was sitting in one of the big armchairs in the drawing room at Cannwood, low and deep, with an unusually big cushion in the back. Reclining on a Saturday evening, a drink somewhere close to hand, I was enjoying watching the children jumping around, dancing to music as they often did in that room before dinner. Iris may have been 11 or 12 in my dream, and she was leaping long-legged in her blue jeans and t-shirt between the big pouffe table at the centre of the room and a large sofa against the wall, grinning widely. The other children were doing their own thing but each with one eye on what Iris was doing. Leaning forward, I grabbed Iris by the forearm as she passed within reach, and I drew her close. We hugged. Basking in the bliss of being with my girl for those few moments, I didn't know that she was dead, and yet somewhere deep down, I did, as is the way with dreams.

We held each other tightly, and I felt an incomparable joy, tears streaming, my face pressed to her right temple. I don't remember ever previously having been aware of being able to smell anything much while dreaming, but on this occasion I was acutely conscious of the smell of Iris's hair. Every parent knows the unique smell of their child. Waking abruptly, my pillow soaked with tears, the smell of my daughter vivid in my recollection, I rolled over, reaching for Jemima in the darkness. I buried my face in her shoulder, sobbing uncontrollably at the remembering, before falling back asleep under the weight of the half-Xanax I'd allowed myself before dinner. The following day I revisited my dream over and over, smiling to myself in an unbearable longing as I toyed with the recollection, torturing myself but unable to resist the urge to feel and press the bruise. I understood why some grieving parents say that they yearn for these dreams, for they are the only place they can be with their lost child.

During my first week back in London, I had made a point of carving out windows of time to walk alone, knowing I'd need that space each day. Mostly I walked up Curzon Street and down into the underpass running beneath that horrible urban motorway, Park Lane, which cleaves Mayfair from Hyde Park. I've often wondered how it must have felt to stroll through Mayfair in times gone by and out to the park across old Park Lane, a boulevard of Parisian splendour lined with some of the finest great houses in London on one side, and an avenue of grand plane trees on the other. My mother had been born in one of those houses, long since demolished and replaced by the Metropolitan Hotel, overlooking the motorway. How could those vandals of 1960s urban planning have blasted an uncrossable six-lane road through a place of such beauty? Emerging from the underpass on the other side and passing through a pedestrian gate into the park, I fell into a routine of walking the full circuit of the Serpentine lake. Sometimes I detoured to buy a coffee from a café at the near end of the lake, by a corner where the water is feathered and soiled by a noisily expectant resident gaggle of Canada geese. More than before, I noticed passers-by: joshing lovers holding each other as they strolled; couples with small children, pushchairs and bread for the ducks; solitary walkers lost in thought or on their phones. Why had all of these people lived when Iris did not? If I cried as I walked, I raised a concealing hand to my eyebrow, or not. Afterwards, I felt better.

I began making plans to see some of the mothers and fathers on my list. Two, I discovered, had found figuring out how to live after their tragedy more difficult than the others, shrinking around their loss, and my conversations with those two scared me. I wondered whether that might be me and whether the rest of my life might be a prison sentence. My goodness, I thought, the rest of my family, my children, my young wife Jemima, they need me back. The remainder of my life may be very long from here, perhaps as much as 50 years; I must rediscover how to live. It struck me that the two who struggled the most had each come to the glum conclusion that what you see is what you get; life is life and death is the end, and there's no more to it than that, no hope of a higher story, nor any ongoing connection. One mother told me in a particularly dispiriting moment that she had 'searched' and found nothing. Deep down, however, this bleak assessment didn't entirely resonate with me.

One autumn morning, after dropping Isaac off at school, I went to meet one mother, a friend of a friend, for tea in her terraced house in Kensington. She had lost her son more than a decade earlier in a freak accident at the age of 14. The boy had been golden: academically gifted, charismatic, beautiful and the apple of his mother's eye. The couple have a second, surviving child, a daughter. Welcoming me into her house warmly, she led me into her front room, where we perched on two sofas at right angles, me in my navy blue suit, she in a crisp, old-fashioned white blouse tucked into a calf-length tweed skirt, hair tied in a round bun at the back of her head. Framed photographs and a collection of glass and ceramic ornaments were neatly arranged on a mahogany side table on one side of the room and some shelves above. A clock ticked in the hallway outside as she poured us both tea. In anticipation of my arrival, she had written a few notes on a piece of paper, which she unfolded carefully as we made small talk. Every bereaved parent has their toolbox, filled with thoughts and ideas that make the ordeal a little more bearable. Iris had been dead less than three months, and I had not progressed beyond the day-to-day struggle to keep myself going. For my own toolbox, I had gathered thoughts and ideas mostly from conversations with other bereaved parents.

I told myself often that even though she had only lived fifteen and a half years, Iris had led a life that was better than the lives lived, I presumed, by a significant majority of girls born throughout human history. She had enjoyed fifteen and a half years replete with love, happiness, a sense of agency, achievement and self-worth, adventure, friendships, and a love of animals and the natural world. Moreover, I felt that Iris had in some way enjoyed her own future, lived in its anticipation, even if not in actuality. When, soon after she died, we discovered a series of mind maps Iris had prepared, plotting her personal development and future, the surge of grief had almost suffocated me, but now these beautiful drawings reinforced the validity of one of my most cherished tools.

I found another of my tools in something Frankie had told me about our relative perception of time. To me, aged 39, his 14 years seemed little, while my own years seemed an eternity; yet, to my mother, who had lived 86 years, my 39 years seemed short. Iris's perception of her fifteen and a half years must have been very different to mine. To her, they were everything, all she had ever known. Simple as it is, I found this idea comforting.

I also thought endlessly about the manner of Iris's death, reassuring myself over and over that it was probably neither slow nor terribly painful. In fact, as the paramedics had explained to me, hers was about as swift and smooth a passage as a person could expect to experience. It could have been so much worse. I was grateful for that.

Never having expended much energy on questions of God or spirits or on what comes after death, I tried at times to find meaning, encountering flickers of solace in the words of some of the many people who wrote to me. Referring to Iris's unlived future, they would say that 'It wasn't meant to be'; or that 'Iris is with God now,' and briefly, I clung to the notion of a higher plan and all that it entails. Engulfed at times by a hallucinating desperation, curled up on the bathroom floor or lying foetal on the bed, I found myself crying out loud, pleading with Iris for a sign, a touch on my shoulder, a giant rainbow in the sky, or to God for guidance on where to find an ongoing connection with my daughter. What I craved more than anything else was to know that Iris's experience continued, that it wasn't all over for eternity, an unending nothingness. I'd go to any lengths to find her, I told Him. As I recovered my senses each time, I found no pathway to accepting the injustice of what had happened. There were times when I allowed myself a kind of selfishness, sometimes after more than one drink. This is my life, and I have a right to do the things I enjoy and to be happy, no matter what bad luck may have befallen anyone else, even my own daughter. Briefly, I felt liberated in such moments, at least partially. Selfishness works, for a time. But inevitably, the pain of grief soon returned with a vengeance.

As our conversation reached its end, I asked if she felt her son was still out there. 'Yes, I do. I know he is,' she replied without hesitation. Tentatively, she unfolded a second piece of paper and handed it to me. On it, she had jotted a name (let's call her Eleanor) and two telephone numbers. 'Eleanor is quite wonderful. She is a spiritualistic medium. Without her, I don't know that I'd have survived losing my son. I go to see her once a year now. It doesn't seem right to impose upon him more often that, wherever he is,' she said.

I sat at my desk, alone that morning in the office, and dialled Eleanor's telephone number from my landline. After two rings, a lady with a crisp Dutch accent answered the phone. Presuming I ought to avoid giving her any information by which she might identify me or my story, I told her that she had been helpful to my friend in the years following her son's death, and I wondered whether she might have a go at similarly helping me. I didn't expect to be so nervous. Eleanor suggested I come to her house in Fulham that very afternoon, at teatime. We agreed on 5 p.m., and I was unable to think of much else that day. I don't know if I really expected anything to happen, but just daring to wonder made my heart flutter in anticipation. The day turned out to be one of the brightest I'd had since Iris died.

I emerged into the orderly grid of late Victorian terraced streets that surround Parsons Green tube station, still wearing my suit. I rang the doorbell of Eleanor's terraced home, and almost immediately the door was opened by a grandmotherly lady who wore a modest, old-fashioned combination of a long skirt, a cashmere turtleneck jumper and pearls. She might have been an Eton house dame, self-confident, upright, elegant and kind, or a retired teacher offering extra tuition after school. I don't know exactly what I had been expecting, but I was struck by how ordinary it all seemed. This seemed like the sort of place where you might expect tea and biscuits, and if extra lessons were being had, they would be something of a pleasure.

Amid the pitter-patter of our small talk – my journey there, the unsettled weather that day – Eleanor directed me to hang my suit jacket on the hatstand in the hallway, beneath which I decided to kick off and leave my black shoes. There was nothing unusual about the front room except for a wooden tray on the round table closest to the window, on which were arranged crystals and stones of various shapes, sizes and colours. On the mantlepiece was a lit candle in a glass jar, which flickered above an unlit gas fireplace alongside a handful of framed family photographs. Above these hung a large painting of a galloping horse. So far, so suburban.

We sat in two armchairs facing each other at 45 degrees on either side of the crystals. Then, without theatre, Eleanor took a crystal in each hand and placed the backs of her hands on her knees, closing her fingers in a loose fist. Eyes shut, she began to speak immediately.

'There's a girl. My, she's a strong character, and she's been very eager to contact you. She wants you to know that she's sorry. I presume she is your daughter?'

My first thought was to wonder whether she had heard my story. I hadn't given her my name, but perhaps our mutual friend had called her following our meeting that morning. Why would she even do that? Nevertheless, the hairs on my forearms and the back of my neck tingled.

What happened next is not a story that is easy to tell. In the world we inhabit, many people are inherently sceptical about the ability of the living to contact the dead or even that the dead continue to exist in any form; indeed, I was sceptical myself. I am conflicted about sharing what was a profoundly moving and essential experience for me at that time, fearful that the telling of it may somehow undermine it. I certainly don't seek to persuade readers of the legitimacy of what came next. What I can say is that it was real for me, and the effect of the meeting was to ignite in me a burning desire to explore what may lie beyond the reality that we ordinarily perceive. Speaking quietly, eyes still closed, Eleanor told me what she was picking up from the girl whose presence she felt so strongly.

'She says that she was always in a hurry, always racing, pushing boundaries. On that day, she went too far. She was being silly; she knows that – she was going too fast, and she's sorry for what happened. But she wants you to know that this was her time; if it hadn't been this way, in that moment, then it would have happened another way.'

'Did it hurt her?' I mumbled. After a moment of silence, Eleanor went on:

'She says the last thing she remembers is being very winded, and then a rising panic at how long it took for anyone to get there. She wanted them to hurry up. Then, she didn't understand that she was dead. She had the feeling she had awoken from a dream. She was confused; she didn't know where she was or what was happening. She saw many people standing around her.'

Speaking up croakily, I asked Eleanor what she could hear that I couldn't. I asked if she could see Iris. Opening her eyes, she looked straight at me and explained simply that she had always been able to invite *contact*.

'Only when I *invite* it do I hear or see these things in the place of my imagination. I cannot explain how it happens, but I can tell you that it is not dissimilar to the feeling brought on by meditation, when you do it properly, creating a space in which intuition, imagination, emotions come to the fore from somewhere deep down. These messages seem to manifest in that place. Next time you come here, I'll show you how you might begin doing it yourself.'

Closing her eyes again, she told me that Iris loves me very much. I struggled not to cry. 'She says she wanted to play tennis with you. She's showing me a bouncing tennis ball. Her smile is soft.' The hairs on my forearms and the back of my neck fizzed once more. 'She tries to speak to you often, but you can't hear her; there's a block.' Eleanor continued. 'Her mother hears her, and one of her brothers, the younger one, but they both think it's just their imagination speaking to them.' I knew that Kate felt she had heard Iris's voice, especially in the early days and weeks, and I had humoured her whilst also envying her for the possibility it was true.

'She says you dreamed of her; she was dancing, like always. You were able to smell her in the dream.' Only Jemima and I knew about my dream. Could this be common to all bereaved parents, dreaming of our lost children, dancing, hugging? Could it have been a lucky guess? Perhaps, but one lucky guess followed another, and another.

'She's with a family dog, not big, brown, with a ball. Now she's showing me a large pink book. She wants you to open it; she's been waiting for you to look at it. She knows you're afraid of opening it, but you'll like it, she says. Please read it.'

Nobody could have known about the pink book of memories and condolences that sat still on Kate's kitchen table and which I had so far avoided reading every time I had been at the house.

'There's a teddy bear under her pillow. I hear a laugh.'

I thought of Kitty, the Hello Kitty teddy, which Iris had held tight at night, now tucked out of sight under her pillow by Kate, who felt that Iris would not have wanted her teenage friends to see it when they came to sit and mourn in her bedroom.

'She's in a place that seems like the sea, she says. All her life, she loved being on the sea, above the waves like she was flying low over the water. That's how everything feels to her now; she is dancing on the water. She understands where she is now.'

I still have a photograph of Iris's neat handwriting in the visitor book at a Corfu hotel, snapped later by a friend, thanking the hotel staff for looking after them so kindly and for the delicious pink smoothies they served at breakfast time. She wrote in the book that she had loved most of all lying on her tummy at the front of the little hotel boat, with the feeling that she was flying over the sea.

'She shows me fried eggs on toast. I see an egg and some bacon. She's laughing again; what a laugh she has. You are the cook, she says. There's a young man with her; older than her but younger than you. They're related. Is he her uncle, perhaps? He also has a wonderful laugh. It must run in the family.'

My brother Rupert, I wondered? 'How did he die?' I asked.

'He drowned in the sea. He has been with her the whole time.'

Eleanor continued after a few moments. 'She was happy when she was finding her way around London. It was all new and exciting for her. Sometimes she stayed up all night exploring the city.'

Not once did it appear to me that Eleanor went down a wrong alley only to backtrack and try another. Each of the things she recorded had meaning, often meaning only to Iris and me.

Nobody could have told her half of these things. During the hour and a half we spent together, we paused several times, and she did her best to answer my backlog of unanswerable questions. She had been sensitive to such incursions all her life, she told me, but with an ability to invite them or shut them off at will. Her mother had been the same. The longer a person has been dead, the less likely it is that she is able to channel them. It seems possible to her that any ability to communicate with the dead may be temporary, lasting a limited period in the aftermath of death. Some people appear to be unreachable for whatever reason. Souls seem to move in groups, like tribes.

'Watch the candle on the mantlepiece,' she said at one point, interrupting herself. The flame appeared before my eyes to grow to twice its previous size, burning upwards, dead straight, before falling back to flicker once more within the waxy rim of its glass jar.

'Only in certain societies in recent centuries is communion with the afterlife a taboo,' she added, explaining that dead ancestors have been celebrated and consulted in almost every society and every culture that has ever existed. Such practices are an accepted part of spiritual life in many religious traditions, especially among the animist societies of indigenous people the world over. Individuals with the gift of sensitivity often fulfil a special role in such societies, and rituals are carried out specifically to invite the presence of the spirits of the dead, sometimes involving the use of psychedelic compounds derived from plant or fungal medicines, which induce a trance-like state. Eleanor explained that whilst she doesn't subscribe to any particular religious dogma, closer to home, both Christian and Jewish mystics, or Kabbalists, 'are aware of what's out there'.

Eleanor was explicit when she told me that my visiting her would offer me no way out of my grief. She could not solve my problem. She seemed to imply that it might not be healthy, even, for Iris or for me, to invite this kind of contact again and again. She said that the best outcome from such an extraordinarily productive session, as she described it, was the reassurance I had received that my daughter is still with me. Eleanor invited me to come back for a lesson in meditation so that I could try to open myself up to the possibility of an ongoing inner connection with my daughter. With that, having agreed to return the following week, I went out into the early evening drizzle. I felt as if the world I had known was somehow cracked open, and something extraordinary beyond had been revealed to me. I felt ecstatic that Iris's existence may not have simply ended on the day of the accident.

I walked on, astounded. Stopping at a newsagent on the corner, I bought myself a packet of cigarettes. I had smoked as a teenager, then given up when Iris was born, and now I was a smoker again. My lungs ached a little, and I knew I would have to stop soon. I crossed the busy road and sat at an outside table in front of a little café. Shakily, I lit a cigarette. The server brought me some tea. I think I was crying, which was nothing unusual at that time. By chance, my cousin Cosima, who I hadn't seen since the funeral, happened to walk past. She sat with me, hugged me, and I began to tell her falteringly what had happened. Smiling, Cosima wasn't in the least bit sceptical. I think that was when I started to wonder how I could have spent my entire life until that point living unquestioningly under the assumption that what you see is all there is, when nearly everyone else in the world has been living in an alternative reality.

My experience that afternoon in that front room gave me comfort in a way that nothing else so far had. It gave me cause to wonder in seriousness whether our conscious existence really is ongoing in some unfathomable way after we die. Perhaps the great majority of humans who have walked the earth through time were not deluded in their belief that there is an existence beyond death. Perhaps it really is possible to communicate with the dead. In the days that followed, I daydreamed incessantly about what may lie beyond our ordinary human perception. Our eyes can view only a minuscule fraction of the vast electromagnetic spectrum that crackles around us. Our ears are capable of hearing less than 1 per cent of the available range of sound. Living our lives within the tiniest of bands of perception, we are, in truth, blind and deaf to much of the physical reality we know is out there, leaving plenty of scope for open minds to daydream of a metaphysical reality beyond even that and to hope. As time has passed, I've come to grasp that learning to accept something so terrible as the loss of your child is difficult without any hope of a grander scheme of some kind, beyond the reaches of our comprehension. The alternative, death and the end of experience in a vast meaningless void, is simply too stark.

A week later, I arrived for our second session, which wasn't obviously different from the first. Eleanor recorded the presence of Iris, but this time she spoke more softly, hesitantly even, guiding me as to how I should sit, where I should place my hands, instructing me on how to calm my mind. She told me that I must do my best to silence my thoughts, or rather to observe them and allow them to drift by like clouds. She told me to imagine myself sitting quietly in a place I love. I selected the wildflower meadow in summer at Cannwood. I pictured myself sitting cross-legged in the middle of that meadow, among the flowers, the sound of the birds singing and the insects humming around me. I did my best not to give free rein to the endless stream of thoughts that kept popping up in my head.

'Iris says she is worried about her grandmothers, especially the older one, your mother. She thinks they've been forgotten in all of this. They're putting on a brave face, outwardly coping, but suffering terribly in silence. Your mother fears her own death. She wants you to pay attention to her.'

She was right, and from that day, Kate and I both made an extra effort to check in on and spend time with both of Iris's grandmothers.

Kate always had a mystical inclination, but it's not something we discussed much when we were married because it was a topic that never resonated with me. From the moment of Iris's death, Kate had considered the synchronicity of the dates – the death of Iris on the anniversary of the death of her own father *and* the birthday of the first children of both her brother James and her sister Alice – a marker of something otherworldly, a signpost that events aren't necessarily random. I believe that Kate drew some comfort from the experience I described to her, and I know that she has since been to see Eleanor, who never asked me for any payment. Even so, after I saw her for the second time, I asked Cosima, who lives nearby, to drop a thank-you card and some money in an envelope through her letterbox on my behalf.

Returning home to Cannwood, I walked with a new sense of attentiveness, feeling for signs. I found fresh poignancy in the shafts of sunlight that broke through the clouds to illuminate the fields and trees. I found new meaning in the beauty of the purple loosestrife that by now was bursting into its autumn colour as everything else died back along the wilder edges of the pond. The spiritual medium had opened my mind to an idea, real to me for the first time now, that Iris may be ever-present all around me. I heard myself talking to the wind and perhaps even meaning it.

'Are you here, Iris? I miss you so much, my little love.'

6

Early Me

And this our life, exempt from public haunt, finds tongues
in trees, books in the running brooks, sermons in stones, and
good in everything. I would not change it.
WILLIAM SHAKESPEARE,
As You Like It

My experience with the spiritual medium was profoundly unsettling, especially as I had never been religious, at least not in the conventional sense of the word. A belief in life after death is central to all faiths, but it was just not an idea I had shared.

Even a close brush with death in my late teens had not changed that. We had been travelling to Kenya when the British Airways jumbo jet on which we were flying was hijacked by a terrified schizophrenic, who had waited for one of the pilots to leave the cockpit before forcing himself between the other and his controls, and plunging the plane towards the Sudanese desert beneath. During the tussle, the plane fell from the sky before climbing steeply as the co-pilot got the upper hand; an aerodynamic stall followed, and the plane fell silently again, this time inverting as it plunged. Passengers, bags and a food trolley were strewn in the aisles. In our cabin, we recited the Lord's Prayer during a momentary lull in the chaos, a stewardess with a broken ankle sobbing in the aisle yards in front of me. Upstairs, aided by a passenger from the front row, the captain had managed to smash through the cockpit door, and the two of them dragged out the hijacker as the co-pilot saved the aeroplane just seconds from the point of no recovery. We landed an hour later at Nairobi Airport amid a phalanx of emergency and military vehicles; the injured passengers and crew were carried out first on stretchers, including the co-pilot, who sat up on two elbows, his white shirt drenched in blood. I stopped to rattle off our story to a news crew on the ground. I remember the hours and days that followed were filled with a sense of extraordinary disbelief that we were still alive. I realised how easy it is to die, so the experience injected a sense of urgency into everything that I did, but not any kind of existential searching.

In so far as I had ever given the idea any thought, my view had always been that we live on through those who carry our genes: our children, nieces, nephews and grandchildren, and through our achievements when alive. Outside school, there just wasn't much religion in my early life. At the Mall, a day school in Twickenham where I spent the first nine years of school life, we sang hymns and listened as occasional bible stories were read to us in assembly, but that was about it. For a brief period, I became fascinated with Jesus, particularly the cruel manner of His death on the cross. Always an obsessive, eccentric child, I remember learning by heart the words of *There is a Green Hill Far Away*, a hymn which still gives me an odd, melancholic feeling in my belly. I was so taken by the story of the crucifixion that I persuaded Steve Hannigan, the young gardener at Ormeley, a Scottish Highlander and one of my childhood heroes, to help me build a replica cross. Somewhat bemused, he agreed, and we nailed together two thick lengths of dark, cobweb-encrusted wood that we found at the back of the garage. I still remember the pungent smell of that wood, which must have once been treated with a chemical preservative. The cross was heavy, but I was just about able to lug it around the garden on my back, labouring up and down until Mimi, who was more than our nanny, a kind of second mother really, shouted down at me to pack it in. She had been watching me from the window of her bathroom at the top of the house and was naturally a little disturbed by the sight of an eight-year-old child seemingly acting out the Passion in the garden beneath her. She hurried downstairs to tell me I was blaspheming, so we dug the makeshift cross into the ground to about my height (and hers) using a spade borrowed from the gardener's shed. We chose a spot under a large evergreen oak at the back of the garden where several weeks earlier, we'd mournfully buried our much-loved but unfortunate puppy Jasper, who had somehow managed to escape the big white gates at the front of the house and had been flattened by a passing car on Ham Gate Avenue.

As a child, I had sometimes wondered if perhaps I was Jewish, which was certainly the assumption of some of my teachers and the parents of some of my friends. I knew I was a *quarter* Jewish because of my father's father, Frank Goldsmith (born Goldschmidt), but the distinction between blood and religion was lost on me. At the age of seven, I was christened by the Church of England, at the same time as my older sister Jemima. My mother walked us around the corner to the little church in Petersham, where it all happened without much ceremony. I'd never been in an empty church before that day, and I remember dashing about the oaky, echoey space and up into the pulpit, peering over the lectern only to see my mother, trying very hard not to laugh and frantically gesticulating at me from behind the aged vicar to come back down. I think my sister had decided to get confirmed at school along with the rest of her group of friends and had needed to be christened beforehand, so my mother had decided to get us both done at once. I had no idea what any of it meant and simply went through the motions. It was all very quick: a prayer, a few words repeated after the vicar by my mother, a splash of water, and that was that. I still have the candle somewhere.

It was at Eton that I was confirmed at the age of 15. All pupils were expected to attend pre-school chapel several mornings a week, during which we would belt out the hymns as loud as we could in a show of teenage exuberance. There was also an irregular but compulsory Sunday morning service, after which we were free to do what we wanted. I did my best to shirk that much-longer service as often as I could. Fully clothed, I made myself pancake flat under the duvet as our boarding house dame did her rounds. Once she'd finished checking all the rooms for miscreants and mess, and when I was sure all was quiet, I'd creep out and make a dash for Windsor and Eton Riverside railway station, hop on the train to Richmond and be at Ormeley comfortably in time for Sunday lunch.

One of the big attractions of getting confirmed at Eton was the promise of several days off school, supposedly time for reflection. I needed no persuading, although my godfather, Evelyn de Rothschild, an imperious, impossibly grand figure (though unfailingly warm and kind to me), did raise his eyebrows on hearing the news. I presume he felt I ought to have been raised Jewish, as well as doubting whether I was doing this for the right reasons, and he brought an air of kindly disapproval to the proceedings on the day itself. In the run-up to the ceremony, one of the school vicars, Mr Mullins, a gentle, bespectacled beanpole of a man, hosted a small group of us at his home each week for tea and cakes made by Mrs Mullins, and a fireside chat about spirituality, morality, Jesus and God.

I don't remember being much of an active participant in those conversations. The subject matter seemed dry to me, remote from my own passions, all of which revolved around the natural world.

Christianity, as I encountered it during my childhood, simply didn't appeal much to me. I found the dutiful recital and celebration of dusty revelations granted to people who had lived centuries earlier uninspiring. I do remember observing my housemaster Mr Fisher one evening before the chapel service had begun, quietly kneeling at the alter saying his prayers, and it struck me as interesting – fanciful even – to see this rational, intelligent man, who was a science teacher, silently conferring with some invisible, all-knowing, all-powerful being. It never occurred to me that Mr Fisher's god had any connection with my god, which was nature. While people like Mr Fisher had to summon their powers of imagination when it came to their deity, I could immerse myself in my own visible god whenever I liked. I would never have used the term *God*, even though my deepest fascination and awe were reserved for nature from the very earliest moments of my life, and all of my happiest memories are associated with nature. As a child and all my life, I have always experienced a sense of expanding gloom whenever I am separated from nature for too long. When I wasn't grubbing around in the garden or the woods, I read books written for children about wildlife: Colin Dann's *Animals of Farthing Wood* series was a particular favourite. I constantly pestered my mother for permission to pursue ever more outlandish habitat-creation schemes. My biggest fantasy was to create a great pond spanning the whole back half of the garden. I daydreamed of the wooden dock I'd build, and of silently rowing in a little wooden boat through willows, whose crooked arms would reach out over the water from the bank. Moorhens would step gingerly from one lily pad to the next;

tadpoles would be so numerous in spring they'd form jet-black slicks across the water like the crude oil leaking from a stricken tanker. I would carefully introduce sticklebacks, minnows and maybe a handful of fearsome pike too, which I'd catch from one of the ponds on Richmond Park, and I was going to install a special nest box to attract kingfishers.

Though the big pond was never to be realised on account of the sandy soil beneath, I planted trees and festooned that garden with nest boxes for birds, built with help from Steve, the gardener. There was a little hardware shop on Ham Parade high street next to the bakery, and the men in blue overalls there took to keeping aside for me the empty wooden boxes in which screws and nails and other bits were delivered in those days. Steve showed me how to carve out a hole the size of a two-pence piece for blue tits, slightly bigger for great tits, and where to position the boxes, generally 3m or 4m up (using an aluminium nail so as not to harm the tree), facing between due north and east to avoid direct sunlight and the wettest winds. For wrens, dunnocks and robins we'd cut out half of the front face of the box and fix it using garden twine inside a thick bush, holly or bay perhaps, or deep within one of the yew hedges that set the formal pattern of the garden. Once they were installed and occupied, I learned to resist the burning temptation to look inside them, not least after one brood of newly hatched great tits was abandoned by their parents on account of my meddling. Their gaping yellow beaks had been outstretched as I peered in and then reached in, the chicks warm and fuzzy in my hand. The following day I returned to find them coagulated into a single cold, hard ball. I was devastated and moped around all day, too ashamed to share my secret with anyone. From then on, I limited my involvement to sitting quietly nearby and simply watching the parents coming and going.

During my childhood, Ormeley was a perpetual hive of activity. The charisma of my mother – kind, generous and elegant – has always had a planetary quality about it ever since she and her siblings had lost their parents as children. Everything seems to be drawn into an orbit around her. An endless stream of deliveries and visitors coming and going, more people at work or sipping tea in the tearoom than could possibly have been needed, each one a lifelong participant in what felt like a commune. Some had grown ancient, like 90-year-old Mr Miners, nearly toothless in his flat cap, who had been the gardener at Ormeley since between the wars and had simply never left, often to the dismay of his successor, who had to put up with frequent bouts of unsolicited advice. Then there was Mrs White, known to my mother as Wags, who came to look after me on Thursdays when I was very young. Mrs White had been a housekeeper and nanny for my mother and her first husband, Mark Birley, in the 1950s, and my mother adored her. Sometimes I visited Mrs White at her house, which was not very far from ours. While she made tea, nearly always fried fish fingers, oven chips and peas, all of which were delicious to me, her husband, a long-faced and long-suffering methuselah of a man named Reg, would heave himself up from his armchair, switch off the flickering old television set and take me wordlessly by the hand to watch the trains that rattled the windows every few minutes. There was an alarmingly flimsy metal footbridge over the railway just across the road from the house, and clambering up the steep steps and onto the flat bridge, we'd whoop and wave to attract the attention of the driver as one commuter train after the next roared past beneath us, seemingly at touching distance. Mr White had a drawerful of medals in the front room, having fought as an infantryman in both world wars, surviving the Battle of the Somme with nothing worse than a burst eardrum.

Maria Teixeira, small, forthright and loving, was our Portuguese housekeeper. Still today, 50 years after they first met, Maria goes in weekly to see my mother and arrange the flowers. Maria's only son David was born just three days before me, our mothers having navigated their pregnancies together, and David was my closest childhood friend. He practically lived at Ormeley, and from time to time, I was lucky enough to be taken off to stay with David and his parents in their spotless white apartment in downtown Lisbon for a week or two. However, it was Steve Hannigan, our gardener, who showed me that an adult love of nature is normal and good. I attached myself to Steve like glue, grabbing the chance to help him in the garden or just tagging along asking him endless questions. I loved joining Steve on his regular lunchtime walk across the woods to Ham Parade high street, where, after placing his bets on various horses at the William Hill while I waited outside, he would buy each of us a pasty at Greggs. On the way home, if it were spring, we detoured to search for birds' nests. Steve showed me how to go about finding them. A pair of wrens like to hide a neat ball-like nest of moss amid the gnarly, earthy roots of a fallen tree. Blackbirds and song thrushes conceal their bowl-shaped nests in dense ivy, bramble or honeysuckle against a thick tree trunk or a wall; you can tell the two apart by the inner layer of smooth, hard mud a thrush uses to line its nest. Steve knew their songs, mimicking the male blackbird so adeptly that the real thing would sometimes come close in furious confusion.

My brother Zac also inspired my love of nature. I still have a framed photograph of us together; me aged five or six with my pudding-bowl blonde haircut and Zac, six years older, a little gawky in a 'Save the Hedgehogs' t-shirt. Zac always had animals at home and at the boarding school, deep in the Savernake Forest, to which he had been shipped, somewhat cruelly, I have always felt, at the age of just seven. I had managed to avoid the same fate, later on, most likely because my mother, grieving the loss of her oldest son Rupert that year, hadn't been able to face sending me, her youngest, away as well.

The first of Zac's animals I remember was a house mouse he rescued as a baby, still pink and blind. He named it Johnny, and it had lived for a full school term in one of his pockets until the teachers decided that Johnny must live at home. Anxious that his mouse shouldn't suffer due to this sudden loss of status, Zac created an elaborate wood and wire-mesh 'mousery' in what had once been a built-in desk and drawers in his bedroom at home. Before long, he rescued another young mouse from somewhere, a mate for Johnny, and soon there were offspring. At first, Zac had been able to keep up with the rate of reproduction, finding homes for the fledgling mice with his friends; my sister Jemima's friends; my friends; even the children of various neighbours; but he was quickly overwhelmed, and then in-breeding became an issue. Parents began complaining that their children hadn't expected to be given white mice with red eyes, a sure sign of in-breeding, some with only three legs. Finally, on one of his occasional visits to Ormeley, my father, who had separated from my mother not long after my arrival and now lived mostly in France with my younger half-siblings, showed up amid the usual whirlwind; rooms that had been shuttered for months were flung open and lit up, and he took one look at Zac's bedroom and decided in disgust that enough was enough. The mice were freed in the garden, the mousery dismantled and the room scrubbed. Zac was appalled but powerless.

There had also been a young blackbird, found spreadeagled on the grass beneath a stretch of yew hedge in the Ormeley garden, featherless and blind, beneath a nest torn to shreds by a mob of magpies. Zac carried it with him tenderly everywhere he went, in one of my father's empty wooden Don Julio cigar boxes, its yellowish beak perennially agape. He fed it worms dug from the soil in Steve's vegetable garden, and it seemed to be thriving, even developing a ruddy quiff on its head and what appeared to be some tail feathers, until one day, all of a sudden, it died. Zac was bereft. He dug a grave under the evergreen oak, solemnly placing the cigar box inside, before snapping at me as I horsed around shirtless in shorts for not taking the proceedings sufficiently seriously.

Zac's *exeat* weekends, when he could return home for a few days, were a hugely exciting time for me. My sister Jemima, already approaching adulthood by the time I was seven or eight, was a more constant presence, caring and funny, but our interests overlapped to a lesser degree than was the case with my brother. Zac and I tended a vegetable garden together and pursued endless wildlife enterprises of various kinds. Often, I slept in the twin bed in his room, which had a funny musty smell on account of the mousery. During the summer months, he would set an alarm for four or five o'clock in the morning, at which time we'd creep outside in the silvery first light of dawn, through a small side gate in the garden wall and onto the golf course next door. There must have been a deliberate policy by the golf course hierarchy to allow scrub-rich margins to prosper alongside some of the fairways, and the place hummed with life. We hunted for lost golf balls to sell later from a little stand at the end of the garden, handing them by the dozen in transparent, sealed bags to golfers through a great wrought iron gate that separated our garden from the fourth tee of the golf course. Mostly though, we looked for wildlife: fox cubs playing in the deserted bunkers, the occasional hedgehog or badger. Once, we saw a male pheasant, magnificent in gold, green and red, unmoving, watching us haughtily from the lower bow of an oak tree. Not used to real countryside where pheasants are commonplace, we gazed awestruck at this splendid creature. It never really occurred to me that we were, in fact, in the suburbs. London seemed a far-off metropolis, a lengthy and tedious drive for appointments with Mr Bradbeer, the dentist at Cavendish Square, a trip that seemed to consume an entire day. To us, the countryside around us appeared far better than *actual* countryside. On rare visits to see an aunt in Dorset, I remember encountering only sheep and rooks in an otherwise dull field bounded by an emaciated hedgerow, though I suppose at the time I simply wasn't looking hard enough.

On the rare occasion during my childhood that I gave any thought to religion, I could not relate to the notion of searching for joy or solace in an invisible, intangible god, an implausible, fearsome, white-bearded man-figure looming over an undefined heaven. It all seemed pure fantasy to me. In contrast to this invisible deity, extraordinary, captivating nature was all around me. Meanwhile, I began to sense a disconnect between the David Attenborough television programmes I adored – which in those days depicted a pristine world teeming with strange and fantastic wildlife – and the reality. I could see that nature was under assault everywhere: habitats being burned and flattened; life in the seas hoovered up by trawlers with nets large enough to engulf a whole town; wildlife across the board disappearing before our eyes. I felt angry. I began to listen intently to my father and his older brother, my uncle Teddy, whose smiling eyes exuded empathy and whose beard made him look like a prophet of the Old Testament. While my father had been building businesses on both sides of the Atlantic, Teddy had been a lifelong pioneer of the environmental movement, sounding warnings as far back as the 1950s about the dangers of deforestation, soil erosion, agrichemicals, big dams and even the threat of global climate change. Teddy had been the founder editor of the *Ecologist* magazine and had stood in Suffolk as an early electoral candidate for the Green Party, where he paraded a dromedary camel borrowed from his friend John Aspinall to highlight the looming desertification of East Anglia from intensive chemical-dependent arable farming. An unruly gaggle of hippies had accumulated around him on the campaign trail, some dressing as Bedouins to accentuate the campaign message, thereby explaining for me an eccentric photograph that hung opposite the loo on my father's bathroom wall at Ormeley.

My uncle Teddy was especially articulate on the cosmic tragedy inflicted on indigenous communities, marginalised, displaced, assimilated and in any many parts of the world, now annihilated. In Teddy's view, the answers to the world's gravest problems lie in the deep spiritual connection that indigenous communities have with nature, in contrast to the stark disconnect that has grown to characterise developed world societies. 'Humanity's last best hope,' was how he put it. In the end, a few years before his death, my father decided to devote himself to the environment. He wanted to wake people up to what he saw to be the overriding purpose of humanity: forging a new relationship with nature. Together he and his brother Teddy created a foundation that, for several years, was one of the most significant sources of funding in Europe for environmental campaigners and nature conservationists.

I suppose everyone who loses a child spends a great deal of time afterwards reflecting on their religious faith, on questions of God, the meaning of life and death and the possibility of an afterlife. My meeting with the spiritual medium in Fulham, who appeared to have connected with the spirit of Iris and seemed to provide a channel through which Iris could communicate with me, plunged me into a prolonged period of such reflection. My experience in her front room had been just too far-fetched, too extraordinary, too inexplicable, too marvellous to ignore. Surely I had been in contact with my Iris. There must be more out there?

During the autumn after Iris died, I walked with an elderly neighbour at Cannwood who described herself as a 'blue dome Christian'. I asked her what she meant by this, and she explained that she finds God under the wide blue sky, or in other words, in nature. In that moment, I understood that I do too, and always have done. My restless, insatiable interest in wildlife, my profound reverence for the natural world: *this* has been my religion. It has been in nature that I have always found my deepest calling and my most powerful feelings of love, purpose and fulfilment. I realised then that I resented the great religions for having come simply to bypass nature in their pathway to God. How can God be eternal, infinite, as we are taught from the pulpit, and yet apparently not present here on Earth in nature? How does a devotee of Christianity, Islam or any other faith reconcile spending their working days plundering the natural world without restraint before showing up at their holy place at the end of each week to signal their devotion to God?

It seems to me that, for Christians at least, everything changed with the Enlightenment, which succeeded in draining the mystery and the magic from nature. Previously Christians tended to see that reality is parallel with divinity and that all things comprise an all-encompassing, immanent God. Early Christian philosophers, most notably St Thomas Aquinas, were unequivocal in asserting that God is to be found in nature. *Pantheology* describes this idea, that God is all things, in an octopus-like plurality. But with the emergence of modern science, Enlightenment philosophers such as René Descartes ushered in a perfect and convenient severing of God from the natural world. God became remote, somewhere else, while nature was transformed in the collective consciousness into a seemingly inexhaustible source of physical resources, there for the plundering by humanity, without any risk of besmirching our conscience. Descartes argued that living things were merely biological machines, even once nailing his wife's dog to a board and dissecting it alive to demonstrate that it had no soul. In his book *Science and Spiritual Practices*, the brilliant modern-day philosopher Rupert Sheldrake argues that the Romantic movement emerged as a fightback against this grim worldview, and a rejection of the separation that ensued. The Romantics successfully encouraged some of us to fall back in love with nature some of the time, he argues. However, we are romantic in our outlook only in our spare time, spent by many of us outside, walking, having picnics and enjoying the sights, smells and sounds of nature. As soon as we are back at our desks, he points out, we revert to a Cartesian mentality, viewing all nature through the mechanistic lens of Descartes. This worldview has since become the dominant one worldwide, and Sheldrake argues that only by re-enchanting nature can we save it, and ourselves.

My fascination with nature has always been more than just a hobby. Occasionally as I grew up, someone would ask me about my interest in wildlife and the environment. 'Oh, you're terribly keen on nature, aren't you?' they would say, as if it were like stamp collecting. I often felt like asking them in return whether they like breathing air or eating food. For me, a love of nature is as fundamental as these things.

In the months following Iris's death, I began to understand that I have always been religious, but in a way that I had never previously chosen to articulate. It has always been clear to me that the magic of nature is worthy of our total devotion. I never used the term 'God', and I had no interest in exploring the questions of souls, spirituality, alternative realms or what happens to us when we die. All of that seemed fanciful to me and a distraction from the cause of turning the tide on humanity's relentless assault on the natural world. I resented religion for that distraction and, worse, for giving cover to seemingly good people who were engaged in destroying nature. Religion seemed to me an accomplice in the destruction. Now, illuminated in the afterglow of the mystical event I had experienced in that front room in Parsons Green, I felt myself open for the first time to a greater magic even than that which we experience all around us all the time. I felt an overpowering urge to explore these questions for the first time.

7

Circle

In the products of the unconscious, we discover mandala
symbols, that is, circular and quaternary figures which
express wholeness, and whenever we wish to express
wholeness, we employ just such figures. . . . The mandala is
an archetypal image whose occurrence is attested throughout
the ages. It signifies the wholeness of the Self. This circular
image represents the wholeness of the psychic ground or, to
put it in mythic terms, the divinity incarnate in man.

CARL GUSTAV JUNG,
Memories, Dreams, Reflections

Someone suggested that we build a stone circle for Iris, in the
Celtic way, at the spot where the accident happened. The only
stone circle I had ever known was Stonehenge, that gargantuan
brooding structure always there beneath the sky as we whizz
back and forth on the A303, the stones just as resplendent in
the slate greys of November as they are in the haze of a late
summer evening. I was introduced via Kate to Dom Ropner,
who had made himself an expert in the creation of stone circles,
having chosen to remember his own sister in this way. Dom
had arrived at Cannwood in his four-by-four one afternoon

that August. Dawdling on my way up from a solitary swim in the pond, lost in thought, I stumbled across him on the lane. I had completely forgotten our arrangement. I hurried across the vegetable garden to pacify my three lurchers, who had bounded over and now surrounded his trembling spaniel, by now on its back, legs akimbo. I apologised for my dogs and suggested we walk straight over and see the spot. We wandered up the lane, me barefoot, eyes down so that I could skirt any sharp-looking loose stones. The cracked, greyish tarmac was pleasantly warm beneath my feet. Dom commented on the beauty of the tunnel, and I looked up for a moment. Shards of light broke through the canopy above our heads, illuminating floating dandelion seeds, little agglomerations of delicate flying insects and other tiny creatures of the summer floating weightlessly in the still air around us. I agreed with him that it was a magical time of year.

I told Dom matter-of-factly that this was the exact route Iris had taken in the Mule that afternoon, turning right at the top of the lane just before the road, through a gap marked by an unusually large field maple, and veering out onto the recently cut grass where, snaking the cumbersome vehicle left to right, she had somehow managed to turn it over and on top of herself. A little older than me, laid back under an Australian-style floppy sunhat, his longish, tousled hair greying at the sides, Dom acknowledged my narration of these events with sympathetic hums, his eyes a little watery. Even as I told the story, I struggled still to grasp the reality that just weeks previously, Iris had lain stricken, pleading with the universe to send help, right here, amid the everyday chattering of birds going about their summer business and the whispering of the long grasses; beneath the gaze of the old oaks along the hedge line who had seen it all happen. It was here, on this grass, that one person after the next and the paramedics had tried in vain to save her. In the end, it had all been over in a moment. I searched for signs of those last moments, as I always did when I came here, but the wheel marks in the grass were gone now, as were the little pieces of plastic left behind by the ambulance crew, which had fluttered about the track for a few days after the accident until they had each been picked up by me or by others who passed by and paused in that place.

Standing stone circles, I learned from Dom, are found across the British Isles, Europe and indeed all over the world. It is hard for us now to conceive how much of a communal effort it took to create these structures. Often the stones are immense. The general view is that for many societies, stone circles have been a place for communing with other realms, with the dead. The circle has been a sacred symbol to a great many people throughout time, representing notions of oneness or wholeness, totality, original perfection, the infinite, eternity, timelessness; even in the hermetic tradition, God, *whose centre is everywhere and whose circumference is nowhere*. None of this meant much to me, but I liked the idea of a beautiful stone circle and, even more so, the idea of a monument that would stand bold for thousands of years. I imagined people millennia from now marvelling at Iris's stone circle, barely changed, without a clue who Iris was. Somehow that idea diminished for me the difference between her fifteen and a half years and an expected human lifespan of 80 or 90 years.

Once a cow field, the gentle slope a little further down from the site of the accident is now a burgeoning young woodland, animated in the spring and summer with birdsong. The slope is bisected diagonally by the track leading to Dreamers Farm, the same track that Iris should have taken to collect Monica that day. When we first arrived at Cannwood, we decided to plant trees here. Poring over an aerial photograph, we had drawn the outline of our new woodland across three and a half fields, adjoining the big old woodland that flanks Cannwood to the south and arcing north-east up to and over the top of the lane along the road to Forest Gate, a neighbouring farm to the north. The trees arrived on a truck and were planted during the bitterly cold winter of 2010, each one a little knee-high whip of a thing planted in its own protective plastic tube. Observing these trees, a broad mix of native species, emerging and growing to tower over us, has been joyful, as has the unravelling of the monotone rye grass between them, now overtaken by tussocky, wild perennial grasses, a smattering of woodland wildflowers that have crept in from the old wood, and various vigorously expanding patches of scrub; bramble, spindle, blackthorn, dog rose, hawthorn, hazel, wild service, dogwood, willow and holly. The whole area has become a haven for small mammals and the kestrels and owls that hunt them, as well as songbirds, grass snakes and wildlife of all kinds.

Once the trees were newly planted in the ground, I had asked a neighbour with a nearby working forest if he might spare me a load of dead wood. A lorry duly showed up piled high with 100 tonnes of fat tree trunks and boughs, no good for the mill for whatever reason, and we made five heaped piles amid the new planting. We wanted to create hiding places and habitat for wildlife, and we wanted the invisible building blocks of a woodland ecosystem contained within the dead wood – the fungi and bacteria, the little bugs, the mosses and the lichens of the old forest – to spill out and colonise ours. Almost 10 years later, Iris's stone circle was to be built between one of these decomposing log piles, now completely surrounded by nettles and covered over by an enormous dog rose, and a little pond we had dug out years earlier along the ditch that runs parallel with the track. I used to bring the children here to play; a little semi-circular patch of open ground adorned with logs to turn over, bugs to catch and hold, a pond to sift and apples to pick in the autumn. Now, this would be a stone circle memorial to one of them, Iris, their ringleader. It was all so hard to swallow.

After looking at the spot, Dom and I walked down the track through the young woodland and turned right at the bottom to make our way along the dead-straight stream that divides Cannwood from another farm next door. A little embarrassed by the yellowing plastic tree tubes, some split now by the fattening trees within, I explained that back then, I hadn't understood that woodland regenerates naturally if you just leave things alone. Seeds are blown in on the wind or carried out into the open by berry-eating birds and other animals. Squirrels and jays choose areas of open ground in which to bury acorns for the winter, many of which are forgotten and germinate into young oaks. Those lucky enough to sprout within the new patches of thorny scrub that bedeck the land are protected from grazing animals and grow tall; hence the ancient saying that *the thorn is the mother of the oak*. All I had known back then was that trees are good, so I had decided to plant several thousand.

When we arrived at the bigger of the two ponds, I suggested that we swim, offering him one of the pairs of navy blue trunks that I always leave hanging on the wooden bench in the summertime. Dom, visibly elated to be in the water, told me he could head down to Cornwall the following week to scour farms at Bodmin for suitable granite stones. The circle must be made of Cornish granite, he said. Apparently favoured by the Celts for these things, the stones are, it turns out, mildly radioactive. Some Bodmin farmers are more than willing to sell to him any big ones that happen to be lying around on their land. A lorry would bring them to Cannwood, accompanied by a crane for hoisting them into position. I'd have to widen the gap on the lane; the big field maple on the corner would have to go. We'd place four smaller stones flat within the circle for seating around a simple fire pit. The largest stone would be on the north side, engraved with Iris's name. I agreed to all this immediately. I thought perhaps one day we might even scatter Iris's ashes amid the stones.

It felt good to have a plan like this, to be doing something tangible to remember Iris. Quietly, I felt more upbeat than usual at dinner in the kibbutz that evening, against the familiar backdrop of stomach butterflies, which waxed and waned but never left me. I fell asleep thinking about the stone circle we were going to build.

Just three weeks later, in September, Dom was back, a day ahead of his lorry and crane. He parked on the track adjacent to the chosen spot and pitched a tent between his four-by-four and the little pond. I liked how he made himself a fire pit by slicing and lifting out a perfect circle of turf, about 20cm deep, which he placed carefully to one side for putting back later. Again we swam, and the following morning the work began. Precise measurement by Dom, marked out with bamboo stakes and a ball of string; a small digger to make the holes, each one much deeper than I expected, a miniature concrete mixer; and in they went, one by one. The huge stones seemed like icebergs, the crane creaking and groaning as it winched them off the back of the lorry and lowered them precariously into the ground while Dom and one of his men frantically shovelled, compacted and smoothed first the concrete and then the earth that was tipped around each stone. I came and went throughout two days, just to sit and watch with little Arlo, two at the time and mesmerised by earth-moving machinery, and then they were gone. In a matter of days, the crumpled grass began to restore itself and grow over the bare patches. We planted bulbs of wild irises around the foot of each stone. Dom returned a few days later to spend an afternoon engraving the largest stone with the words *Iris Annabel Goldsmith* above three watery lines, the emblem of Aquarius, Iris's constellation. I loved it; everyone did.

Each evening I made my way out to the stone circle, the three lurchers streaking ahead in front of me through the long grass. They seemed to take on an air of serenity as we approached the circle, sitting patiently by at a small distance, ears cocked to the wind. I felt sure they sensed my sadness, and I wondered if they knew the reason, if they were aware that Iris had died in this place. I allowed myself to daydream that perhaps these dogs sensed her presence here. Each one had grown up with Iris, who loved them; Olive, the mother of Elvis; Elvis, the father of Tarka; Tarka, the mother of a brood of boisterous puppies on the yard. As the days grew shorter and the leaves on the trees began to take on their autumn hues, and wispy cirrus clouds accumulated high above, pink and amber in the last light of day, it felt as if all of this, draped in Iris's colours, was her stage. I liked to stay a while until, one by one, the birds fell quiet in the fading purple light, the last of which always a blackbird, alone singing its languid, luscious song in the descending darkness. I felt close to Iris here. Sometimes I sat quietly just thinking about her, the things she did or said, her little giggle; sometimes, I railed at the injustice of it, my forehead tight, teeth and hands clenched, mind whirring; and at other times, I just cried, grateful to be undisturbed.

After my visit to the spiritual medium that autumn, I found myself pleading with Iris to make her presence known to me, just once. I tried to quiet my mind as Eleanor had told me, eyes closed, sitting on one of those flat stones. I didn't know what I was expecting to conjure. Might I hear her voice, as Kate felt she had? I wished for that more than anything. Or a faint caress on the back of my neck? Perhaps a rainbow might arc spontaneously across the evening sky? The word 'Iris' means rainbow in ancient Greek, and rainbows were her favourite thing, so that would make sense. I found that my mind was prone to wandering and more resistant to being quieted than I had expected. Why hadn't I brought my glass of whiskey and a cigarette with me? My chest hurt a little – I shouldn't have started smoking again. Maybe it wasn't my lung, and I'd pulled a muscle in my ribcage bowling cricket balls that afternoon? Isaac's batting was getting good; he might be really good when he's older.

And so I thought of taking meditation classes. Mostly I thought of where Iris was. Where do they go when they die? This question seemed vital to my own ability to continue living. I would never come to terms with the idea that her entire experience had been permanently extinguished in the blink of an eye.

I need to start reading, I thought. Perhaps I'll contact the kindly vicar, Father Justin, who had christened the smaller children and whose handwritten letter had been the first to arrive after the accident, soon lost amid the mayhem on my side of the bedroom in those early days. If you can hear me, my girl, I love you with all my heart, and I miss you, I thought, as I sat amid the great stones. Disturbed by Tarka, now restless, a pair of mallard ducks exploded from the rushes at the unkempt field margin, jolting me. I got up, buttocks cold and a little numb from sitting on the hard, uneven stone surface, and made my way back along the path in the half-light towards the warmth of the house and dinner.

I wrote to the church the next day, explaining the circumstances and that I would hugely appreciate an opportunity to meet with the vicar for a cup of tea. The reply came back that Father Justin had retired and moved away but that his predecessor, Father Mark, still lived in the area, in his eighties now, and would be delighted to come and see me at

Cannwood. The two of us spoke and made a plan to go for a walk together on that Saturday afternoon. I had in mind to walk down the lane, round the regular loop and through the big wood, along the towering oak cathedral, up through the younger trees in their tubes and to stop at the stone circle for a rest. I didn't know how good he'd be on his feet, but I need not have worried.

The day arrived, and shortly after lunch, I greeted the sprightly, white-haired former vicar on the lane, a west countryman wearing a pair of spanking new outdoor walking shoes, and we set off as planned. We talked a little about our shared love of nature, specifically our interest in rewilding as a way of reversing some of the ecological losses he had witnessed in his lifetime. I told Father Mark that since the loss of my daughter, I was thinking of throwing in the towel on my attempts to produce grass-fed beef profitably here, and going the whole hog on restoring nature across the farm. It turned out some time later that once nature had begun to run riot, I'd return to producing beef, but in a much wilder way, with longhorn cattle free to roam where they want, eat what they want, sleep where they want, in a burgeoning wood pasture. I interrupted our conversation periodically to point things out, as I always do; a new pond recently excavated; some common snipe flushed by the dogs from some pooled water among the rushes, darting airborne in zigzags away from us; an area of bare soil at the woodland edge freshly rooted by either a very big badger or a wild boar.

Father Mark had lost a daughter too. She had died in her thirties following a short illness a decade earlier. We shared our stories of loss and grief, and it gave me some comfort to see the sparkle in his eyes, his ability to talk freely about the tragedy that had befallen his own family and the lasting joy that he is now able to find in his life. Our conversation turned to religion. Father Mark had experienced a low-key, very English kind of epiphany several decades earlier, long before the death of his daughter, which had led him to quit his regular work in logistics and devote his life to giving succour and support to others. He had come to understand that this was 'his calling', as he put it, having found that engaging with individual people in their time of need, and with their troubles, brought him closer to God. As we spoke, it occurred to me that perhaps the letter of the law laid down for Christians mattered less to Father Mark than the urge to follow an inner calling to help others.

I told Father Mark that gratitude and a boundless love of nature had been the sum total of my own spiritual life. Now, reeling in the aftermath of an event so bluntly awful as the death of my brilliant teenage daughter, out of the blue, I was searching for more. On my bedside table, a stack of books grew higher each week. Books on parental grief, life after death, our soul's purpose, evidence suggestive of reincarnation, Jewish Kabbala, spiritual mediumship, the Buddhist wheel of Dharma, Sufism, near-death and out-of-body experiences, Tolstoy's *Confession*, Jung's *Memories, Dreams, Reflections*; I was looking for answers. Without mentioning my experience with the spiritual medium, I told Father Mark that often I catch myself asking out loud, 'Where are you, Iris?' I wanted to know where she is now and what happens to us when we die.

'Do you believe that our spirit remains connected, however tenuously, to this earthly realm? Are there ghosts?' I asked.

On all of this, as we sat in the solemn quiet of the stone circle, Father Mark simply affirmed that the only certainty is that we live on after death; how, where and in what shape is an unfathomable mystery. My itch went unscratched.

Since the accident, I had received regular text messages from Vipula Kamburugamuwa, known to friends and clients

as Vip Kam. For years Vip had been the boss at the Belgravia
Garage on Eaton Mews, buying, selling and fixing cars: Aston
Martins, Lamborghinis, Rolls Royces and, for a while when I
lived in that neck of the woods, my dented Volkswagen Golf
GTI. Small, bald and immaculate in his two-toned, cufflinked
shirt and sharp Savile Row suit with a cigarette permanently
between thumb and forefinger, Vip had in his eye the glint
of a man who knows well how to look after himself. One of
the best-connected men in London, he simply knew everyone,
and we had stayed in touch. A Buddhist of Sri Lankan descent,
Vip had called repeatedly that summer, insistent that I go with
him to visit his monk at a monastery in Acton. The London
Buddhist Vihara had been the first Sri Lankan Buddhist
monastery outside Asia, established in 1926 by revered Sri
Lankan Buddhist revivalist Anagārika Dharmapāla, who
himself had been the first global Buddhist missionary and the
first to preach the *Dhamma* in three continents: Asia, North
America and Europe.

Having politely palmed Vip off during that summer, not
long after visiting the spiritual medium, I found myself
clambering into his electric G-Wiz outside the tube station
at Hammersmith. We pootled through the caricature leafy
suburbs between Hammersmith and Acton before pulling up
outside a handsome, red-bricked Edwardian building with
sash windows, set back from a broad street. Smiling broadly,
Vip pushed open one half of the heavy front double doors
and beckoned me into the silent entrance hall, which was
reminiscent of the reception at my prep school. The hall
was illuminated with the kind of blue-ish strip lights used in
municipal buildings; a large side table proffered a selection
of leaflets advertising events, classes and various causes.
Delighted, Vip pointed me towards a wooden door off to one
side, partially open, behind which was a large open room,

bare except for the spartan chairs stacked along one wall and an immense robed Buddha in gold leaf at the far end, half smiling, plump lips closed, the hands folded in the lap.

I was peering in through the gap in the door when, with a tap on my shoulder, Vip introduced me to his monk. Smiling broadly, he didn't offer me his hand. The monk was younger than I had expected, wrapped round and around in robes dyed in bright orange, the colour of illumination, the highest state of perfection, Vip told me later, explaining that it was the Buddha himself who decided that his followers were to wear robes of orange. The monk led us along a drab corridor and into an office lounge, a desk at one end, a semi-circle of ornately cushioned cubes for seating at the other. Vip chose a little sofa beneath the window and said nothing. I thanked the monk, now seated perfectly still opposite me across a rectangular glass table, calmly waiting for me to speak. I told the monk that my teenage daughter had been killed in an accident in July and that I was intrigued by the Buddhist understanding of death and reincarnation. I told him that certain experiences since the event, including dreams, had led me to believe that my daughter may remain present in some way.

Before coming, I had read that Buddhists use the term *saṃsāra* to describe a continuous cycle of life, death, and rebirth, without beginning or end, in which we are all cosmic participants. It was an appealing idea. Buddhists believe each rebirth is temporary and impermanent: you are born, then you die, only to be reborn elsewhere in a new body. All of this takes place in accordance with your own *karma*, the Buddhist spiritual notion of cause and effect, whereby your intentions and your actions during one life directly influence the circumstances and outcome of the next one. Good intentions and good deeds give you good karma, and therefore happier rebirths, whereas bad intent and bad deeds are bad karma, in which case you may find yourself at a disadvantage in the next life.

It is not only Buddhists who believe that after death, the soul is reborn. Reincarnation is central to the beliefs of Hindus, Jains, Sikhs and numerous animist or pagan societies the world over, from Australia to Africa to the Americas. Upon his arrival in Britain, Julius Caesar recorded that the spiritual guides he encountered among Celtic tribes, known as druids, taught their followers that their souls 'pass after death from some to others'. So, too, did some of Ancient Greece's most prominent philosophers, most notably Pythagoras, Socrates and Plato, whose work *Phaedo* is seemingly aimed solely at making the case for reincarnation. While mainstream Christianity and Islam, the world's most widespread religions and the only two whose followers seek proactively to convert others to their belief system, do not subscribe to the idea of reincarnation, great swathes of their adherents do, from Christians and Muslims across Africa; Catholics in the Philippines and other parts of Asia; and whole defined groups within and around these two faiths. Alawites, Druzes, Rosicrucians, Cathars, Neoplatonists, Orphists, Hermeticists, Manichaeists and Gnostics, Islamic Sufis, modern-day spiritualists and of course Kabbalists, of both the Jewish and the Christian variety, have all been committed to the belief of the transmigration of our souls after death.

After a long pause, the monk inhaled deeply and began to talk, his perfect English spoken with the same lyrical Sri Lankan accent as Vip. He explained that one of the key values of Buddhists is an understanding that all living things, causes, conditions and situations are impermanent. Impermanence, known to us as *anicca*, is the idea that everything eventually disappears once it has originated. Impermanence is constant, all around us, from one moment to the next. Directly related is *anatta*, which is the idea that truly *self* cannot exist. Since everything is both in the process of decay and entirely connected to everything else, the self cannot exist in saṃsāra. Vip nodded as the monk spoke, and each time he looked over at me to smile encouragingly, I smiled back as if I had understood perfectly.

The Buddha himself is said to have had difficulty explaining the idea of anatta to his followers, concluding that it can only be experienced, not described. Obtaining an awareness of the Buddhist concept of anatta, that we are in unity with everything else, brings liberation from the *push-pull* of our individual appetites, passions, ambitions and fixations and the external world's domination of us in general. In grasping the notion of anatta, as we pass from one lifetime to the next, we conquer the so-called three fires of greed, hatred and delusion and thereby come to achieve a state known to Buddhists as *nirvana*, in which the cycle of birth, suffering, death and rebirth comes finally to an end. Nirvana is the goal of all Buddhists. I wondered if the anatta idea of the unity of everything and the absence of self might be described as the opposite of a much later pronouncement by Descartes, 'I think therefore I am.'

I asked the monk whether Buddhists believe it is possible to communicate with souls when they are on the other side. Smiling, he replied that certain individuals seem to be sensitive in such a way as to be able to communicate with the souls of the departed, but for most people, he told me, such communication is confined to the world of dreams. At this point, our conversation drifted into a lengthy discussion about Buddhist rites and rituals. When a Buddhist dreams of a departed loved one, it seems that the dream can carry one of two meanings: either the departed soul is content, in which case the dreamer must give thanks with offerings at the temple, or the departed one is making a plea for help, in which case the dreamer must make extra offerings or perform rituals such as chanting and candle burning, with or without the participation of the monks of the temple, to ramp up the karma of their lost loved one. For billions of people, it has been a known truth that our soul comes and goes from the world as readily as I travel back and forth between Somerset and London.

Afterwards, I sat beside Vip in his little electric car as we scooted and weaved through the mounting traffic. After nearly 50 years in England, it was time for Vip to move back home to Sri Lanka. He told me proudly that he was building a house in Colombo, and I was welcome to visit him there whenever I liked. 'One day,' I promised him, meaning it. Vip suggested that I look up the work of a Canadian-born psychiatrist named Ian Stevenson, who devoted much of his life to the study of near-death experiences, reincarnation and the idea that emotions, memories, and even physical bodily features can be transferred from one life to another. I looked him up. Stevenson had worked for the University of Virginia School of Medicine for half a century, including chairing its department of psychiatry for more than a decade. As founder and director of the university's Division of Perceptual Studies, Stevenson became known for his research into cases he considered were suggestive of reincarnation. Over more than 40 years in international fieldwork, Stevenson investigated with rigour 3,000 cases of young children from all over the world who claimed to remember past lives, and came to the view that certain phobias, philias, unusual abilities and illnesses could not be fully explained by heredity or the natural environment, and that reincarnation might provide a third, contributing factor.

Stevenson co-founded the Society for Scientific Exploration and produced hundreds of peer-reviewed scientific papers and numerous books on reincarnation. I ordered one: *Twenty Cases Suggestive of Reincarnation* (1966). I also thought about ordering his immense two-volume *Reincarnation and Biology: A Contribution to the Etiology of Birthmarks and Birth Defects* (1997), but decided against it. This book reported 200 cases in which birthmarks and congenital disabilities appeared to correspond to a wound on the deceased person whose life the young child was said to recall. Stevenson wrote a shorter version of the same research for the general reader, *Where Reincarnation and Biology Intersect*, and I now have this sitting on my table. Stevenson never committed himself fully to the position that reincarnation does occur, just that 'reincarnation is the best – even though not the only – explanation for the stronger cases we have investigated.' There was one case I found especially striking:

> When Thusitha was about three years old she heard someone mention Kataragama, and she began to say that she was from there. She said that she lived near the river there and that a dumb boy had pushed her into the river. She implied, without clearly stating, that she had then drowned. (Thusitha had a marked phobia of water.) She said her father was a farmer and also had a boutique for selling flowers which was near the Kiri Vehera (Buddhist stupa). She said that her house was near the main Hindu Temple (Devale) at Kataragama. She gave her father's name as Rathu Herath and said that he was bald and wore a sarong. Thusitha did not give a name for herself in the previous life and indeed gave no proper names apart from 'Kataragama' and 'Rathu Herath.' She never explicitly said that she had been a girl in the previous life, but she mentioned frocks and also objected to having

her hair cut; so her parents inferred that she was talking about the life of a girl.

Tissa Jayawardane learned of this case in the autumn of 1985 and visited Thusitha and her family for the first time on November 15, 1985. Having recorded the above statements and some others he went to Kataragama. Here we should explain that Payagala [where the girl lived] is a small town (population in 1981: 6,000) on the western coast of Sri Lanka south of Colombo, and Kataragama, a well-known place of pilgrimage, is in the south-eastern area of the island, in the interior (Obeyesekere, 1981; Wirz, 1966). Kataragama is approximately 220 km by road from Payagala. It is also a small town (population in 1987: approximately 17,500) and consists almost entirely of temples and supporting buildings together with residences for the persons who maintain the temples and supply the needs of the pilgrims. A moderately large river, the Manik Gangs, runs through the town. T.J. went first to the police station where he inquired for a family, with a son who was dumb. He was directed to a double row of flower stalls along the pavement of the main road to the Buddhist stupa, known as the Kiri Vehera. (The vendors at these stalls sell flowers to pilgrims for their use in worship.) Upon inquiring again among the flower vendors he was told to go to a particular flower stall, and at that one he asked whether a young girl of the family had drowned. He was told that a young daughter of the family had drowned in the river some years earlier, and one of her brothers was dumb. According to T.J.'s notes, Thusitha had made 13 verifiable statements and all but three of these were correct for the family with the dumb child who had lost a girl from drowning.

In the second phase of the investigation (in December 1985), G.S. learned about 17 additional statements that Thusitha had made, and he recorded these. The two families still had not met (and, so far as we know, this is still true), so that, as mentioned earlier, we consider our record of these statements uncontaminated by any contact between the two families. Two of these 17 additional statements were unverifiable, but the other 15 were correct for the family of the drowned girl. Thusitha said that her father, in addition to being a farmer and selling flowers, was also a priest at the temple. She mentioned that the family had had two homes and that one of them had glass in the roof. She referred to the water in the river being low. She spoke of dogs that were tied up and fed meat. She said her previous family had a utensil for sifting rice that was better than the one her family had. She described, with imitative actions, how the pilgrims smash coconuts on the ground at the temple in Kataragama. Western readers unfamiliar with Sri Lanka may not immediately appreciate the unusualness of the details in several of these statements. For example, there are plenty of dogs in Sri Lanka, but most of them are stray mongrels who live as scavengers; few are kept as pets. Also, most Sinhalese who are Buddhists would abhor hunting, although Christian Sinhalese might not. It happened that the family of the drowned girl had neighbours who hunted, and they fed meat from the animals they killed to a dog chained in their compound. This would be an unusual situation in Sri Lanka. Another unusual detail was that of a glass (skylight) in the roof of the house. Devotees at Hindu temples other than the one at Kataragama may smash coconuts as part of their worship; however, Thusitha had never had occasion to see this ritual.

In the third phase of the investigation, I. S. (accompanied by G .S. and T. J.) went to Thusitha's family and then to Kataragama. Each family was visited twice in this phase, once in November 1986 and again in October 1987. We learned that the girl who had drowned, who was called Nimalkanthi, had been not quite two years old when she died, in about June 1974. Nimalkanthi had gone to the river with her mother, who was washing clothes there. She was playing near her mother with two of her brothers one of whom was the dumb one. Her mother apparently became absorbed in her washing, and then suddenly noticed that Nimalkanthi was missing. The brother who could speak could not say where she had gone. Nimalkanthi's mother raised an alarm, a search was made, and Nimalkanthi's dead body was recovered from the river. It is unlikely that the dumb brother had pushed Nimalkanthi into the water, but all three children had been playing around just before she disappeared. It seems probable that she lost her footing and slid or fell into the water; she could not swim. Thusitha's statement that the dumb brother had pushed her into the river thus remains unverified, and it is probably incorrect. However, the brother may have pushed her playfully just before she drowned accidentally. Two of Thusitha's verifiable statements were definitely incorrect. She said that her father of the previous life was bald, but Nimalkanthi's father (whom we interviewed) had a good head of hair. She said his name was Rathu but it was Dharmadasa. There were, however, two bald men in the family – Nimalkanthi's maternal grandfather and a maternal uncle – and Nimalkanthi would have seen them often. And a cousin by marriage, whom Nimalkanthi saw from time to time, was called Herath (not Rathu Herath). Thus one could argue that Thusitha's memories included some confusions of the adult men in her family, but we do not wish to emphasize this explanation.

In each case, the recollections of the child seemed to fade after the age of six or seven. For a while, these stories were mesmerising, although after reading through several of Stevenson's case studies, I felt I had taken in the point. Perhaps Iris will have a second chance at life in the world, I thought. That would be good. This was a fruitful path of discovery.

8

Caledonia

The essence of nature is wholeness, a wholeness woven from infinite complexity. Trying to save nature piece by piece doesn't make sense even if we had all the time in the world, and we most certainly do not.
DOUGLAS H. CHADWICK

Three months before Iris died, my friend Anders Povlsen and his wife Anne lost three of their four children in a terrorist atrocity on the island of Sri Lanka. They were killed on Easter Sunday 2019 when three churches and three hotels in the capital Colombo were targeted in a coordinated series of Islamist suicide bombings. Smaller explosions followed at a housing complex in Dematagoda and a guest house in Dehiwala. Hundreds lost their lives, including beautiful, innocent, nature-loving Alma, Agnes and Alfred Povlsen, who had been downstairs at the Shangri-La Hotel that morning, waiting for their parents and sister Astrid to join them for breakfast. It is hard to imagine a more devastating loss. Like so many others who knew this family, I thought of little else for weeks on end. I agonised over what to say to Anders. Eventually, I simply sent him my love in a short message a week after the event.

Anders is a rewilding pioneer; a strong but gentle man of few words who, with his wife Anne, is devoted to the cause of nature restoration. Anders and Anne are now Britain's second largest landowners after the Duke of Buccleuch, having pieced together an immense tract of land in Sutherland in Scotland's far north and another at Glenfeshie in rugged Inverness-shire. The big plan was to restore vibrant nature across these hills and valleys, while showing that a living landscape provides more opportunities and more jobs than a depleted one. Anders has always been one of my heroes. Like so many Scandinavians, he harbours a deep love of nature, which was why he and his family had been exploring Sri Lanka's wild places in the days before the terror attack. I knew that if Anders were to get through the horrendous trauma inflicted upon him, finding solace in the great outdoors would be key. I didn't see him until many months later, after Iris's accident. Now we were both members of that wretched club of parents who have lost children. A few weeks after Christmas, I flew to Scotland to spend some time with him for the first time since our lives had been changed forever.

I flew into Inverness airport, the plane bumping lower before popping out beneath a menacingly grey ceiling of clouds that slanted low over the treeless hills and glens, bleakly beautiful to the horizon in all directions. I've been a fearful flyer all my life, and typically I'd have been gripping the sides of my seat, but this time I felt mournful. Whether it's the air or the pressure, or simply the moment of thoughtful solitude up there in the sky, flying has a way of bringing emotions to the surface. Earlier, as the plane had soared out of Heathrow, banking east high over countless tiny reflections that flickered one after another on the ground below, my thoughts had turned to Iris, as they so often did. I imagined her sitting near me on the plane, that perfect little round face cocking me a sympathetic half-smile from across the aisle as the two younger boys scrapped in their seats on my other side. She was always eager to be travelling somewhere, anywhere, headphones on, book in hand, a packet of mints tucked away somewhere close at hand; everything arranged around her exactly as she liked it

A Land Rover awaited me in the blustery cold outside the airport, driven by Thomas McDonnell, the architect of an ambitious plan conceived more than a decade ago to reduce the number of red deer dramatically on Povlsen-owned land, thereby allowing wildflowers, scrub and young trees to emerge for the first time in several generations. In a matter-of-fact way, Thomas explained as he drove how he and Anders had decided to shoot a lot of deer, 'on sight really', during the season and how they had stuck to their guns in the face of a barrage of furious opposition from some neighbouring landowners and the wider Highlands landowning community. Ever since Queen Victoria acquired Balmoral Estate in 1852 and her husband Prince Albert headed into the glens with his rifle, clad in a ridiculous Sherlock Holmes hat and tartan plus-fours, Highland landowners have loved stalking. Their desire to maintain as many red deer as possible on their great estates has resulted in the ongoing treelessness of the landscape today.

In the past, the Highlands of Scotland were a far wilder place than the landscape through which I drove that day, with a rich and dark history that has always fascinated me. In his seminal work *British Animals Extinct Within Historic Times* (1880), Victorian naturalist James Edmund Harting, drawing upon earlier accounts, described the wilds of Scotland as they were in Norman times:

> *As for Scotland, we can scarcely over-estimate the wildness that everywhere prevailed, when in the south a vast forest filled the intervening space between Chillingham and Hamilton, a*

distance, as the crow flies, of about eighty miles. Including within it Ettrick and numerous other forests; and further north the great Caledonian wood, known even at Rome, covered the greater part of both the Lowlands and the Highlands, its recesses affording shelter at one time to bears, wolves, wild-boars, and wild white cattle.

The original inhabitants of the Highlands were animists, worshipping deities that were divine manifestations of different aspects of nature. Highlands folklore, elements of which survived long after the arrival of Christianity in the fifth and sixth centuries after Christ, revolved around these 'nature Gods', set amid the triadic Celtic cosmos of land, sea and sky. Like pagan societies the world over, the original Highlanders were intricately and spiritually connected with the rich and mystifying tapestry of nature around them. For pre–Christian Highland people, nature was represented by the goddess Ana, embodying the spiritual essence of the natural world: wind, wisdom, death and rebirth. Another Highland god, the Cailleach, was said to be the mother of all the other gods and goddesses, a divine hag, a one-eyed giantess with white hair, dark blue skin and rust-coloured teeth, at once creator and destroyer, gentle and fierce. The Cailleach was believed to have shaped the mountains as her stepping stones using a great hammer that she always carried in her hand. According to ancient Highland tradition, the Cailleach reigns unchallenged from Samhainn, the first day of winter, ushering in snow, storms, torrents and floods until the first day of summer, known as Bealltainn, when she willingly cedes to Brìghde, who rules the summer months. Confusingly, the Cailleach and Brìghde were considered two faces of the same goddess.

The indigenous Highland people turned to shamans for spiritual guidance. These Druid spirit walkers taught reincarnation and recounted tales of Gaelic heroes, who travelled into the otherworld, returning laden with wisdom and power that brought healing to the land and skill to artisans, hunters and warriors. King Arthur's legendary journey by ship to Annwn, the underworld of the British Celts, in search of a mysterious cauldron of inspiration and rebirth, as recorded by the thirteenth-century Welsh poet Thomas ap Einion, is typical of a Celtic otherworld voyage undertaken by sea, known in Gaelic as *immramma*.

The Highland people lived with their shaggy cattle amid an ancient wood pasture mosaic dominated by grand Caledonian pines, across an immense mountainous wilderness known as the Caledonian forest. Today just scattered tiny fragments of that great forest remain in what has become one of the most ecologically depleted landscapes in all of Europe. The collapse of the ecosystem in this part of the world can be traced to the time of the Clearances in the mid-eighteenth to mid-nineteenth century, when thousands of Highlanders were brutally evicted from their homes to make way for vast sheep estates. The Clearances tore apart communities that had lived on and worked the same land for centuries, as landlords forced them out of their crofts as part of the Scottish Agricultural Revolution.

The story of the Highland Clearances and the treatment of Scotland's original inhabitants by the English, told and retold by people from all sides has been the subject of countless dramatisations, each offering a different interpretation. Before travelling up to see Anders on what would be only my second visit to the Highlands, I had tried to come to a view on the bare bones of that troubled history. I understood that following the Jacobite Rising in 1745 and the infamous Battle of Culloden the following year, the very last pitched battle ever fought on British soil, the victorious British government set about declaring one law after the next designed to curtail the power of the clan chiefs and dismantle the ancient Gaelic culture that underpinned it. They even outlawed clan tartans and bagpipe music. The path was cleared for great swathes of land across the Highlands to be acquired by new outsider landlords set on replicating agricultural models employed in the English lowlands. George Granville Leveson-Gower, later the Duke of Sutherland, and my own mother's direct ancestor, brutally evicted a large number of Highland communities between 1810 and 1820, burning their cottages, harvesting the best timber trees from the glens and bringing in enormous numbers of sheep from outside to graze on the deserted landscape. Refugees were resettled and forced to subsist on small tenant farms known as crofts, primarily on barely cultivable land along the coasts. In 1846 an outbreak of potato blight caused a famine of epic proportions, and great numbers of Highlanders chose to emigrate to Canada and Australia, the cost of their fares covered in many cases by the same landlords that had forced them onto the margins.

The Clearances coincided with the eradication of many of the wild animals that had existed in the forest alongside the Highland people. Among those lost were the four considered to be keystone species of the Highlands. Keystone species are those whose role in the ecosystem is disproportionately vital and on which, therefore, all other species depend. In the same way that each arch of a medieval bridge is supported by a keystone which, if removed, causes the arch to collapse, we now understand that the health of ecosystems also hangs upon certain species, whose activities create so-called trophic cascades that benefit all the others.

Principal among the Highlands' keystone species is the native Highland cattle and, long ago, its ancestor, the fearsome black, long-horned wild ox, or *aurochs,* which may have survived in the wild until after Roman times. The browsing, grazing and trampling of these large-horned cattle prevent the darkness of the tree canopy from eventually closing over the landscape, instead engineering open, sun-dappled glades and grazing lawns in which wildflowers, berry-laden scrub and small fruit trees may flourish. Then there's the pig, kept domestically for millennia, and its untamed ancestral species, the wild boar, nature's gardener, whose incessant rootling and disturbance of the ground exposes the bare soil to the benefit of delicate wildflowers, butterflies and songbirds. A third keystone species is the beaver, which, by damming up even the smallest brooks and streams, holds water in the landscape in permanent pools that hum with life of all kinds. Finally, and most importantly, is the wolf, the apex carnivore whose hunting maintains healthy populations of wild herbivores, keeps their numbers in check and controls their behaviour, such that herds are endlessly on the move, never stopping long enough to over-graze or over-browse one spot.

Nearing Glenfeshie, I asked Thomas for his views on wolves, a singularly controversial subject in Scottish circles. He told me that wolves had managed to cling on in the Highlands in the face of unrelenting persecution until the eighteenth century. A few stragglers may have survived into the early Victorian era. Once they were gone, the population of their main prey, red deer, began to explode. At the same time, wool produced at a much lower cost and imported from across the British Empire rendered the homegrown wool trade uneconomic. Gradually, as a consequence deer stalking replaced sheep as the main economic activity on the great estates. Landowners encouraged the proliferation of red deer to make for easy sport, feeding them through the winter. As we drove, we saw hordes of them, smaller than they should be, huddled on the bare hillsides on either side of the road. Red deer evolved to exist in woodland, but now, after two centuries of intense overgrazing by sheep and then deer, there was no woodland here.

Turning off the main road into Glenfeshie after a long drive through the surrounding landscape is like moving from black and white into technicolour, even in winter. It is as if the hills and valleys here are reawakening after a long sleep. Thomas beamed as he pointed out emergent juniper, hawthorn, dog rose, blackthorn and other scrub up the hillsides. Amid the grass and heather, I could see young Scots pines, rowans, birches and even oak trees, crisp brown leaves clinging to their whip-like stems, defying the elements. Even up on the ridgeline, where it was said trees would never grow, new saplings were springing up. We wound our way along a neatly compacted dirt road that follows the River Feshie, a tributary of the mighty Spey, as it cascaded along the rugged valley floor. Awestruck, I half expected to glimpse a secretive lynx hiding in the broken – but still proud – ancient trees along the middle reaches of the glen.

Eventually we pulled into a gravelly yard before a wide, two-storey Victorian lodge built of slate, complete with decorative turrets and castellations, warmly lit from within and encircled by a handful of crooked old pine trees. In the warmth of the Land Rover, I had been so lost in my enthusiasm for the sweeping beauty of the landscape that the day had given way to night unnoticed. It was bitterly cold as I climbed out of the car. At the open front door stood Anders: tall, thick-set, wearing dark corduroys and a cardigan the colour of claret. He was waiting to welcome me with his hands on his hips, feet slightly apart, the Henry VIII beard exactly as I had remembered. We hugged briefly without saying much. His hair and beard seemed a little greyer; his cheeks a fraction hollower, the eyes sparkling darker. He knew now, as I did, the desperate depths of grief that await any one of us in the abyss of possible freak events. We went inside, where I kicked off my shoes in the hall and left them with my bag by the door. Thomas and I walked single file behind Anders through to a warmly decorated sitting room where a fire was blazing and exuberant tartan throws covered enticingly fat sofas and armchairs. We sat down, the three of us, and I glanced at the titles of the coffee table books placed neatly on the low table between us: *Birds of East Africa*, *Wildlife of Britain*, and an enormously wide and heavy book of wildlife photographs by David Yarrow.

Thomas talked to us more about the ongoing rewilding of this part of the Highlands, Anders chipping in with a supporting comment here and a roll of the eyes there, emphasising the politics and the difficulties they had encountered getting all this done. We talked about the new lodges, the bothies and the growing stream of visitors who come not just for the stalking, now much more arduous and authentic than elsewhere, but to revel in a mythical landscape under comprehensive restoration. There are more people working at Glenfeshie now, and undoubtedly a reinvigoration of the local community is underway. Even some of the most resistant neighbours, instinctively wary of outsiders and of change, are now coming around to Anders' vision. We talked about a growing number of other great estates across the Highlands adopting a similar approach. Hugh McLeod, chief of the ancient McLeod clan, announced his plan to rewild a great swathe of the Isle of Skye, describing the desecrated land surrounding Dunvegan Castle as a human-made 'lunarscape'. The craft beer company Brewdog has acquired an estate with the explicit goal of rewilding the land and, in the process, capturing carbon from the atmosphere and developing nature tourism. Even more exciting, across some of Scotland's most iconic landscapes, all kinds of landowners – public, private and NGO – are stitching together habitat on restored land across millions of acres, of which Cairngorms Connect and the Affric Highlands are just two examples. Anders had been among the first – an inspiration.

After a short dinner of venison with crispy roast potatoes, Thomas rose to wish us goodnight, making his way out into the darkness for home and leaving Anders and me alone for the first time together. I asked how he was coping. We found all manner of similarities in the journey we had each endured since I had last seen him. Amid the chaos and the darkness, Anders and Anne had found comfort in the notion that we are part of a mystery beyond our understanding and that the souls of his children persist, beyond the senses, in some way that is unfathomable to us now. Like me, Anders soon found deep, meaningful solace in the magic of nature, first in the vicinity of his home in Denmark and later in Scotland too, when he returned. Now, not quite a year on, his tragic experience compelled him with a fervour greater than ever to bring positive change to this huge landscape. Both of us had found a lifeline in doing what we could to restore nature in a broken world at a time when our own world was broken. Anders directed me to my room, where I slept deeply before being woken with a start by my alarm clock. Six o'clock. After a cursory breakfast of cereal and black coffee, we left Glenfeshie before first light, Anders at the wheel, taking me back to Inverness airport. After a few minutes, a red deer hind leapt from the juniper and across the road in front of the headlamps. Swerving to avoid the frightened animal, Anders told me that he was surprised by this encounter: few red deer remain at Glenfeshie. He explained that once the forest has recovered a little more, they will allow numbers to increase.

I broached the subject of wolves.

'The politics here make it hard to imagine that wolves will be brought back any time soon,' he replied. 'But there are wolves in Denmark again after two hundred years. Did you see? They came across from Germany and have settled in a well-populated part of West Jutland. The area is suburban, almost. This is big news back home.'

I reflected on the hysteria around wolves in British rural society, especially here in the Highlands, surrounded by innumerable deer and vast open spaces, perfect for wolves. I wondered why there is such a deep-seated aversion to the idea of living alongside charismatic wildlife in this country. The technical word for an irrational fear of wild animals is *zoophobia*. A good number of British people are, at heart, zoophobes, often without even knowing it. More species are widely considered to be an intolerable nuisance than not. All too often, species are castigated as vermin, the animal equivalent of the weeds of the plant world; both are singled out for eradication.

The writer George Monbiot has quipped that wildlife in Britain generally falls into one of two categories: *game*, which are animals we pay to kill, and *vermin*, which are animals we pay other people to kill. With some blurring of the lines between the two, there is a truth to this. Virtually every mammal depicted on the tatty wildlife calendar that hangs in my children's playroom is considered by someone to be a pest. Badgers stand accused of spreading disease to livestock as well as eating all the hedgehogs, while their smaller mustelid cousins – the pine martens, polecats, stoats and weasels – are all considered voracious pests by gamekeepers and farmers alike. Hedgehogs love to scoff the eggs of game birds. Even tiny, inoffensive moles, so lovely in their jet-black velveteen coats, are considered an annoyance with their restless burrowing and tunnelling, an activity that is vital in the turning over and aeration of the ground, the softly sieved soil of molehills a perfect germination bed for the seeds of wild plants. I have never forgotten visiting my older brother Zac at his intimidating boarding school in the Savernake Forest and seeing from the car window the tiny black corpses of dozens of moles strung along a barbed-wire fence beside the long drive. I just could not understand why people would go to so much trouble to massacre these sweet creatures. We are raised in a culture of relentless killing, and few people question it.

Otters eat all the fish, as do the lanky, secretarial herons that stand motionless at the water's edge at dusk and dawn. Other much-maligned fish guzzlers include seals, goosanders and the witchy, jet-black cormorant, a seabird relic from an ancient age, before the evolution of waterproof feathers, which hangs its wings out to dry on either side of its body after venturing into the water.

By the same token, foxes are seen as a menace to poultry and game birds, and their night-time shrieking is particularly unappreciated by city-dwellers. If some people had their way, there'd be no wildlife more charismatic than a blue tit in our landscapes.

When it comes to deer, disliked by farmers for munching and flattening crops, the zoophobes have a point, but only because our ancestors eradicated the predators that once effectively controlled their movements and population. The irony, of course, is that many of these so-called vermin species have thrived in the absence of predators that would otherwise keep their numbers far lower. The list of enemy species goes on. Wild boar are almost universally loathed and perceived as dangerous when, in fact, they pose very little threat to humans unless they feel directly threatened. Beavers are accused of flooding fields, roads and even homes, all while making a terrible mess along the riverbanks (more on beavers later). Corvids – ravens, rooks, crows, magpies, jackdaws and jays – as well as buzzards, eagles and all raptors, get in the way of the shooting industry and are accused of devouring songbirds as if we humans have played no part in the disappearance of birds from the landscape. Rabbits build huge, Hogarthian warrens from which they emerge to eat all the grass. At the same time, their larger brown hare and mountain hare cousins are slaughtered in enormous numbers every year for harbouring ticks that could jump across to the hordes of grouse we otherwise line up on the moors for blasting out of the sky each summer. Screeching gulls are reviled for swooping low to steal ice creams from the hands of children, and red kites similarly terrify picnickers as they circle and dive and demand their share. Our hostility towards wildlife extends even to the bullfinch, a strikingly gorgeous songbird, because its diet includes fruit tree blossom in spring. Even though it is on the Amber list of conservation concern after steep population declines in the last century, some fruit growers are still granted licences to control its numbers.

Plans to reintroduce Britain's lost species never fail to elicit howls of protest from a vocal minority. It took 30 years of persuasion before legendary rewilder Roy Dennis managed to gain permission to restore majestic white-tailed eagles to the Isle of Wight, where the last pair had nested in the eighteenth century and from where they soar once again now on their eight-foot wingspan, hunting geese, grey mullet and even foxes, it is said, up and down the south coast of England. Today, an ill-tempered debate persists over plans to reintroduce wildcats, once known as *woodcats*. These are not much larger than domestic tabbies but were brutally eradicated from all but the remotest corners of Scotland in the nineteenth century.

Perhaps we've lived so long without much wildlife in the British Isles that we've become accustomed to a sanitised environment, yet we present ourselves to the world as great wildlife lovers. It is we British who make the most extraordinary nature documentary films; David Attenborough is our national treasure. Our wildlife conservation organisations, which do invaluable work all over the world, are among the oldest, biggest, and best anywhere; and we endlessly lecture other nations on the importance of protecting what remains of their fauna. Yet the notion of reintroducing lynxes or wolves, our apex carnivores, is dismissed as the fantasy of ecologists, even though our remoter landscapes rank among the least densely populated areas in all of Europe.

Without fuss, just across the channel on the Continent, bears, lynx and particularly wolves have made a remarkable comeback from near extinction. A few tiny refugia wolf populations that clung on in the wildest mountain ranges of eastern and southern Europe have quietly spread outwards over several decades, and wolves are now found in every mainland European country. Wolves have even made it back to Normandy, which is half the distance from Cannwood as Cannwood is from Findhorn in Scotland, where the last British wolf is said to have been killed. There are wolves in Belgium, in the Netherlands, Europe's most intensively farmed and densely populated country, and even in the tiny financial centre of Luxembourg, where residents have taken to watching them through binoculars from the outdoor dining terraces of certain country hotels and restaurants. The stereotypical image of wolves as dangerous and frightening and needing vast tracts of wild land turns out to be all wrong. We thought the wolves and the eagles only lived in the remote mountains and that they could not co-exist with us, but it turns out they were only confined to the high ground because the last few survivors were driven there by humans. Co-existence with wolves is not only possible but desirable. Without them, our wilder places and farmland become overrun with deer and other hungry herbivores, and the entire ecosystem falls out of balance. It occurs to me that wolves are totemic. Until we find peace with them, and learn to live alongside them, we will not find any harmony with the wider nature around us.

The list of missing species that have been reintroduced to the British Isles is beginning to lengthen. Red kites, great bustards, white storks, white-tailed eagles, common cranes, cirl buntings and choughs have all been brought back. Wild boar brought themselves back by escaping from specialist farms in the 1980s and 1990s. Beavers, pool frogs that sing loudly during the breeding season at night, sand lizards, large blue and chequered skipper butterflies and short-haired bumblebees are also back in England. Now there is a growing clamour for more from a public enlivened by a rewilding movement offering a vision of great, untrammelled optimism, of landscapes richer in nature than they have been for centuries.

It is becoming conceivable that Europe's mysterious big cat, the lynx, may even make a return to Britain. The Scandinavians call lynx the ghosts of the forest, believing that they see without being seen. The Celts of Britain worshipped a god named Lugus, the Celtic equivalent of the pan-European deity known to the Greeks as Hermes; to the Scandinavians as Odin; to the Slavs as Svarog and to the Romans as Mercurius. Some suggest that the name Lugus derives from lynx, the last of which are thought to have disappeared from Britain at least a millennium ago. Lynx do not harm people and rarely take livestock, instead ambushing small deer in woodland. It is only a matter of time before the magical notion of their return to Britain becomes a reality. The lynx, an intrinsic part of an unimaginably intricate web of life which we have now depleted beyond recognition, was here long before we had even developed language. We need lynx back not only to help reduce the number of deer overgrazing woodland across Britain but because it is our moral and sacred duty to bring them back. Only when we begin piecing back together what we have broken and, in the process, learning how to co-exist with species that may appear to be inconvenient, will we begin to restore harmony in our relationship with nature.

In some parts of rural Europe, such as Romania's Carpathian Mountains, Italy's Apennine mountains and Asturias in northern Spain, the return of iconic wildlife species has made nature tourism the mainstay of the local economy. Asturias is a particularly beautiful place, with a climate and topography surprisingly similar to Britain's western uplands. I visited with Frankie and Isaac in August 2018, in part to experience for myself a vision of what our uplands might one day be. Iris had chosen to stay with friends further south, where we'd meet her a few days later. We took the regular flight that leaves Gatwick for Oviedo each Thursday. A lot of the people on the plane wore khaki-coloured trousers and carried waterproof rucksacks, quite different from the other flights from Britain to Spain I'd taken.

From an ecological perspective, Europe's Atlantic coast, stretching from Scotland's western Highlands and Islands down through Wales, Cornwall, France's west coast and north-western Spain, is a world in its own right. Stormy skies and no shortage of rain make this region Europe's coastal temperate rainforest zone, now a vanishingly rare habitat of which only fragments remain. Long after the fertile lowlands of Europe were converted to feed a growing human population, south-west Europe's coastal uplands, mostly inhospitable for arable farming, changed little. As in the Highlands of Scotland, the local population lived in much the same way for generation after generation, eking out a living principally through the extensive grazing of hardy upland cattle among the trees. In more recent centuries, however, the hills were cleared to supply shipbuilders, housebuilders and industrial furnaces. Larger wild animals were picked off one by one until prevailing economic forces finally swept ancient upland communities away. As in Scotland, much of the land was given over to sheep.

We were met at Oviedo by a local naturalist and wildlife artist named Luis Frechilla, a small man with friendly, eager eyes, who drove us from the airport up to a mountain village called Tablado, in the heart of bear country. During the twentieth century, the economy of Asturias was underpinned by two industries: open-cast coal mining and sheep, both of which fell into sharp decline; the coal because coal is dying everywhere, and the sheep because, as any upland farmer will tell you, running large flocks up and down hills is not a business that works well in today's world, at least not without hefty subsidies. Young people moved out to the cities to find work. Whole villages and great swathes of the landscape were simply abandoned. Then something remarkable started to happen. For the first time in living memory, the formerly barren hillsides of Asturias became cloaked in the colours of countless flowering plants. Tree saplings began to appear, seemingly out of nowhere. The birdsong intensified.

Soon wildlife too began to return: chamois, roe and red deer, wild boar, Iberian wolves venturing down from the Pyrenees, eagles and vultures. The handful of Cantabrian brown bears that had clung to a precarious existence in mountain strongholds crept down and began to multiply. And then the tourists came; first, a trickle, principally bird-watching enthusiasts from Britain and Germany, but the numbers grew. Quick to spot an opportunity, the Asturias regional government, supported by the national administration in Madrid, set about creating protected areas. They put in place funding to support the grazing of traditional cattle in the hills, to rebuild the ancient circular dry-stone structures known as honey castles used to protect beehives from bears, and to provide grants for local businesses gearing up to cater to the influx of tourists. They began to promote Asturias to the world, even adding the moniker Paraiso Natural (Natural Paradise) to the name of their principality. As the natural environment flourished, so did the rural economy.

In Tablado, we stayed in a small *casa rural*, a tiny family-owned hotel with just four bedrooms, one of a dozen such businesses in the village, all catering to nature tourists. A burly, chain-smoking young man named Victor, son of the proprietors, took us out wildlife watching each day, loading up with a basket containing coffee and the traditional Asturian fare of bread, cheese, cured sausage and *casadielles*, or walnut doughnuts, made by his mother for the trip. We were relaxed about not seeing a bear in those first two days in the hills surrounding Tablado because there was so much other wildlife. The place was alive; we were never bored. There was beauty in all directions. We swam in the icy water of the Rio Cares and ate like kings at a different tavern each evening. After a time, Luis took us deeper into the mountains, heading for the huge Somiedo National Park. There we stayed in the small town of Pola de Somiedo, where the mayor told me over breakfast one morning that the town, once a backwater, now receives 125,000 visitors a year. The tourists come to experience an actual national park of the kind that we simply do not have in the British Isles. By comparison, our national parks are largely bare, stripped clean of wildlife and grazed treeless by sheep or deer. Pola de Somiedo, which buzzes with energy, sits in a large valley enclosed by steep slopes that, if cleared of nature, could easily be in the Highlands of Scotland or in Wales' Cambrian Mountains. The iconic capercaillie, a huge grouse-like bird that is on the cusp of disappearing from the British Isles, thrives in this valley, as do wildcats, which we spotted on several occasions stalking their small prey out in broad daylight amid the wildflowers.

The main thing to do in Somiedo is hike up to a rocky viewing spot high on the mountainside to scope for bears. We waited and waited, Luis and I drinking a local red wine from two metal cups, Egyptian vultures wheeling high overhead, until finally, at dusk – to hushed whoops of excitement – a young bear lolloped out from the chestnut trees into a large clearing on the other side of the valley and began foraging for bilberries and wild strawberries. Our hearts sang. From the hillside, I had sent a message to my friend Anders: Asturias might be the template for the recovery of the Highlands.

9

Wilding

*The tree which moves some to tears of joy is in the eyes of
others only a green thing which stands in the way. Some
see nature all ridicule and deformity, and by these I shall
not regulate my proportions; and some scarce see nature at
all. But to the eyes of the man of imagination, nature is
imagination itself. As a man is, so he sees.*

WILLIAM BLAKE

Iris and I shared a love of icy frosts and the wide blue skies
of 'proper winter days'. On snowy days she made a point of
sending me a blizzard of photos and the kind of frustratingly
short video clips that teenagers love to share. As Iris's 16th
birthday loomed in late January 2020, six months after the
accident, a particularly mushy, warm winter had settled over
us: weather to match my gloom. A year earlier, two so-called
beasts from the east in quick succession had blanketed the
British Isles each time in a metre of snow. Sometimes I re-watch
the clips Iris sent me from Wycombe Abbey. There she was,
ploughing through the fresh snow with her friend Carys, fat
snowflakes tumbling from the sky all around them. The two

were hopelessly dressed for the weather, Iris beaming in a soft red and white Christmas hat, I remember pointing out to her at the time. 'Hi, Dad!' laughing as first, she ran, then fell and rolled, virtually disappearing beneath the snow.

Though I didn't like the oppressive grey weather that first winter without her, I was quietly glad about the lack of snow. There was comfort in studiously avoiding all sorts of things Iris would have loved. Fishing with Frankie for muddy pikes in the drizzle on the lake at Stourhead was fine. Whereas a fruit smoothie drunk on the doorstep of her favourite place in Barnes, making cupcakes in the kitchen at Cannwood, music blaring, or drinking a cold beer at a fun little party in London … the very idea of these things filled me with longing and dread. My very ability to indulge in such pastimes seemed profoundly unfair. Deep down, I knew that these aspects of my life would need to resume at some stage and that I would come to do them again, not least because I owed it to my family, but not yet. I made a point of defiantly rejecting anything that might underscore the injustice. Why was I alive still at the age of nearly 40 to enjoy for the umpteenth time things that for Iris had been shiny and new, while she was just gone, her life over before it had even really started?

I stopped listening to music altogether. When I stumbled upon music being played elsewhere, the effect on me was often giddying. A soaring *Ave Maria* that played on the radio in the dentist's waiting room sent me into a spiral of grief; so irresistibly beautiful I found myself mesmerised by it, unable to tear myself away until, eventually, I had no choice but to creep out and hide sobbing in the lavatory by the receptionist's desk. While melancholic music was particularly crushing, lively music transported me to memories of bouncing around with the three children when they were small, doing my best not to spill a beer in one hand while spinning Iris by the hand with the other. Some songs reminded me of driving them to their prep school in my old Golf on a Wednesday morning, which was always my morning to drop them off. Iris tended to sit in the front next to me, queen bee of the car. I took to playing the music of a particular time or from a single musician, telling them between songs as much of the story as I knew. Immaculately turned out in her school uniform, hair tied back in a ponytail, Iris would look ahead and listen intently, periodically turning sharply to rebuke or swipe at the two boys noisily pulling and pushing at each other in the back. We played Buddy Holly, who had died alongside fellow 1950's singers Ritchie Valens and the Big Bopper at the age of 21 when his small plane crashed in a field in Iowa – a day forever remembered as *the day the music died*, as remembered in the Don McLean song. We played Desmond Dekker and the birth of ska; early Bob Marley, Lee Scratch Perry and the emergence of reggae; Elvis, of course; Roy Orbison; Fats Domino; sometimes the Rolling Stones, whose hit 'She's a Rainbow' had been for us *the Iris song* since she was a toddler. Now I found that most music made the missing of Iris too much to bear. Movies had the same effect; there was always a trigger that sent me outside the room, tears brimming.

It was in the run-up to Iris's birthday that winter, the first after her death, that I was walking with her younger brother Frankie along one of the rough field margins at Cannwood, picking our way between the verdant, berry-laden hedge and the barbed-wire fence designed to keep the cattle penned in their field. We were looking for edible mushrooms for Jemima (chicken of the woods, ceps and other edible boletes are the ones that grow most prolifically at Cannwood), but mostly we were focused on not tripping over the ferocious tendrils of bramble spilling out from the side of the hedge.

'Why can't the whole of Cannwood be for nature?' Frankie had asked me at that moment, 'Not just the edges of the fields and around the ponds?'

Whilst most of the farm remained dedicated to the conventional rotational grazing of 40 Poll Dorset sheep and the same number of White Park cattle, I had made efforts to create more space for nature around the edges. The new woods were substantial at one end of the farm; the hedges were now overgrown and becoming massive; the ponds, and more recently, the still-muddy rewiggled stream and wetland that now snaked along the valley bottom – all these were great habitats. When the time had come to replace some of the old field boundary fencing, we had moved the new fences inwards to create more space for nature, a long open ride that ran the length of the farm between the old woodland and the fields. This had been Iris's idea. Her chestnut brown Welsh hill pony, Ben, had arrived one Christmas when she had been seven or eight. The pony was Kate's initiative in what was to be the last year of our marriage, so in due course, the burden of looking after this new addition to the burgeoning menagerie at Cannwood had fallen on me. Iris had been so excited by Ben's arrival that she had led him straight through the back door of the house, through the boot room and right into the kitchen, where he stood wide-eyed, poised at the edge of panic in the space between the Aga and the kitchen island. Unaccustomed to handling horses, I froze, heart-pounding, braced for disaster, while Kate calmly took hold of the lead rope and brought the pony outside. Simultaneously appalled and relieved, I skulked off, wanting nothing more to do with it.

Nevertheless, I arranged for three dilapidated stables tucked at the side of the big shed to be cleared out, fixed up and painted a deep green. Great care was taken not to disturb the ceiling encrusted with the mud-cup nests of swallows, now vacant for the winter. Kate began teaching Iris how to ride immediately. It hadn't started well. First, I heard the shrieking and the rapid-fire clackety-clack of hooves on tarmac before I caught a glimpse of Iris clinging round the neck of the galloping pony as he tore up the lane, low to the ground, the two ponytails, hers and the horse's, pirouetting in unison away from me. There being nothing much I could do, I stood rooted to the spot and watched through my fingers as somehow she managed to persuade the pony to slow to a canter and judder to a halt before they reached the road at the end of the lane. Iris slid off and led Ben back down the lane towards Kate and me, doing her best to appear breezy, her little round face streaked with tears. A local girl named Catherine, who lived and worked at a nearby horse livery, agreed to come in each day for an hour or two to look after the pony when we were away and to continue Iris's riding lessons.

I didn't have quite as many interests in common with Iris as I did with the two boys, and in any case, girls, it seems, get bored of their fathers as adolescence looms. I pretended not to mind when Iris forbade me from hugging her at the start or the end of the school day. Before long, I wasn't even allowed to walk with her from the car to the classroom unless there happened to be more stuff than usual to carry between the two, in which case she let me walk several paces behind her. During weekends and long holidays in Somerset, I wasn't part of the plan. Iris and her friends made music films in the garden with their phones, baked cakes, or tarted themselves up with make-up pinched from Jemima's cupboard. Iris rode out every day on Ben, sometimes with one of the Dreamers girls, each of whom also had a Welsh pony, or on her own. They spent hours beforehand and afterwards brushing their ponies, cleaning them, feeding them carrots, apples or Polos, leading them here and there, and dressing them in blankets when the weather turned. One day, I decided to get myself a horse, so I could go out riding with Iris. This was quite a leap for me.

I'd ridden horses as a young teenager, but only American style, without a hat, guiding the horse one-handed, my other hand gripping a large wooden pommel at the front of the saddle. Even this I had only done during the handful of Easters I spent with my father at Cuixmala, his ranch-turned-nature reserve on Mexico's Pacific coast. In the last years of his life, he had acquired and was restoring nature on a huge area of degraded land, now part of Mexico's official national park network, known as the Chamela-Cuixmala Biosphere Reserve, the largest extant piece of Pacific semi-deciduous tropical dry forest in Mexico. Hundreds of thousands of invasive eucalyptus trees were removed, wetlands were rewetted, and ocelots (wild cats native to that part of the world) and crocodiles were reintroduced with help from legendary wildlifer John Aspinall. The number of turtles returning to nest on the beaches, now protected by a rotation of guards, soared. Growing squadrons of pelicans glided just above the crest of the waves rolling into the beach. Eventually, even the jaguars returned. The place teemed with life in a way I'd never experienced anywhere else.

By far the best way to explore the reserve was on the back of a horse, and when it came to riding, we were thrown in at the deep end. The stables were overseen by a wiry, five-foot-five moustachioed horseman named Liberado, who was probably in his mid-sixties by then and rumoured to have several wives and a number of children scattered among the local villages. I was enthralled by Liberado, and my father adored him. Setting out, Liberado led the way, soon singing loudly under a gigantic Mexican hat, astride a stallion named Ojos Blancos, on account of the whites that were visible all around his almond eyes, a feature that gave the horse a deranged look. I rode a grey gelding named Gabilan in an American saddle, which is much wider and deeper than the European kind, rather like an armchair. I quickly got the hang of it, mostly because the horses just fell into line behind Liberado. One word from him was enough to stop the whole troop, or set it into a gallop. These were some of the most intimate moments I spent with my father. We rode out at sunset, mostly in silence, wandering single file behind Liberado along sandy paths beside the water, marvelling at unending columns of birds floating in to roost: roseate spoonbills, egrets, cormorants of various kinds, white ibis, magnificent frigate birds, great blue and green herons and yellow-crowned night-herons, all jockeying for space in an escalating cacophony on islands of mangrove amid the lagoons. Giant crocodiles silently stalked the water beneath, just the eyes and the tips of the tails visible above the water, waiting for a bird to make a mistake and slip within reach.

After Iris got her pony, I found an American quarter horse named Jessie, trained to follow instruction the Mexican way. I rode Jessie using an English saddle but with the single rein I'd learned to use in Mexico, and it worked fine. Jessie was quick, and I am a coward, so I went out each time with clammy cold hands and returned, legs trembling a little, ecstatic to have made it back still in one piece. Much braver and more competent than me, Iris found the whole thing hilarious. Mostly I rode behind her, walking, trotting or galloping either along the hard bridlepath that bisects Cannwood or at a canter along the new grass ride that ran parallel. Both ways took us up into a huge wood belonging to the Duke of Somerset that stretches along the entire length of the ridge above the valley and all the way into Wiltshire. The wood is criss-crossed with tracks and paths fringed with foxgloves, nettles and comfrey. Whenever Jessie got too close to Ben's backside, he kicked back, sometimes making her rear up. If I complained, it triggered an argument, so I learned to keep quiet and to keep the horse back. This plan for spending time with Iris as she entered her teens worked. We rode together all the time, sometimes chatting and laughing, sometimes just riding side by side in silence. I haven't yet ridden Jessie since Iris died.

When they were little, one summer, I took the three children, Iris, Frankie and Isaac, to visit my friends Isabella Tree (Issy) and Charlie Burrell at their home, Knepp Castle, in Sussex. Issy and Charlie are the original pioneers of rewilding in Britain, an idea now widely popularised by their extraordinary project at Knepp. Two decades ago, they made the momentous decision to give up what had become an exhausting battle to make a success of an intensive arable and dairy farming operation on their 3,000 acres of heavy clay, handing their entire farm back to nature. The big idea at Knepp was a simple one, derived from the work of Dutch ecologist Dr Frans Vera, who argues that in ancient times, Europe was never, in fact, blanketed in the kind of dense closed-canopy forest that we imagine. Vera believes that large herbivores are the principal factor in creating rich habitats and that the disturbance created by great herds of wild ox, bison, horses, boar and deer, which once roamed Europe and the British Isles, has been entirely overlooked by ecological historians.

In her bestselling book *Wilding*, Issy describes 'the great forest misconception,' the mistaken notion that the British Isles were once covered in closed-canopy woodland, such that 'a squirrel could have run from John O'Groats to Land's End on the tops of trees.' This is the stuff of fairy tales, she says, and dense forest should not be the goal of those dedicated to nature restoration. 'Many of our shrubs and trees – including hazel, wild apple, wild pear, wild cherry, rowan, dogwood, common privet, Scots pine and oak (that quintessentially English tree) – are light-demanding species that cannot regenerate in closed-canopy conditions,' she writes. These species 'point to a much more open landscape – a wood-pasture system driven by free-roaming herds of grazing and browsing animals, where trees regenerate out in the open, within thorny scrub. This is the landscape described by Oliver Rackham, our late, great woodland expert, as the *wildwood*. It is the landscape of the New Forest and all the other hunting forests of medieval England – a dynamic mosaic of gigantic open-grown trees and groves of all species and ages, grazing *lawns*, water meadows and thorny scrub. Paradise for wildlife.'

Knepp turned out native, domestic proxies for the keystone species that were once prolific and whose activities underpin the entire ecosystem. They chose hardy breeds that can live outside all year round without supplementary feeding. Old English longhorn cattle were used in place of aurochs; Tamworth pigs for wild boar; and Exmoor ponies for Europe's long-extinct wild horse, the tarpan. Red and fallow deer were added to the mix. At Knepp, all these animals are free to roam where they like, eat what they like, sleep where they like. Across the entire landscape, a shape-shifting wood pasture has grown up, rich in scrub and wildflowers, a mosaic of habitats teeming with wildlife in an abundance that we are unused to seeing today. Issy's book charts the astonishing natural recovery that is unfolding at Knepp and the surging return of species that are disappearing almost everywhere else in the British Isles: turtle doves, nightingales, purple emperor butterflies, kingfishers, all five British species of owl and countless other species are present at Knepp in numbers that seem unprecedented. Populations of insects and small mammals are skyrocketing, and with them, everything that depends on them for food.

On the day I visited the farm with the children, small then, we piled into Charlie's military-green roofless jeep and set off, bumping over ground rendered uneven by the rootling of pigs the previous winter. A wet spaniel in the back seat did its best to rest its drooling muzzle on my shoulder. Exhilarated and engulfed by the warmth of the breeze all around us, I felt as if we were exploring England's version of the savannahs of East Africa, famously among the most beautiful and vibrant landscapes in the world. Perhaps on some deeper level, I felt I'd been in this kind of place before; everything felt right and beautiful. Great flocks of goldfinches scattered between islands of scrub as the jeep bounced through the tussocky grass. In the back with the spaniel, the children strained for a better view, howling with excitement when we spotted not one but three vivid blue kingfishers zipping by in succession along a river that had been liberated from its straightjacket and was now free to meander, broad, shallow and slow, across its own floodplain.

Charlie stopped the jeep amid scattered shoots of sallow near the water's edge to show us not kingfishers but purple emperors, one of Britain's rarest and perhaps most beautiful butterflies. It was not long before an iridescent butterfly bigger than I expected floated by and settled on a leaf in front of us. Charlie carefully examined one whip of sallow after the next before producing tenderly in his hand a fat emperor caterpillar for us to peer at before he placed it back where he had found it. The species had never previously been recorded at Knepp. Now the farm is the most important hotspot for purple emperors in Britain. 'It's because of the *sallow*,' Charlie said, explaining that sallow, which is hybridised wild willow, is the favourite food of purple emperor caterpillars. Most landowners dislike sallow and weed it out, but once upon a time, sallow had all sorts of uses, from tools to wicker-ware and winter fodder and even as headache medicine (aspirin is derived from salicin, a compound found in sallow bark). Charlie explained that the seeds of sallow, which appear in great blooms of fluff every few years, need bare, wet soil in which to germinate; in other words, precisely the conditions created by the rootling of pigs. The tremendous abundance of sallow that has appeared at Knepp has led to an explosion in the number of purple emperors. Where conventional conservation had primarily failed, the hands-off approach to nature restoration at Knepp had worked miracles, all the while upending our most basic understanding of the complex, enigmatic life cycle of the purple emperor butterfly.

The brilliance of the Knepp project lies in how little human interference was needed for the transformation to occur. The story of Knepp's resurgent purple emperors is just one example of how Charlie and Issy's project has turned nature conservation in Britain on its head. Lying out a rug, Charlie produced a wicker basket from the back of the jeep, and the children descended on the bread, cheese and cold-sliced (Knepp) ham and beef within. Two huge longhorns lay chewing the cud a short distance away on the other side of the water. Sitting there in the shade of that massive oak, immersed in the thrumming of insects and a cacophony of birdsong all around us. I reflected on quite how disappointing the rest of Britain is by comparison, how quiet, how colourless. I felt a powerful urge to bring people here, to show them what Britain can be, if we so choose.

Most people are aware that the natural fabric of the British countryside has been degraded and depleted over the centuries, but few realise the full extent of the catastrophe that has unfolded, particularly in recent decades. Depressingly, the British Isles now rank among the most nature-impoverished places on Earth. Expectations diminish from one generation to the next as each passing generation becomes conditioned to what they know during their own lifetimes, in a process known as *shifting baselines*. We simply have no inkling of how much we have lost. Countless species have vanished altogether, and those that do remain frequently exist in isolated, often tiny fragments of remnant nature, largely thanks to the care of a handful of dedicated nature-friendly farmers and conservationists. Personal accounts from earlier centuries describe seas rich with life, meadows and woodland glades carpeted in wildflowers and thronged with songbirds. That's why rewilding has captured the public imagination. Rewilding offers a route, for the first time, to meaningful, landscape-scale nature restoration, a way to start reversing the losses. In her book, Issy talks of the differing reactions of their neighbours and other locals upon first being shown around the changing landscape. The couple found that young people were often wide-eyed and enthusiastic, while the middle-aged were appalled by the mess. Those over 80, however, grew misty-eyed, reminiscing about the landscape of their childhood. Not so long ago, much of the British Isles was cloaked in a richly dynamic natural tapestry exactly like this, particularly where the land is not well suited to arable farming, across the south, the west and the north.

Not everyone is convinced by the new rewilding movement. Some see rewilding as a threat to traditional farming communities that have managed our landscapes for centuries, fretting that it could even lead to their disappearance altogether. Nothing could be further from the truth. Britain's remoter landscapes were grazed extensively by native cattle of the kind found at Knepp for centuries before intensification, and a return to this kind of traditional farming will be essential to the process of nature recovery on agriculturally marginal land. Alongside stewardship payments from the government and a thriving nature tourism business, Knepp sells more than 100 tonnes of prime 'wild' beef, pork and venison each year. After my first visit to Knepp, I reflected that the term 'wilder farming', rather than 'rewilding', might be a better way to describe the changes a growing number of people long to see across swathes of Britain.

Our visit to Knepp stayed with me, and in the years that followed, I leapt at any opportunity to go back, forging a close friendship with Charlie and Issy. Though I was inspired by what they were doing, at the time, I imagined Cannwood to be somehow different, too small for this kind of approach. In due course, however, while doing my best every year to make our little nature-friendly but conventional lamb and beef enterprise at Cannwood work, I saw that, across much of Britain, modern livestock farming of the kind I was attempting is simply not viable. Most of the food grown in Britain is produced on only a fifth of the land, predominantly the rich arable landscapes of the east. The environmental cost of trying to make more intensive farming work everywhere, no matter how suitable the land, has been catastrophic. It only happens because of oodles of government subsidies, which are now finally being phased out and replaced with a shiny new system that will reward farmers for restoring soil and nature on their land. Against this backdrop, there is now a huge opportunity to begin the process of bringing nature in Britain back to life.

It is the uplands that have been most tragically depleted. Tens of millions of sheep have almost entirely stripped hills and valleys of their green mantle. Trees, scrub, wildflowers and birdsong are largely absent, except in small pockets. People think of our upland National Parks as great nature reserves, but they are not. Indeed, there is often less wildlife in these parts of our country than in the surrounding areas. A little more than a year before Iris died, in spring 2018, I was invited to stay with Julia Aglionby, chair of the Uplands Alliance, near Carlisle in England's far north. I wanted to see the Pennines, as bleak a landscape as you'll find anywhere in Britain until you arrive at a huge farm called Geltsdale, where Julia brought us to meet her friends, the tenant farmer Tom Wilson and his wife Julie. The Wilsons decided in 2010 to swap their intensive sheep enterprise for a herd of native longhorn cattle. As we sat in his kitchen over steaming mugs of tea, Tom acknowledged the environmental impact of sheep farming. Managing a herd of several thousand sheep had been hard work. So when a local Natural England representative suggested switching from sheep to cattle and a much wilder way of farming, Tom decided to try it. Frans Vera visited Geltsdale to discuss options, and a deal was struck with Natural England on a stewardship scheme.

The transition wasn't easy. Initially, the family missed their sheep, but they soon fell in love with their beautiful, shaggy longhorns, and today the awakening landscape is a sea of wildflowers dotted with emergent scrub and young trees of all kinds. A small river fringed with the fresh growth of willow, aspen and alder babbles through a valley-bottom vivid with colour. Amid the melancholic cry of curlews wheeling overhead and birdsong the likes of which I've never heard anywhere else except at Knepp, I found Geltsdale mesmerising.

It was in that moment, in the winter after Iris died, picking my way along a thin strip of vibrant, unkempt nature between the hedge and the barbed wire, that – prompted by Frankie's simple question – I decided we would set out to emulate Knepp in our own small way at Cannwood. Later it transpired that two of my neighbours were also moving in a similar direction, and I began to imagine that our place might even come to an inkblot of natural regeneration expanding outwards from the Brewham Valley. Brewham lies at the heart of the ancient Forest of Selwood, once a great wood pasture straddling the Somerset–Wiltshire border, extending south of Frome almost into Dorset. Brewham itself, in the heart of the forest, has a mystical past dating back to the Druids; indeed, *Druley,* of Druley Hill, which overlooks Cannwood, is an alternative form of the word Druid. In more recent centuries, Brewham harbours a murky history of witchcraft. In his book *The Witches of Selwood Forest,* local historian Andrew Pickering records accounts of black sabbath meetings of two covens of witches, one centred upon Bayford and Stoke Trister at the southern end of the great forest and the other close to Cannwood, at Brewham. A formal accusation for maleficent witchcraft was made of almost 30 women and men between 1658 and 1690, and according to Pickering, 'Until its suppression by higher authorities, the Selwood Forest panic looked set to become one of the most severe witch-hunts in English history.' Most likely, these witches were merely men and women who had managed to hang onto some of Britain's pre-Christian spiritual association with nature and who were living in small forest-dwelling communities. It was often witches who had retained a detailed knowledge of the medicinal value of the plants and fungi of the forest, treating common ailments and providing general medical care and midwifery in the community. Such people suffered violent persecution across Christendom, and Selwood was no different.

Not long after my rewilding plans came to light, one of my neighbours, a landscape designer named Lulu Urquhart, who has become famous for working with rather than against nature in her beautiful designs and who even went on to win the Chelsea Flower Show with a garden modelled on a beaver wetland, suggested that the reason so many people in and around this area are now actively working to restore the once-rich natural tapestry of Brewham, for her a holy place, is because the land itself is calling out to be healed. I felt no inclination to dispute this lovely idea.

After a visit from Charlie Burrell and discussions with our local Natural England advisor and some of our neighbours, the work at Cannwood began in earnest at the start of spring in

2020. The sheep were sold before spring lambing, as were the White Park cattle, magnificent though they had been. We'd have longhorn cattle back, but not yet. Chris and Garry set to work removing fences. I watched for hours as the tractor grabbed one end of an entire fence and just pulled it out like spaghetti, miles of it, before bundling it into coiled, jagged, rusty piles, which were later loaded into skips and carted away. We found layer upon layer of fencing, as if nobody had ever removed an old fence before adding a new one. It took us about a month to get rid of it all, and then we opened up wide gaps in the hedges dividing one field from the next. A little creative destruction was acceptable, I felt, given that these hedges are not particularly old, having been added as a way of enclosing the ancient Selwood forest during the Victorian era. In any case, an explosion of new scrub was just a while away.

By the time the intensity of the work began to peter out, spring was in full flow. Wild daffodils and early purple orchids were the first flowers to appear, twinkling in the morning dew across fields that, fenceless, gateless, and now connected by wide open gaps in the hedges, already gave the impression of an open landscape, a wildwood miraculously in the making. The old oaks that line the hedges contributed to the scene, offering a glimpse of Selwood as it might once have been. Looking east, up to the end of the wooded ridge running the length of the Brewham valley, you can see King Alfred's Tower, built in 1769, before Selwood was divided into the patchwork quilt of fields that characterise the landscape today. The Hoare family built the tower to commemorate the spot where King Alfred of Wessex amassed his troops in Selwood Forest before heading out to conquer the eastern kings and crown himself the first king of all England. A patch of newer brickwork about halfway up marks where a light aircraft hit the tower during the Second World War, killing both pilots. I began to conceive a plan to work with landowners to restore streaks and patches of nature across the old Forest of Selwood.

That spring, absorbing entirely new perspectives of Cannwood as I walked across fields recently opened up, I imagined how much fun Iris would have had riding here now. I searched the ground for tiny scrub and tree saplings pushing up through the grass. Within weeks, nature across the farm already became more unruly; and I began to notice larger flocks of birds, as if somehow the word was out. I thought of Iris constantly. I still have a video she sent me, aged eight or nine, of a great flock of starlings she had managed to catch on her phone whilst out alone with Ben, the pony.

'Look, Dad, I'm right by the starlings,' she says in the video, breathless, overcome with awe. 'I'll get them to fly. And look, they're going up! Look how giant that is! I was right next to them!'

In her video, the starlings lift collectively off the ground to form a genie-like figure above her, shifting its shape as it moves off down the valley before the birds settle, chattering in a row of large oaks. I return to watch that little video over and over. The wonder she felt at this magical spectacle and the joy in her voice, these things fill me with such pride. I know that I played a part in instilling in her a love of nature that, in moments like those, gave her deep happiness. I am glad she experienced the fulfilment that comes from awe in the face of nature's beauty during her short life. The wilder corners of the farm reverberate with memories of Iris. I decided that in rewilding Cannwood, in giving nature a free rein to run riot, the presence of Iris's spirit would resonate even more strongly here, in the place she loved most. My heart skipped a little as I imagined the scene, nature reawakening in all its glory, the colours and the music unfurling, patterns overlayed on patterns, an intricate tapestry coming together, perfectly infused with her spirit.

10

Beavers

*Let yourself be silently drawn by the strange pull of what
you really love. It will not lead you astray.*

RUMI

*I used to swim with these beavers in a beaver pond when
I was 10. I went back when I was 11 and found there
were no more beavers. I found that trappers had taken
them all, so I became quite angry, and that winter I began
to walk the trap lines and free animals from the traps
and destroy the traps.*

PAUL WATSON

I took the Northern Line up to Hendon one clear-blue frosty
morning at the start of 2020, feeling more chipper than usual,
on my way for a private audience with an orthodox rabbi. I
had walked through Regent's Park several weeks earlier with
a young friend, Ollie, a devout Jew, and had been stirred by
his views on our purpose in life, on death and on what comes
afterwards. Ollie had offered, somewhat tenderly, to take me to
see a famous rabbi, tipped even as a future chief rabbi, he had
told me. Ollie and I met on a nondescript residential street,

suburban almost, the two of us in almost matching navy-blue woollen overcoats, Ollie in his usual yarmulke, the velvet skull cap worn by devout men of his faith.

We walked briskly together to a synagogue tucked behind a pair of heavily reinforced wrought-iron gates. It was set back a little from the street in a small, modern quadrangle shared with a religious primary school. A burly guard in a black bomber jacket and warm gloves gave a broad grin as he cranked open the gates to allow us through. I felt a momentary sense of shame and outrage that here in Britain, these people feel the need to protect their primary schools and places of worship in this way. We passed through a sea of small children tearing noisily about, bouncing off each other in a playground, their skull-capped teacher, little more than a teenager himself, seemingly resigned to his total lack of authority over them. By contrast, the silence of their classroom, through which we walked to greet the rabbi, was deafening; little chairs neatly pulled up behind matching desks, a single large whiteboard on the near-end wall, floor shelves along the length of the room stacked with wide sets of identically bound books with spines in Hebrew.

Entering at the same time as us from the other end, the rabbi was a bear of a man, of probably 40 or 45 years old. I couldn't help admiring the lustre of his jet-black beard as I shook his hand and introduced myself. Without saying much, he led us through a door at the back of the classroom and up a fire-escape staircase to the first floor, back in through another door and straight into a simple office of the kind you might find in a local government building. As we entered, Ollie reminded me in a whisper that the rabbi was hugely respected among the Jewish community of north London.

There was no small talk. I told the rabbi about Iris and the accident, and as I spoke, he wept, without fanfare, expressionless behind the great beard, save for a creasing of the kindly eyes. He reached for a tissue from a cardboard box on the desk and wiped away a small accumulation of tears from each eye. After a long silence as the three of us digested the awfulness of the story, I asked the rabbi whether Jews believe we die according to a higher plan, and I asked where Jews believe we go when we die, and how those of us who live on in the aftermath are supposed to respond. The rabbi thought for a moment and then began to speak slowly, thoughtfully, in a rich baritone.

'I'm so sorry for your tragedy. We cannot know why such a thing should have happened. We do everything in our power to sustain life and avoid dying because each and every moment of life is sacred. Life houses our soul's presence in this world, which is an integral part of our soul's divinely ordained purpose. On the other hand, the moment of death is accepted as the will of the one True Judge, who alone knows when our soul's mission in the physical world has been fulfilled. But it is our soul, not our body, that is the *true* self. Our body will inevitably fail and disintegrate, whereas our soul is eternal and indestructible. The period of physical time in which our soul resides within our body is just one phase—though a most important one—of its existence, an existence which precedes physical life and extends long beyond it. The soul of Iris, who you loved so much as a physical being on this earth, continues to exist after her death, continues to be aware of what is going on in the lives of those she loves and continues to be the beneficiary of your love and of the good things you do on her behalf. The thing now is for you to begin the work of honouring Iris.'

I asked the rabbi for his views on the kabbalistic belief in the reincarnation of souls. I told him I had a plan to meet a teacher of Jewish kabbalah later that week and that I was interested to know whether orthodox Jews approve of Jewish mysticism.

'The idea of reincarnation holds huge appeal for me,' I told him. 'It would make me happy to believe that Iris will have another chance to enjoy a life here in the physical world.' The rabbi surprised me with his open-mindedness on ideas of reincarnation, describing kabbalah as a sacred and important part of Judaism. These ideas have been studied and debated among Jewish theologians for thousands of years, he told me.

'But it's a sensitive area of discussion and needs careful handling,' he added.

Among some Jews, it is forbidden to study kabbalistic ideas before a certain age, or even at all, and among most, there's a sense of disapproval towards kabbalists who strip away and discard the whole panoply of Jewish traditions and teachings, indulging only their adherence to the kabbalistic ones at the centre. With that, Ollie and I said our thank yous and our goodbyes before scurrying downstairs, out and across the bustling high street for a breakfast of kosher croissants and orange juice.

A week later, I took a black cab in the drizzling darkness to the Kabbalah Centre, which occupies, from top to bottom, a handsome Regency building on Stratford Place, off Oxford Street. Before my new-found interest in matters of death and the soul, all I knew of kabbalah was that it was a sort of a cult, perhaps in the same bracket as Scientology, and I had been wary. Having learned that, in fact, kabbalah is the term used to describe the ancient Jewish mystical tradition, as Sufism is to Islam, I visited a knowledgeable friend of a friend to find out more. We drank whiskey, too much, in the half-light of a first-floor north-London pub saloon, and he gave me a number to call. Now here I was, directed by a male receptionist up a series of staircases to the top floor where David, a kabbalist teacher and rabbi, was waiting for me. Fit, wearing an open-neck shirt and jeans, dark-haired with greying sideburns, clean shaven,

David told me he was fresh back from a day spent sports fishing off the Sussex coast; sea bass, from a kayak, with photos on his phone to prove it. It looked cold and wet out there, the sea a menacing shade of brown. Rather him than me, I thought. A father of young children himself, David was clearly affected by my story but serious and eager to get down to business and begin his own story, a description of the greatest secret of the universe, whose origins, he told me gravely, predate all the great religions.

Gilgul neshamot, he told me, is the term used to describe the wheel of souls; *gilgul* is the Hebrew word for wheel and *neshamot*, the souls. The wheel of souls describes an ongoing process of reincarnation as understood by Jewish kabbalistic mystics. David spoke in remarkably similar terms to those used by the Sri Lankan Buddhist monk I had met in Acton before the winter. Our souls cycle through lives or incarnations in a series of different human forms through time. According to kabbalists, each life in this world unfolds according to a particular mission. From generation to generation, lights ascend and vessels descend in a process known as *tikkun*, or messianic rectification, along near-identical lines to the Buddhist concept of samsāra. In urgent tones David explained, perhaps a little disconcertingly, that the human soul comprises three parts, the *nefesh*, the *ru'ach* and the *neshamah*, words which I jotted down in a little notebook as he spoke. The nefesh is found in all humans, entering the body at birth. This is the lower, or animal, part of our soul, linked to our instincts and bodily cravings, and is the source of our unique physical and psychological nature. The next two parts of the soul are not implanted at birth but develop according to what we believe and how we behave during our allotted time. These are said to exist only in those who are 'awakened spiritually'. Ru'ach, which translates literally from the Hebrew as the breath of

God, is the middle soul, containing our moral virtues and our ability to distinguish good from evil. Neshamah is the higher, or super, soul, separating us from all other forms of life. This part relates to our intellect, enabling us to perceive the presence of God and allowing us to enjoy and benefit from an eventual afterlife. In most of us, as I understood it, the neshamah is absent, or perhaps he meant dormant.

Making us both an instant coffee and placing some raisin shortbread biscuits on the low table before us, David went on. In kabbalah, all creation is understood to be a descending chain of spiritual worlds of cause and effect. I didn't understand.

All physical and spiritual creations only exist due to a divine *ohr*, or light, which emanates from God's will to create and which glows within all things, he explained.

In other words, a shard of God exists within us, and if the light is withdrawn, then we cease to exist. One of the great Jewish mystics, a medieval kabbalist, named Isaac Luria, taught that even stones possess a subtle form of soul, coming into this world to receive a rectification of sorts, as he put it. Kabbalists like Luria, and David sitting opposite me, consider there to be two aspects to God: God in essence, transcendent, unknowable, limitless divine simplicity beyond revelation; and God in manifested form, through which He creates and sustains and relates to this world. They speak of the first as the *infinite* or the *endless*. Of this impersonal aspect of God, nothing can be grasped by our feeble minds. However, the second aspect of God, as understood by kabbalists, is accessible even to our limited perception, in nature, for example, dynamically interacting throughout spiritual and physical existence and bound up in each of our lives.

'Iris and you, and all the ones around us that we love, are on a big journey much longer than this small chapter,' David assured me eagerly, fixing me with his peregrine eyes. 'Iris loves you. Everything you have experienced is part of a great plan far beyond our understanding.'

I found myself welling up, wishing it to be true, grasping at the notion, abstruse as it might have been, that somehow Iris and I would be connected again. Staring at my shoes, I managed to hold back the tears, doing my best to figure out a plan for a dignified exit. We agreed to meet again, and I thanked him while backing towards the door, breathing carefully, in through the nose, out through the mouth. I skipped two steps at a time down to the grand hallway and out in the cold dampness of the night.

David and I met on several subsequent occasions, sometimes for a walk around Primrose Hill and through Regent's Park, sometimes in my living room at home. I liked him, and I was fascinated by the stories he told me, stories that have been distilled through three millennia. Sometimes we drank whiskey and talked about fishing. I promised to arrange for him to go spinning for perch and pike with Frankie at Stourhead someday, perhaps that coming summer. David urged me to buy the Zohar, the kabbalist holy book. Yes, of course, I told him, wiring a modest donation to his teaching centre. Several days later, a van pulled up, and the driver hauled several heavy cardboard boxes into the narrow hallway, kicking children's wellington boots and a loose umbrella aside to make space. The books, all twelve of them, bound in crimson leather, entirely in Hebrew, now occupy the top shelf of the children's playroom. There's a sequence in which I'm meant to scroll through them day by day, but I think David understood that he'd lost me at this point. The presence of the books in our home will bring us good fortune, I'm told, and that's good enough for me.

Lying awake in bed, Jemima asleep beside me, I allowed my mind to wander across the wild ideas laid out by some of the people I had met. They are far from alone in their beliefs. Of all the humans who have lived across the aeons, an overwhelming majority have *known* of the existence of souls and an afterlife. People intuitively sense that there is more out there than the reality we ordinarily perceive, beyond the senses, something mysterious, eternal and unfathomable. We glimpse divinity in the natural world around us – in the sun, the moon and the stars above; in the love that we feel for others and for the world; in the innate sense of purpose that calls us, and in our dreams and the imaginings and creativity that bubble up from deep within us. Different groupings of humans have merely differed in their interpretations of what all this means and how to respond to it. I thought of the Indian parable of the blind men and the elephant, where a gaggle of blind men, none of whom have ever met an elephant previously, learn about the elephant by touching it with their hands. Each of them feels a different part of the elephant, but only one part – a thigh or a tusk. Soon each blind man begins to describe the elephant as he finds it, and each description differs wildly from the next. In escalating anger, the blind men accuse each other of lying and come to blows. A great brawl ensues.

I found it pleasing to wonder how the other creatures of the world may relate to the universe. The Germans have a word for this, *umwelt*, meaning lifeworlds, the world as it is experienced by a particular organism. We can barely imagine the kind of consciousness experienced by a butterfly during its short life, or by a bison, or a bowhead whale wandering Arctic seas accruing wisdom for more than two centuries. Undoubtedly, we are not the only species to maintain intimate, complex, emotional relationships with each other. Scientists are now able to identify the meaning of the clicking and the singing of sperm and humpback whales, using artificial intelligence in an attempt to eavesdrop on their conversations. Could animals be consciously connected to the universe, perhaps with a greater clarity even than we consider ourselves to have? There is an unmistakeable magic in the piercing, wraithlike eyes of a wildcat peering out from the boughs of a tree. It is impossible not to be drawn by the profound *knowing* that emanates from the eyes of a matriarchal elephant. Stories abound of wild and domestic animals portending natural disasters, howling or making their way to the higher ground. Rupert Sheldrake once carried out a series of experiments that sought to show that dogs, cats and horses seem to know when human members of their family are about to arrive home, even switching up schedules and vehicles and finding that the animals' behaviour demonstrated a kind of clairvoyance that is simply unexplainable by science.

What about plants? Is an oak tree conscious? Why not? We are only now beginning to understand the ways in which plants are connected with each other via compounds released into the air, warning each other, for example, of approaching danger. The arrival of a giraffe at one acacia tree triggers the flooding of bitter chemicals into not only its own leaves but those of its neighbours. At the onset of an attack by aphids, other plant species appear to summon aphid-eating wasps by way of a chemical signal.

Rupert Sheldrake's brilliant son Merlin has written in his book *Entangled Life* of great mycorrhizal fungal networks in the earth, through which whole communities of trees and other plants are seen to disseminate information, including via electric pulses. We are learning that plants even use the network, known colloquially now among some scientists as the 'wood wide web', to share energy and nutrition with each other. The fungal mycelium, out of which these networks are made, appears to be conscious, demonstrating memory and intent, to the extent that the younger Sheldrake suggests it is not the plants that are in charge of the web but rather the fungal web itself.

An unfathomable realm of inter-species and inter-kingdom communication and cooperation exists. Some fungi are found to co-opt the minds of animals. Merlin Sheldrake describes one such species, *Ophiocordyceps unilateralis*, which produces a spore that drops onto an ant passing beneath, becoming a branching filament which burrows in and forms a mycelium growing through the ant's body. Only the ant's brain remains unpenetrated by the fungus. In time, the ant is compelled to leave the nest and climb a stem to a precise height, in conditions of a precise humidity, before clamping its jaws to the underside of a leaf. Mycelial threads emerge from the ant's feet, binding the ant to the plant, and as the fungus digests the ant's body, a slender fruiting mushroom emerges from its back and releases spores onto new ants passing beneath. This story is perhaps not so implausible to anyone who has experienced an altered state of consciousness after consuming 'magic' mushrooms, a practice central to the religious experience of many indigenous peoples the world over.

The older Sheldrake, Rupert, goes beyond the physical, believing that *all* things, human and non-human, are, in fact, bound by a kind of vast, timeless collective consciousness in whose *morphic resonance* we may find truth.

Months before my meeting with David, not long after the accident, I had travelled to Oxford for the advisory board meeting of the Oxford Martin School. It had been one of the first meetings I had attended after returning to work. I found myself alone and tearful during the lunch break with the great physicist and astronomer Professor Lord Rees. Casting his eyes down towards the table, the old man began to speak. He referred to a letter written by Einstein to the family of Michele Besso, his lifelong collaborator and closest friend, just a few days after learning of Besso's death. In that letter, Einstein wrote: 'Now he has departed from this strange world a little ahead of me. That means nothing. People like us, who believe in physics, know that the distinction between past, present, and future is only a stubbornly persistent illusion.' Einstein was describing what some philosophers call the *block universe*, the idea that reality is a static four-dimensional space. Every entity has a *world line* in the fourth dimension, time, which our consciousness samples along the way as we travel through it. But there's a sense in which past and future times are all out there. He told me that he finds this a comforting way to envisage the world, and mortality, because it gives a permanence to things that appear to be transient. He offered me a simple example:

> *If you cultivate a beautiful garden for a few years, which is then abandoned and overgrown, the block universe is timelessly imprinted with a patch of beauty, occupying a few acres in space, and a few years in the time-dimension, with which your own world-line is intertwined. We are all bounded in space and time, but in the other perspective we are* always there.

An alternative, somewhat competing idea is that of a *growing* block universe, in which the present moment is considered to be like a moving spotlight. As time passes, more and more comes into being, and so the block universe is said to be growing. The growth of the block happens in the present, a very thin slice of space-time. In either scenario, Iris is still out there. However, if the block is growing, then the question arises as to whether the future is, in fact, foretold in any sense, or is unpredictable and random. Physics, in which I far from excelled during my school years, seems to lead inevitably somehow to metaphysics, with scientists such as Professor Lord Rees and even Einstein finding themselves pondering the existence of some great originating dynamic, a clever play on words by Rees. All I really wanted was to come to a view on whether Iris is still out there somewhere, whether I have any hope of meeting her again, and whether her death was the result of random chance or part of some grand, unfathomable plan. Perhaps Iris is far ahead of me now and knows the truth, wherever she is. Eventually, lying sleepless, I began to feel the need to drag my thoughts to a simpler, happier place. On such occasions, I often thought of one of my favourite species: the beaver. I counted them in my mind in the way insomniacs are supposed to count sheep. When she was in an attentive mood, Iris had been kind enough to pay some attention to my latest obsession, while Frankie and Isaac were always been undiscerning in their Tiggerish enthusiasm for any outdoor adventure I suggested.

It was Charlie Burrell who first made me aware that beavers had once been widespread in Britain and across Europe, not the North American kind, *Castor canadensis*, but their European cousins *Castor fiber*. Our ancestors wiped them out several centuries ago, every last one. I found that the more you learn about the extraordinary way beavers create new wetlands and breathe life back into the land, the more fascinating they become, and now beavers have become a kind of obsession for me. Charlie, my brother Zac and I did whatever we could to support Derek Gow, a man who knows everything there is to know about beavers. He is breeding them in captivity on his increasingly wild farm in Devon, and leading the campaign for their return. Derek is a former sheep farmer on Dartmoor, a thickset Scot with a warm smile nestled behind a beard of immense proportions. You might say Derek has even grown to look a little like a beaver. He has a persistent, attention-fixing way of articulating the case for radical nature restoration and the return of beavers; a man with a big laugh and a taste for good Scotch.

Like a growing number of farmers and landowners across Britain, Derek decided around a year before I did to emulate the Knepp way of doing things on his farm, Coombeshead. In

2020 he swapped his sheep for an intimidating herd of Heck cattle, jet black with the kind of fearsome horns you'd expect to encounter at a bullfight at Seville or Cordoba. He ripped out his internal fencing, got in a handful of Exmoor ponies and some wild boar, and his farm is well on the way to looking like an African savannah. The key, Derek explained to me when I last visited, is to ensure a perfectly pitched battle between the vegetation now growing up with vigour all over his farm and the grazing herbivores that keep it in check. Too many animals and the scrub and trees will not grow; too few and, eventually, you'll have a dark, closed-canopy woodland. Derek does a profitable sideline in water voles, which he breeds in their scores within a large purpose-built shed for reintroducing to suitable habitat in landscapes undergoing restoration elsewhere. It was his work with water voles – he has reintroduced tens of thousands into the wild – that led Derek to beavers. Like so many other species, water voles, whose numbers have collapsed in Britain, thrive in beaver-made wetlands.

Frustrated by an inability to move ahead with species reintroductions in the United Kingdom, with policy historically dictated by varied special-interest groups, some individuals have taken it upon themselves to undertake guerrilla releases of several formerly extinct species. Otters made their way back from just a tiny relic population clinging on at the brink of extinction in remote west Scotland, and now thrive in every county in Great Britain. It is impossible to believe that they did so without surreptitious human help along the way. Similarly, having been absent for over three centuries, wild boar are back in several parts of Britain thanks to unlicenced releases during the 1990s, with populations expanding outwards from the Sussex Weald, the Forest of Dean, Lochaber in Scotland and several other forests. So it has come to be that small but growing numbers of beavers have established themselves in recent years on several river systems in Scotland, the Welsh borders, Kent, and the West Country stretching from Cornwall all the way to Bristol at Avonmouth. Evidence of the presence of beavers, and even direct encounters, have become increasingly common on the Rivers Avon and Frome in Somerset, and I knew of family territories not far from Cannwood.

A local birdwatcher tipped me off that one beaver family was living in an enormous lodge overhanging a tributary of the River Frome amid some rough woodland. During the first warm weekend during the spring of 2020, I went with Frankie and Isaac to find the lodge. We drove several miles east to the suggested spot and parked in a lay-by. Entering a small wood overgrown with willow and alder, we had to crouch to follow a narrow packed-earth pathway leading along an escarpment by the stream. Here the babbling water was shallow, not quite a river, periodically dividing on either side of a string of sinewy islands. The ground beneath the trees was carpeted here and there with the little yellow stars of lesser celandine. After almost an hour of walking, clambering, following the water, a long way from the car now and with no signs of beavers, we came to a smaller trickle of water running perpendicular down from the wooded higher ground into the stream. It was not much more than a ditch. Lo and behold, a young willow, neatly gnawed through at the base, had fallen clean across the water. Isaac spotted it, a sure sign that beavers were here. We knelt, the three of us, to run our fingers over the tooth-marked grooves of the stump. I picked up a small handful of pale wood shavings and allowed them to fall between my fingers back to the ground.

We changed direction and headed uphill towards the source of the water, following an increasing frequency of felled young trees and cleanly severed stumps, tooth-marks clearly visible in everything they had done. Soon we saw further up that the tiny brook was stopped up with a series of neatly constructed dams. Running ahead of me, the boys had to skirt around the scalloped pools behind each dam that formed a string all the way up the hill. Pausing to catch my breath, I saw that the earth around each pool had been excavated to give the ponds breadth. In some places, the beavers had dug out canals stretching away from the stream into the wood, where they had continued their coppicing of the smaller trees. All around was bursting with life, the healthiness of this wet woodland ecosystem illustrated with the strings and bundles of toadspawn and frogspawn in the pools. It may have been our imagination, but the birdsong seemed richer and fuller in this place, and the sunlit water's edge was lined with the fresh growth of willow, hazel and alder, artfully coppiced as if by a team of skilful gardeners.

Jubilant, ecstatic, we felt as if we were the first humans to have discovered paradise. At the top of the brook was a larger pond, human-made, we presumed, and on this among the bullrushes was a massive dome of sticks, plastered with mud on one side. Shoots of bracken, willow and bramble grew through the whole structure, which overhung the water. The lodge was awesome, a sight not seen by people in Britain since the Dark Ages, I told the boys. Beaver lodges, I had read, are home to countless other species: nesting birds, hibernating reptiles and amphibians, hedgehogs and small rodents all use beaver lodges for cover.

Beavers were entirely eradicated from Britain centuries ago. Being highly territorial, they live in small family groups comprising a single pair and their kits, along with an assortment of adolescent offspring who tend to hang around until their second or third year. Water is their principal means of escape, so while their food – the bark, twigs and shoots of trees, shrubs and other plants – is to be found on land, beavers never travel far from water. Life, therefore, is straightforward for beavers with prized territories along broad stretches of water, but when these areas are occupied, young beavers looking to establish a territory of their own must make their way up into the streams and tributaries, like the one in which we found ourselves now. It is here, up in the bronchioles of a river system, that beavers really make an impact. Without adequate deep water, beavers must set about creating it themselves, using stones, branches and mud to construct small dams, behind each of which they dig out a pool that fills with water. Before long, the stream resembles the flooded steps of an immaculately terraced rice paddy. These beaver-made wetlands abound with life.

Streams engineered in this way to form successions of beaver pools along their length are not only of enormous benefit to wildlife, they also replenish the water table while protecting us from flooding, seasonal drought and even wildfire. In the absence of beavers, winter rainfall brings torrents of water that flash down creeks and streams all at once, bursting the banks of our straightened and dredged waterways and causing flooding further down the catchment. Floods, in turn, give way to dry, lifeless gullies (and hosepipe bans) through the summer once the water has gone. Beaver dams dramatically slow and regulate the flow of water, holding it back in great volume, giving nature time to cleanse it of sediment and impurities such as the harmful nitrates and phosphates used in farming, and releasing it, clean, down the catchment through the year.

Across the Northern Hemisphere, even as far east as Mesopotamia and the Levant, where it was considered a grave crime to harm a 'water dog', our ancient ancestors understood that the humble beaver is the key to the healthy functioning of land and water. Native Americans revered their own North American beaver, referring to them as 'little people' and holding the great beaver society that existed alongside them in the highest esteem. Apart from humans, no animal so earnestly and capably engineers its environment to suit its own ends, such that we can scarcely conceive of the vast influence beavers once had on our landscapes. It is reckoned that a quarter of a billion beaver dams across North America created wetlands accounting for as much as a tenth of the continent. One writer suggested that America ought more aptly to have been named Beaverland. Then the Europeans came, and trappers fanned out across the land, nearly always the first of the colonisers to arrive in each place. They worked their way along rivers, streams, across wetlands, swamps and estuaries, searching for every last beaver; such was the value of their fur. By the time the explorers, cartographers, photographers and hordes of settlers arrived in their footsteps, the beavers were long gone, wiped out across virtually all of America, and with them, their dwellings and dams and canals, and all trace of that great parallel society. With the beavers went the water, life drained out of the land, and the vast western states, worst affected by the loss, became much more arid and bare as we know them today. Recent satellite imagery shows that the steady return of beavers to America's western states after an absence of centuries is quite literally greening the desert, as great ribbons of beaver-made, fire-break wetlands appear across the landscape. This has not gone unnoticed in California, where the legislature recently signed into law an Act specifically mandating and funding the restoration of beavers across the state.

Europe's indigenous beavers suffered a similar fate, albeit centuries earlier. In Europe, trappers sought not only their fur but also the yellowish oil, castoreum, that beavers exude from sacs beneath their tails. This oil was in such demand for use in cosmetics that the value of a single European beaver throughout history was roughly equal to a year's earnings for the average peasant. By the time of the First World War, only tiny remnant populations of European beavers remained, in a handful of marshy and mountainous reaches of eastern France, Germany and Russia. Since the beginning of the last century, both species of beavers have been granted legal protection in a growing list of places on both sides of the Atlantic, while the value of their fur has diminished. Consequently, beavers are staging a remarkable comeback. Carefully planned reintroductions have taken place across Europe and North America. While numbers remain at a tiny fraction of their former level, there now exist perhaps two million beavers in Europe and ten million in North America.

Opposition to the return of beavers primarily arises from misunderstanding. There are worries that migratory fish such as salmon and trout might be unable to make it past beaver dams, which ignores the fact that these fish co-evolved over millions of years with beavers. You could say it was the beaver that taught the salmon how to jump, and young salmonids depend on the cool, stable pools and gravel spawning beds created by beavers. Some people object to the perceived mess that beavers make along the water's edge. Considering that most of our land is stripped, cultivated, tidied and managed by humans, it seems only fair that we might allow nature a bit of free rein along our watercourses. As I gazed upon the beaver-made wetland on a spring day, it occurred to me that beavers know what they are doing. Everything we are told presupposes that nature is chaos while we bring order. In fact, the opposite is true; nature is order, while we bring chaos. Beavers restore order to our landscapes, and a growing understanding of their importance for mitigating flooding, drought and wildfire and for breathing life back into our depleted ecosystems has led to calls for their restoration right across Britain. For me, the return of beavers, along with all they do, is cause for celebration and for hope. The beaver believer movement, a symbol and a tool for the restoration of nature in Britain, is one of my great passions and among my first and last thoughts each day and a reason for optimism and joy in a world without Iris.

11

Levels

Yes, I will be thy priest, and build a fane
In some untrodden region of my mind,
Where branched thoughts, new grown with pleasant pain,
Instead of pines shall murmur in the wind:
Far, far around shall those dark-cluster'd trees
Fledge the wild-ridged mountains steep by steep;
And there by zephyrs, streams, and birds, and bees,
The moss-lain Dryads shall be lull'd to sleep;
And in the midst of this wide quietness
A rosy sanctuary will I dress
With the wreath'd trellis of a working brain,
With buds, and bells, and stars without a name,
With all the gardener Fancy e'er could feign,
Who breeding flowers, will never breed the same:
And there shall be for thee all soft delight
That shadowy thought can win,
A bright torch, and a casement ope at night,
To let the warm Love in!

JOHN KEATS,
'Ode To Psyche'

The woodland floor was already carpeted with early spring flowers when a sombre-looking Boris Johnson issued the nation with what he called a 'very simple instruction'. A novel coronavirus was sweeping the United Kingdom, and the public would have to stay at home to save lives and protect the National Health Service. In a historic announcement, on the evening of March 23, the prime minister imposed an unprecedented national lockdown. A week earlier, sensing what was coming, Jemima and I had settled into what felt like a new kibbutz at Cannwood, eight months after the last one, but this time with our friends Gerald and Kate Wellesley, who had rolled up a day after us in a hatchback groaning with luggage, their second daughter just 10 days old. Once the schools were closed, Kate and her boyfriend Paul similarly hunkered down with my two boys at Beech Cottage on the other side of King Alfred's Tower, brooding on the ridge between us.

We knew we were among the lucky ones, none more so than me. This was an opportunity to withdraw from the world for a few months and immerse myself in nature and my family. I knew it would be restorative. I had found myself less able than I had expected to bear the stresses of life back at work in London which, despite offering relentless, fulfilling distraction, seemed to deprive me of time to grieve and to heal. I had begun to feel frayed and more easily tearful, and I hadn't been coping well. Back at Cannwood full time, I found a visceral contentment in communal living, each of us making a point of playing a part during each day. We brought firewood into the house, picked vegetables and herbs from the early beds in the vegetable garden, and gathered eggs each day from the rickety garden shed now used for a mobile chicken house in the orchard, the whole thing welded onto the chassis of a long-gone caravan, which we shunted monthly around the farm at night while the chickens roosted inside. Jemima, so talented with food, made lunches and dinners. I took to marshalling the children on adventures outside, announcing a 'who can find the most interesting thing' competition at a different spot each day, just as I had done with Iris and her brothers a decade earlier. I spent as much time as possible outside, carefully scheduling big gaps on days I otherwise spent meeting people on a screen.

I joined Chris Couldrey and Garry as often as I could to help in their work transforming Cannwood around us. I helped as they thinned out the trees of a small plantation woodland planted behind the big pond by the previous owners, writer Polly Devlin and her marvellous husband Andy Garnett, two decades earlier. We stacked the thicker boughs beside the track for firewood and all the rest in linear 'dead hedges', perfect cover for wildlife living among the remaining trees. We moved the pigs around the farm, and we hammered wooden posts into the ground at random across the fields. This had been Chris's idea. Birds would alight on these, he supposed, depositing seeds in their droppings at the base of each post, where patches of scrub would later grow up. I decided finally to remove the plastic tree guards from the bottoms of the young trees in the newer woods. I set myself a target of one trailer-full per day, wearing thick gardening gloves, and using a machete in one hand to hack a way into the thorns and a box-cutter knife in the other to slice the tube away from the trunk of the young tree inside. Sometimes a bundle of earwigs would tumble out of the bottom, or a startled field mouse. Various local friends of Chris's and mine needed little encouragement to come and help. Over several drizzly days in late March, we formed small working groups in line with the current guidance to put up variously shaped nesting boxes for birds, bats and wild bees, and to plant a thousand trees – in biodegradable cardboard tubes this time – along the road in a widely spaced belt. Jemima and the two little ones came back and forth on a quad bike loaded with hot tea and chocolate biscuits. There was a wartime feeling about the whole thing, our faces rain-flecked, each one of us as exhilarated by the novelty of the lockdown as we were apprehensive about the emergent pandemic.

Over time, a feeling grew that amid the suffering and the loneliness of the Covid situation, people everywhere were experiencing an upwelling of love for nature. Locked down, people had little choice but to explore their own immediate locality and its patches of greenery each day. As our human world shrank back, nature expanded. Video clips circulated of dolphins playing in the deserted silence of Trieste harbour in Italy, of the mighty Himalayas seen through clear air from northern India for the first time in decades, of wild boar trotting the deserted streets of Berlin. For a while – we had no idea how long it would be – the pace of life slowed for everyone, stopped even, granting us time to reflect on the magic of the world and on what truly matters in our lives. The disappearance of traffic offered a glimpse of how clear the air can be when the roads are deserted, how rich the birdsong sounds when unwanted noise dies down, how delirious with wildflowers the road verges become if they are left unmown. During that first national lockdown, people were reawakened to the vitality of nature and its importance in our lives, amid the unfurling of a spring that seemed especially vibrant that year.

I took every opportunity I could to walk, delighting in the pace at which nature was now reclaiming what had once been fields. We mowed long, straight paths through the newly open landscape, a way of bringing order amid the chaos perhaps, and I walked these endlessly, alone or with Jemima, who was by then heavily pregnant with our third child, mostly very early in the morning and last thing in the evening. The Japanese have known for centuries that spending time immersed in nature, using all of our senses to connect with the environment, is good and healthy and staves off ill health. The Japanese practice of *shinrin-yoku* translates literally as 'forest bath'. This is what I did; I bathed in nature, now running riot across this landscape. In those moments, I felt good. Each night after dinner, I walked with the dogs, always passing Iris's stone circle. The wind in Somerset has a habit of often giving way to an eerie stillness at night, and when the sky was clear, I looked with an expanded sense of wonder at the stars peppering the vastness of the sky above. On some evenings, the landscape was bathed in the silvery glow of the moon, bright enough for me to glimpse a roe deer or a wild boar skittering away from the sound of the dogs and into the trees. It was on these walks that I most yearned for some sign from Iris. I don't know quite what I expected. Mostly I just missed her, ached for her, wished with all my might that she was not gone, that the accident hadn't happened. Why couldn't she just have emerged injured, a lesson learned? How could we have been so unlucky?

Two weeks into April, baby Vita arrived. We gave her Iris for a middle name; Vita for the miracle of her own survival. On our way to London for a final routine scan, we were alone on the motorway, a pair of red kites presenting an apocalyptic vision as they feasted undisturbed on a flattened pheasant in the deserted middle lane on the opposite side. Within an hour of arriving in London, Jemima had found herself in an emergency room, the baby narrowly saved and whisked to intensive care. I spent the first couple of nights in the car outside the hospital, my mind looping over the possibility that I might lose two daughters in the space of a year. As the days passed, brave Jemima met the situation with courage and optimism, insisting that we walk the Serpentine each morning after she had seen the doctors on the ward. We took to stopping on the way back for an Afghan kebab with a black coffee on Church Street behind the Edgware Rd. Eventually, two long weeks after leaving Cannwood, we were able to return with tiny Vita in Jemima's arms, not unscathed, but alive, gratitude and relief coursing through our veins. The whole episode soon took on the feeling of a dream.

Day or night, my walks at Cannwood generally followed the water, from pond to pond or along the rewiggled stream. We seemed now to have water everywhere. In Somerset, the ground is nearly always wet underfoot, and the further west you go, the wetter it gets. The name Somerset itself is thought to be a derivation of 'the land of summer' or 'the summer settlement', a place only habitable during the summer. Really, the name refers to the Somerset Levels, which lie just 20 miles to the west of Cannwood, once an immense, mysterious wetland to rival France's Camargue at the mouth of the Rhone or the Danube Delta or Spain's spectacular Guadalquivir marshes at Doñana, where Andalusia's great river reaches the Mediterranean to the west of Gibraltar, at the end of a long journey through the arid hinterland, and the cities of Granada, Cordoba and then Seville.

I had always wanted to visit Doñana, a place stalked by secretive Iberian lynx, the spotty, smaller, rabbit-eating cousin of our own Eurasian lynx, long since wiped out in the British Isles. A long time ago, when I was still married to Kate, we decided to go. It was October, and we travelled via Seville. Iris, Frankie and Isaac were small at the time. After two days exploring the aching romance of the city, we lugged bags and children through the rising heat of the early morning to a small dock on the river, down a metal-framed staircase and onto a worn-out Sunseeker. The boat was crewed by a thick-set Sevillano with an impressive moustache and a baseball cap. He greeted us warmly, taking two bags out of my hands. He spent the winter months each year captaining container ships on the high seas, he told us, and summers taking tourists up and down the river and out dolphin watching in the Bay of Cadiz. Two large cold boxes sat in the middle of the rear deck, one stacked high with bottles of San Miguel beer, the other with Serrano ham, Manchego cheese cling-filmed in thick-cut square slices, a set of purple figs, each one tenderly wrapped in thin paper, and several large loaves of white bread of the kind that in Spain they call *barra*, similar to a French baguette but wider and shorter.

As the boat set out, we felt sublimely happy; Iris was lying on her tummy at the very front, her face over the water. Accustomed as we were to the comparatively sterile landscapes of Britain, the river seemed alive. Great shoals of barbel – small, carp-like freshwater fish – leapt clean from the glassy-flat water before the bow wave of the boat, and we glided past sandy banks dotted with pond turtles basking in the Spanish sun. In the shallows were groups of flamingos and spoonbills nonchalantly sifting the water for food and in the poplar, willow and aspen that fringed the riverbank meditated large gangs of brilliantly white egrets. However, I noticed that even here, the river was granted little in the way of space, with cultivated ground right to the edge on either side as the water snaked through the flatlands towards the delta.

Our pagan ancestors believed that rivers have souls and revered them. The rivers they worshipped in the distant past were very different from the ones we know today. Instead of a single channel, broad and deep and often artificially straightened, rivers were made up of multi-braided, intertwined, shallow channels that meandered across the whole floodplain. In a way, the floodplain *was* the river. Today, though much diminished, individual rivers still loom large in our collective psyche, defining places that are meaningful to those who live nearby. To Liverpudlians, the Mersey is sacred; to Londoners, the Thames; to Parisians, the Seine; to the Romans, the Tiber – in which beavers have recently been discovered for the first time in more than a millennium. Given their enormous importance, it doesn't seem unreasonable to allow these rivers a little space in which to find their own course through the landscape and to let them reconnect with their original richly flowered floodplains.

Instead, we have straightjacketed our rivers with concrete banks, weirs and dams which block the migratory passage of fish such as salmon, shad, trout, eels and the enormous sturgeon, known as the royal fish, all of which have consequently declined catastrophically. These man-made structures, many of which serve no useful purpose, also disrupt the movement of fertile sediment along the river, with an ecological impact that we are still far from grasping but which includes the accelerating loss of sandy deltas and beaches downstream. Dams also cause catastrophic water loss, as huge quantities simply evaporate from the reservoir surface, while preventing the recharging of vital aquifers beneath ground, both downstream, and also upstream, because the sediment accumulating on the reservoir bottom forms an impermeable concrete-like crust. A growing river rewilding movement is now springing up across Europe. Stories abound of dams being removed and even blown apart, natural meanders being restored, and whole rivers, newly liberated, returning to life.

On the Guadalquivir all those years ago, I was appalled to see crudely ploughed arable fields crumbling into the otherwise-clear water. Then suddenly, everything changed: the river grew boundlessly wide, sandy islands began to appear around us, and following the western bank, we marvelled at a landscape transformed. As far as the eye could see, farmland gave way to an enormous marshy wetland, the coiled tributaries of the river intricately patterned through islands of sedge, rush and reed, sandbanks emerging like the backs of breaching whales along the flow of the river. Further back, the landscape was studded into the distance with mighty umbrella pines, each twisting upwards from its own small patch of ground above the marsh. A column of buzzards, vultures and eagles of various kinds took advantage of a huge tubular shaft of ascending warm air, circling endlessly higher into the vastness of the azure sky. We saw no lynx, nor deer, nor even a wild boar as we passed through this astonishing, seemingly endless wetland, but it was enough just to know they were out there, playing their part, nature in full flow, complex beyond wonder, across thousands of flooded square kilometres. Soon the brown of the river began to give way to blue, the islands thinning, the banks of the river receding from us yet further on either side and, all of sudden, dolphins appeared, too many to count, twisting and turning beneath the water at the bow and beside the boat, more still further out, breaching and occasionally leaping from the water. We were giddy with joy. The delta, we were told, is rich in nutrients and therefore heaving with fish, so the dolphins form great pods here.

During the last century in Britain, we have destroyed nearly all our remaining wetlands, large and small. Considering the extent to which earlier generations had already striven to convert wetlands into something they felt was more immediately useful, the losses are immense. Today, only fragments remain of the great wetlands Julius Caesar would have encountered on his arrival in Britain nearly 2,000 years ago. These waters have been drained, dredged, straightened, engineered and ploughed almost out of existence. It is now hard to imagine the amazing runs of salmon that once arrived each year in British rivers. Eels were so numerous that eyewitness accounts describe the water of the Severn being almost displaced by great shoals as they began their epic journey from ponds, lakes, streams and rivers across Britain to breed and die in Bermuda's far-off Sargasso Sea.

Among the greatest of Britain's lost wetland landscapes is the Somerset Levels, known to some as the Vale of Avalon, once a vast, shimmering inland sea, framed by the Blackdown Hills to one side and the Mendips to the other and bisected by the Poldens. According to folklore, the Somerset Levels were a hiding place for King Alfred of Wessex at Athelney following the fall of his kingdom to the Vikings during the Easter of 878 AD. The presence of several monasteries and churches at Glastonbury is linked to the legend that Jesus Christ came here, having travelled to Britain with the merchant Joseph of Arimathea, later one of the disciples, a legend immortalised in William Blake's epic *Jerusalem*. They are said to have visited Glastonbury, an ancient town built, like the other elevated settlements that dot the Levels, on top of what was once a natural island known as Glastonbury Tor, the name a reference to the glass-like appearance of the water that once surrounded it. This landscape has been considered sacred since early Celtic times because of its confluent position on one of Britain's most significant ley lines, which are said to link the sacred sites of England. Ley lines are often likened to the Chinese feng shui idea of beneficial alignment, or to the energy associations of Aboriginal songlines.

Had Christ really been in the Vale of Avalon, his experience would have been radically different from mine when, at the end of the lockdown, I made the short drive west to see what remains of this natural wonder. On a particularly warm and bright morning, I climbed into our newly leased electric car, which felt more like a smartphone with seats and wheels than a car, and slipped silently up the lane and onto the open road. Though nature has been substantially subdued in this part of Somerset, the rolling landscape still has a chocolate-box kind of beauty: a giant patchwork quilt of neat fields, each one bright green at that time of year, with an occasional square of woodland on a hillside or valley bottom. Even the roads here have a poetry to them, framed with verdant hedges as they dance in tune with the contours of the land. Soon, heading west, undulations give way to a flatness, the latticework of fields broadening into much larger ones bordered by fences instead of hedges. There are fewer trees, I imagine because of the deep peat beneath. As I approached a town named Street, the map told me I was in the Levels. I stopped in a lay-by on a natural elevation to get my bearings and take in the view. The landscape seemed somehow concave, sinking from the middle outwards. I saw black and white Friesian dairy cows freshly turned out from their winter sheds, several expansive fields of maize, and a large flock of sheep grazing some higher ground. A canal ran dead straight away from me into the distance. There was little to suggest that this had once been a marvellous inland sea. Just a blink of an eye ago, in evolutionary terms, wild ox and horses, boar, red and roe deer, lynx, wildcats, beavers, pine martens, cranes, marsh harriers, white-tailed eagles, vast aggregations of wading and sea birds and even Dalmatian pelicans abounded here; the water thronged with salmon, trout, all kinds of fish, extraordinary numbers of eels and even pond turtles.

The Somerset Levels are fed by the rivers Axe, Brue (which, like the Frome, originates at Cannwood in the Brewham valley), Parrett, Tone and Yeo, all of which have been engineered beyond recognition, in works carried out mostly since the Second World War with the sole aim of transferring their flow into the sea as fast as possible and creating an artificial area of dry ground for farming. A human-made river, the Huntspill, was built during the 1940s with sluices at both ends to serve as a sixth major drainage channel. Those who worked on the project failed to dig the Huntspill as deep as had originally been intended, making gravity-fed drainage from the surrounding landscape impossible. As a result, the water must be pushed uphill at great expense by the continual action of pumps. A seventh major drain running between the River Parrett and King's Sedgemoor Drain, named the River Sowy, was completed in the 1970s. For miles around, the landscape is artificially drained by a vast network of smaller *rhynes* that are pumped up into the major drains. Much of the peat that underlies the Somerset Levels has been removed, using giant machines, to sell as fertiliser, leaving behind ugly pockmarks across the lower reaches of the landscape.

It's hard to conceive of a place more comprehensively dominated, manipulated and transformed away from what nature intended for so little gain. What was once western Britain's great mist-shrouded, sacred wetland has been converted into 140,000 acres of dull, low-grade, unprofitable farmland, all of which is slowly collapsing into a mire of drying peat in a process that produces a greater volume of greenhouse gas emissions every year than all of the rest of Somerset combined. As the peat dries out and the ground sinks ever lower, the effort required to keep out the water becomes ever greater. The eye-watering cost is borne by taxpayers, though few know anything about it. To me, the whole thing is an ongoing, bewildering act of vandalism.

That morning, I was on my way to meet naturalists from the Somerset Wildlife Trust, Natural England and various other organisations doing their best to restore life to the Levels. Their efforts are focused on a place that has come to be known as the Avalon Marshes, recently declared Britain's newest super nature reserve, where they have cobbled together and rewetted several thousand acres. The unmarked road leading to Shapwick, at the centre of the initiative, is long and straight, and runs above the level of the surrounding farmland. I pulled up in the gravel car park at the Avalon Marshes Centre and, finding all the buildings shut, made my way to a garden at the back where a gaggle of people with binoculars round their necks and sturdy boots on their feet chatted enthusiastically, each one as delighted as I was to be seeing people outside our so-called lockdown bubbles. Once we were over the awkwardness of greeting each other without handshakes, we settled down at a series of pub tables pressed lengthways together. We had come together to explore how we might collectively catalyse change in this extraordinary, misused landscape. I was full of questions. Pointing to a ridge in the distance, Georgia Stokes, chief executive officer of the Somerset Wildlife Trust, told me that Neolithic people once lived on the higher, drier ground around what is now Shapwick Heath. Using neatly carved fenceposts pinched from the dwellings of the beavers that once abounded here, they built a vast grid of wooden walkways across the flooded, reedy ground. Some of these are still present today, preserved in the peat and exposed now once again. The small but growing patchwork of connected reserves here at the centre of the Avalon Marshes offer a glimpse of what could be. The rhynes have been stopped up here, and water levels have been allowed to rise despite unrelenting political obstruction from the internal drainage boards. Life is already flooding back in.

The discussion over, we set off to walk along an abandoned railway line raised above the surrounding ground. Soon we were looking out over a mosaic of habitats; channels of water snaking through broad beds of reeds, areas of open water and small elevations of land carpeted with wildflowers beneath stands of willow and alder. The birdsong was rich and varied, different here from anything I knew from Cannwood, rare wetland birds singing from somewhere hidden within the green. The air was heavy with the fruity, pondy, cut-grass fragrance of springtime. Two marsh harriers glided lazily overhead. The *booming* of bitterns can be heard here for the first time in generations, and even majestic cranes, eaten by nobility and royalty to near extinction centuries ago, are breeding here once again. The Avalon Marshes is a place like no other I've experienced in Britain.

Across most of the British Isles, it is farmers who have shaped the land for millennia, and the task of restoring nature will inevitably be led by farmers today. Across our more agriculturally productive landscapes, a regenerative farming revolution is taking shape. Arable farmers are combining ancient wisdom with modern technology in a concerted effort to rebuild soil, restore the health of nature and feed the nation. Farmers on the best soils are returning to age-old seasonal rotations that combine grazing livestock with arable farming. Even ploughing and the consequent loss of soil is becoming a thing of the past as no-till practices, whereby seed is sown directly into the undisturbed earth, take hold. Across much of the rest of the country, in more agriculturally marginal landscapes, and particularly in upland national parks, I believe the future lies in *wilder* farming. Here the replacement of hordes of sheep with more modest numbers of traditional native cattle, grazing and browsing and trampling across the land, offers a pathway for restoring the wildwood, our lost great wood pastures, just as I saw beginning to take shape at Geltsdale.

There are some places, however, where current management runs so contrary to the grain of nature that wholesale change is needed. The landscape of the Somerset Levels, representing both an ecological catastrophe and an economic folly, falls into this category. I feel passionately that the pumps must be shut down, the drains stopped, the rivers rewiggled, and the water allowed to return to where it belongs. A whole new way of living needs to emerge here: an increased focus on nature tourism; traditional, extensive summer-only grazing by native cattle, water buffalo even, and perhaps some semi-wild horses; the harvesting of reeds for building material and soil conditioner; the pathway oiled with so-called natural capital payments to landowners for their help in reducing flooding, delivering cleaner water and taking measures that store carbon from the atmosphere. Perhaps this is a place where the government should even be prepared to buy land from landowners unwilling or unable to take on the change.

I drove back wistfully, reflecting on the extent of the nature lost in Britain and daydreaming at what might be once again. Many other countries are becoming bolder in their efforts to restore lost wetlands, from Florida's disfigured Everglades to the Indus Delta of Pakistan, which was drained under the British Empire. So too should we, starting here. Soon I was wending my way through the tight lanes and fields of Selwood, and home, wandering along the rewiggled stream with Vita strapped to me, thinking of Iris, wondering how much she'd love the big changes we were making at Cannwood since she left us.

12

Bustards

I grasped the meaning of the greatest secret that human
poetry and human thought and belief have to impart:
The salvation of man is through love and in love.

VIKTOR FRANKL,
Man's Search for Meaning

It was during the lockdown that we first spotted a red kite at
Cannwood. Silhouetted against the rising sun, an unusually
large shape caught my attention; a lusciously bronze pterodactyl
of a bird, seeming much larger than a buzzard, the angelic
wings streaked white and black, the tail unmistakably kite-
shaped. I was sitting with Eliza and Arlo on a circle of mown
grass among the buttercups beside the pond, and we gawped
as the great kite hung languidly against the breeze above us,
scanning the ground for movement before arcing away over
the woods. Red kites have become a familiar sight across some
of Britain, but having never seen one at Cannwood, this was
an exciting moment for us.

Red kites were once so numerous across Britain that
Coriolanus's London was 'the city of kites and crows', but
along with most other predators, large and small, they were

persecuted with remorseless determination. Precious few escaped, and egg collectors whittled the remainder down to just a handful of individuals in the wilds of central Wales. Then, 30 years ago, in one of Britain's first rewilding projects, conservationists secured permission and funding to bring a handful of individual red kites to Britain, in crates loaded onto a British Airways flight from Spain. The first consignment of birds was released in the Chilterns, followed by more each year for several years. Before long, the kites were successfully breeding, and the population began to grow outwards in all directions. Now here I was, three decades later, in Somerset's Brewham valley, gazing at one of likely 10,000 red kites in Britain today, the first to show up around here in centuries.

Although they will hunt small animals, red kites eat mainly carrion if they can find it, fulfilling a clean-up role occupied in warmer climes by vultures, and new populations thrived around motorways strewn with roadkill. It was rewilder Derek Gow who gave me the idea of building a *sky table* at Cannwood to attract kites and other raptors that might be passing through. Chris Couldrey built it in rough wood among the young trees planted a decade earlier towards the top of the farm, and the finished table stood 2.5m tall. It looked like something out of Jack and the Beanstalk: not exactly a thing of beauty in itself, but the sight of these magnificent raptors swooping down to the platform would more than make up for the resemblance to a cast-off from a pantomime set.

When it was complete, we needed bait. Someone told me they'd seen a dead roe deer by the side of the dual carriageway a few miles east of Cannwood, so I set off in a van to retrieve it, hoping it would prove sufficiently tempting. It wasn't long before I spotted the carcass, spreadeagled on the hard shoulder. I pulled over, donned a pair of thick rubber gloves and, pursing my lips, set about my grim task. Holding my breath, I heaved the rigid carcass onto a small tarpaulin spread out in the back of the van. Back at Cannwood, I was even more repulsed as I carried the dead deer up a stepladder and onto the platform, where it sprawled supine, tongue lolling. I took to creeping up close to watch magpies, crows, rooks, jackdaws and even once a raven pulling apart the glistening entrails, bickering and scrapping as they worked. They feasted, but there was no sign of the kite. So far, nobody has seen it go anywhere near the sky table, but it has stuck around; a young male, we think, and we are hoping more will arrive.

Not so very long ago, it was far more common for the carcasses of wild animals and domestic livestock to be left out in the open. The flesh, bones and proliferations of attendant insects were not only food for raptors and other carnivores but also for all kinds of smaller animals. Even tiny blue and great tits could be seen picking at the exposed fat of a dead animal. The fur would be gathered by birds and small mammals as nesting material, and as the carcass gradually disappeared, it would enrich the soil beneath, leaving a verdant green imprint long after all physical traces of the unfortunate creature had gone. It seems dead animals are every bit as vital a component of the ecosystem as dead wood. All that changed in the late 1980s as a result of bovine spongiform encephalopathy (BSE) – a disease of the brain which affects cattle and became known as mad cow disease. Following a disastrous outbreak in the United Kingdom, the European Union made it illegal for landowners and local authorities to leave livestock carcasses out to be dealt with by nature, as they had been forever. There was now a duty to remove them as soon as reasonably possible. This diktat was handed down even though the epidemic had nothing to do with livestock carcasses left out in the wild, instead having been caused by the bestial stupidity of a factory farming industry that had taken to grinding abattoir waste and dead animals into feed for living ones. It has long been established that a specific transmissible agent known as a prion is spread by cannibalism in mammals, causing their brains to degenerate. Yet here were herbivorous cows being fed dead cows, pigs being fed dead pigs, and ground-up dead chickens being fed to giant sheds of miserably confined chickens.

The most visible effect of the disappearance of carrion from the landscape was in southern and eastern Europe, where griffon and bearded, cinerous and Egyptian vultures – whose populations had already been dwindling due to persecution – suffered a sudden and dramatic collapse in numbers. Thankfully certain parts of Europe have since been granted a derogation, allowing farmers to leave fallen livestock out. With a bearded vulture having made the journey from the Alps to Britain, to huge excitement, and now circling the skies of Lincolnshire and Norfolk, there is even talk of doing something similar in our remoter landscapes here in Britain. In the meantime, another environmental catastrophe makes up somewhat for the disappearance of carcasses from the landscape: roadkill. Innumerable animals of all kinds end up splattered along British road verges, including up to a third of all hedgehogs every single year, numbers of which have fallen by more than 90 per cent during my lifetime.

Many of the United Kingdom's remaining wild places have been carved up by busy roads. In *Wilding*, Isabella Tree argues that the impact on wildlife, 'not just in terms of roadkill, but in the far more insidious effects of physical and genetic isolation, is almost completely overlooked.' There is a solution that does not require everyone to abandon their cars. It involves creating safe passages for wildlife over or under roads. Elsewhere in Europe and in some of America's more enlightened places, work has begun to reconnect the landscape by building beautiful green wildlife bridges, complete with grass, scrub and trees, over the busiest roads, and underpasses beneath others. We have a small handful of these in Britain, but not nearly enough. The Netherlands alone has built 30 in recent years, with another 20 in the planning, and they work. Cameras have shown a steady stream of wildlife crossing back and forth: deer, wild boar, badgers, foxes, hedgehogs and even wolves safely moving unimpeded once more through the landscape. To me, these initiatives are essential in any wider effort to stitch back together the depleted natural fabric of our island. They're also basic common decency in our relationship with the non-human creatures with whom we share the world.

I daydreamed now, as I had throughout my childhood, on the things we ought to be doing to restore nature to the kind of rich abundance our ancestors once knew. Above all, throughout my life, I have yearned to restore lost species to Britain. The disappearance of so many extraordinary species from our country appalled me, especially given that most of the losses were the result of deliberate, calculated acts of eradication. Setting about to extinguish certain species from our shores, often the most charismatic and wonderful ones, seemed like a kind of godless vandalism by our predecessors, and I was sickened by the notion that there could be any resistance to putting it right today. I longed, unrealistically, for pine martens and wild boar in the woods at Ham and Richmond Park and felt in their absence vital cogs missing from the exquisite complexity of the clock. Aged about 15, I won a prize for the best letter to *Country Life* magazine, in which I suggested that some of their readers may have lacked imagination in demanding the eradication of the small pockets of wild boar that had sprung up following farm escapes in the great storm of 1987. I argued that wild boar have just as much right to be here as we do; that they play a vital role as woodland gardeners, turning the soil and creating the right conditions for wildflowers and other delicate plants to germinate; that boar are exciting to hunt and delicious to eat; and all in all that we should be overjoyed to have them back after so long. *Country Life* sent me a green Schöffel coat as a prize. I still wear it today. In the following edition, the ageing Duke of Wellington penned a curt but amusing reply to the editor asserting that any wild boar turning up at Stratfield Saye would be shot by his keepers.

Red kites and wild boar are just two examples of species that have returned to our island, and a rewilding movement growing in popularity and confidence is pushing for the reintroduction of more. Often it is the energy and determination of individual campaigners that makes these things happen – as is the case with the return of the world's heaviest flying bird to England. It is thanks to the incredible dedication over nearly three decades of a man named David Waters that the enormous great bustard is back. These wonderful creatures were wiped out of the United Kingdom by trophy hunters two centuries ago. I wanted to see the famous bustards of Salisbury Plain and to pay my respects to David, so one day, I took Frankie and Isaac to meet him. It was summer now; the lockdown was all but over, and I found on certain days like these that rays of optimism, happiness even, were beginning to break through the clouds of my grief.

We drove east along the A303, then followed the reassuringly precise directions David had provided for when we left the main road. Salisbury Plain is immense. Sometimes known as 'Greater Stonehenge' because of the prehistoric icon at its centre, it is the largest unbroken expanse of chalk grassland in north-west Europe. Though I had driven back and forth past Stonehenge countless times, I had never paid attention to the area around the monument. From the main road, the surroundings had always seemed bare and uninteresting to me. I was wrong. As we turned off, I found myself gazing at a vast expanse of grassland: 200,000 acres of grand, gently undulating terrain sparsely adorned with occasional pockets of thorny scrub and juniper, some of the best and last of its kind in England. Americans often refer to the midwestern prairies, or the fragments that remain, as 'big sky country', and this is how Salisbury Plain felt on the day of our visit. Everything was on a different scale from any place in England I had seen. Scattered settlements are occupied mainly by military families, and the Ministry of Defence owns most of the plain itself, the distant rumble of artillery sometimes reaching us at Cannwood 30 miles to the west.

David – tall, upright and broad-shouldered – strode towards the car as we pulled up. Beaming behind a magnificent Victorian-era mutton chops moustache and sideburns, he looked every bit the former military man that he is. He wore an immaculately polished pair of brown boots, dark green moleskin trousers, a checked country shirt and a brown waistcoat jacket. Since leaving the army 30 years ago, David had devoted almost every waking moment to restoring the great bustard to Salisbury Plain, a feat deemed near impossible by an overwhelming majority of conservationists. Through a combination of sheer determination and resourcefulness, he had made it happen. We crunched over the rough ground from the car towards a collection of green cabins; an office and a messroom for David and his team, which backed onto a series of sheds and pens housing young bustards.

Salisbury Plain has been extensively grazed by domestic livestock for centuries and by their wild antecedents before that. In recent decades, some parts have been ploughed or converted to the monotony of so-called 'improved' pasture for intensive farming, but for the main part, the plateau remains in good shape. Soon the A303 that slices the landscape in two will run through a tunnel beneath the ground, described already by some conservationists as Europe's largest wildlife crossing, and there are calls for a more ambitious landscape restoration plan across the plain. As I looked out, I felt a frisson of excitement at the thought of great herds of domestic native cattle or even wild ox and horses roaming once again across the grasslands surrounding Stonehenge, in an echo of the savannah that was once known here by our own Mesolithic ancestors.

Today the plain is a haven and last refuge for wildflowers that thrive on this kind of terrain, a kaleidoscopic array of which stretched away from us in all directions. These flowers have strange, romantic names from a time when such things mattered to more people: devil's-bit scabious, saw-wort, ox-eye daisy, chalk milkwort, fragrant orchid, frog orchid, lesser butterfly-orchid, bee orchid, autumn lady's-tresses. Some varieties are now found only here: the tuberous thistle, early gentian, bastard-toadflax, burnt-tip orchid, round-headed rampion, field fleawort. Others, rarer still, grow only at one of the last strongholds for wildflowers that thrive; little mouse-ear, sea mouse-ear, dwarf mouse-ear.

The cabin rocked a little as David followed us up the foldaway metal steps, directing us inside to sit on a surprisingly plush sofa that ran around one end of the cabin. The small windows were all jammed wide open, and a warm breeze wafted through the office. A stuffed bustard watched us, glassy-eyed, from a corner table; a huge male as tall as a farmyard turkey and almost as round, its long neck and face grey, the chest and tailfeathers a vivid shade of orange, the undercarriage white. An assistant prepared mugs of tea, a burly-looking countryman of few words whose name I didn't catch, and David began his story of blood, sweat, tears and bustards. Leaning forward with an elbow on one knee, he spoke earnestly of his love for this 'marvellous' bird. His mission had begun on the icy Russian steppes, one of their few remaining habitats. From the post-Soviet government of Boris Yeltsin, David had secured some kind of licence to collect their eggs, and had spent weeks away from his long-suffering family trying to retrieve as many as he could. It was thankless work, punctuated by more failure than success. He transported his precious cargo back to the United Kingdom in specially designed briefcases, carried onto the plane as hand luggage, but there were endless setbacks: chicks eaten by foxes and stoats, little to no support or engagement from sceptical fellow conservationists, and disinterest at best from government officials. Dispirited but undeterred, he pressed on, mortgaging his home to cover mounting costs. Having tried and failed with Russian eggs, he sought permission from Spanish authorities to collect eggs there. This marked a watershed.

A handful of hand-reared fledglings released into the wild survived, and then some more. Then there were nests hidden in the grass, tentative and without much luck, before one year later, a few wild-born bustard chicks appeared on Salisbury Plain. They were the first in Britain for two centuries. At the time of our visit, more than a hundred adult great bustards wandered the plain, and the number is growing each year. David sensed our impatience to get outside. My boys were getting fidgety. Slapping both knees to indicate that the preamble was over, he stood up and announced that our first stop would be to see the new hatchlings in the pens behind the cabin. Then we would go out onto the plain to look for wild bustards.

David gave us our instructions as we made our way around to the back of the cabins. From the moment they hatch to the time they are released, the young bustards must never set eyes on anything that looks like a human. Therefore, we would have to dress like adult bustards, much to Frankie and Isaac's amusement. David's wingman went to fetch a pile of hooded, bag-like suits of various sizes in grey and orange, along with matching boots and gloves. Of course, we looked ridiculous, but David's experience showed that the fancy dress works. Nonetheless, the young bustards were momentarily alarmed by our appearance. As we opened the wooden door to their pen, they hurtled around their shed in fright, dashing into an outdoor pen beyond. Doing our best to look unthreatening, we crept out after them and sat in a semi-circle on the floor. It was not long before curiosity got the better of them. Egging each other on, they came within touching distance. Around a month old and gangly, they would eventually be released into a huge, safely fenced outdoor enclosure, a kind of halfway house, before finally flying free into the wild.

Half an hour later, we were inside a rickety wooden hide on a slope, seated on a row of stools and peering through a horizontal slit out at the sweeping landscape below, binoculars pressed against our faces. With the enthusiasm of a schoolboy, David pointed out a faraway flock of black and white lapwings tumbling over each other in the wind. Much nearer, two skylarks were in full song, rising and falling alternately like two yoyos in the sky above a nest tucked away in the grass beneath. A kestrel darted by, and then we saw them: wild bustards, a dozen or more picking their way through the longer grass along the opposite ridge. Even from this great distance, they were magnificent, easily big enough to see off a fox or any other potential predator brave enough to try. I thought I heard David's voice crack at the joy of showing us the sum of his life's work out there on the plain. Everyone had said it was impossible, yet here the birds were, right before our eyes. It was an extraordinary achievement by one man, whose obsession with these birds derived from an inner calling that he obeyed unrelentingly.

David's happiness and fulfilment shone out in a way that prompted me to reflect on some of the ideas I had encountered since Iris's death. After the accident, a deluge of letters arrived at Cannwood. Some came attended by books offering wisdom on how to comprehend my loss. Among these were several copies of *Man's Search for Meaning*, the seminal work of psychiatrist Viktor Frankl, who had miraculously survived years in the concentration camps of the Holocaust. Having to witness who among his fellow inmates lived and who did not, Frankl came to believe that, whether they know it or not, all people are motivated by an inner *will to meaning*, and it was in the honouring of this that often dictated who made it and who did not. Frankl wrote of his experiences in the camps:

> *Woe to him who saw no more sense in his life, no aim, no purpose, and therefore no point in carrying on. He was soon lost. The typical reply with which such a man rejected all encouraging arguments was, 'I have nothing to expect from life anymore.' What sort of answer can one give to that?*
>
> *What was really needed was a fundamental change in our attitude toward life. We had to learn ourselves and, furthermore, we had to teach the despairing men that it did not really matter what we expected from life, but rather what life expected from us. We needed to stop asking about the meaning of life, and instead to think of ourselves as those who were being questioned by life — daily and hourly. Our answer must consist, not in talk and meditation, but in right action and in right conduct. Life ultimately means taking the responsibility to find the right answer to its problems and to fulfil the tasks which it constantly sets for each individual.*

After the war, Frankl developed *logotherapy*, the practice of healing inner suffering by helping individuals look within and discover their own unique purpose. Frankl's will to meaning offers a way of surviving trauma and leading a happy and fulfilled life. Burning with purpose, David Waters and his bustards showcase this theory. Throughout the time we were together, David spoke lovingly of the sacrifices made by his wife and of her unquestioning support of him over three decades, stating that it was through her love that he had retained the confidence to do what he did. This is the second significant insight offered by Frankl, who believed that it is through love that human beings find and act out their own will to meaning. He writes that:

> *Love is the only way to grasp another human being in the innermost core of his personality. No one can become fully aware of the very essence of another human being unless he loves him. By his love he is enabled to see the essential traits and features in the beloved person; and even more, he sees that which is potential in him, which is not yet actualized but yet ought to be actualized. Furthermore, by his love, the loving person enables the beloved person to actualize these potentialities. By making him aware of what he can be and of what he should become, he makes these potentialities come true.*

As we drove home, my thoughts turned again to Iris. We, her family, had loved her with every ounce of our being, and in the light of our love, we had seen her brilliance, her dedication, and her huge potential. During the years we had with her, Iris had been supported and encouraged, and she had truly shone. This idea that Iris's life, short though it had been, was steeped in purpose, and the achievement of potential from start to finish gave me comfort, of sorts. I found myself smiling, bittersweet, as I thought of her and the life she had led.

13

Anniversary

The anniversary of Iris's death loomed large in my mind. The date was 8th July 2020. Throughout the previous year, anticipating the eighth day of each month also brought a chill wind. I tried to tell myself that dates are meaningless, pushing the dread to the back of my mind; nevertheless, a gloom descended as each milestone approached. I found myself scrolling through pictures and videos of Iris, missing her even more than usual throughout each day. Every second month I posted a photograph of a meaningful moment on Instagram, and beneath each, I wrote a short letter to her. Describing in writing these bright little memories – addressed to Iris each time – had helped in some way to ease the pain. I eventually came to understand that the anticipation of milestone days was worse than the days themselves turned out to be.

Not long after the accident, Kate had discovered a series of mind maps Iris had jotted, concerning preparation for her future. Kate had found them on the side table by her bed. At the centre of each diagram was a fluffy cloud drawn around a single word; on the first, 'English'. Arrows extended outwards to smaller clouds, forming a task list: 'Re-read Jane Eyre,' 'Try writing poetry,' 'Read essays to develop structure,' 'Read Walter Scott, Sylvia Plath, *Brave New World*.' The cloud at the centre of the second sheet was marked 'Languages'. She planned to 'Watch Spanish Netflix shows', 'Focus on adding to vocabulary' and 'Read Spanish newspapers.' The third sheet was about 'University,' the satellite clouds mulling the merits of the American institutions, 'Yale, Harvard, Princeton, NYU', versus 'Oxford, Cambridge, Edinburgh, Bristol, UCL'. She had selected as A levels and possible future university options: 'History, History of Art, English, Spanish and Biology', with a note to herself on the importance of 'Volunteering'. Mysteriously a fourth had 'SCs' at its centre, 'Social Connections' perhaps? 'Lunches with Dad'; '*The Ormeley Environment Dinner*', a biannual fund-raising dinner Zac and I had organised with others for a few years. I smiled at that page. Quite right – they'd have loved you, I thought to myself. At the centre of the fourth was 'Law', with plans for upping her knowledge of current affairs, volunteering overseas, joining the school debating society and exploring whether to go straight into law or do a conversion course. On the fifth, 'Fitness', with boxing on a Sunday, daily visits to the school gym, Saturday Pilates, cutting out sugar, and sit-ups in her room all part of her plan. A sixth note entitled 'Art' envisaged visits to galleries, exploring 'experimental ideas in art', visiting the Chelsea Arts Club with Great Aunt Sabrina, and reading about surrealism, romanticism, impressionism and post-impressionism. It was almost unbelievable: Iris had everything mapped out in fine detail. On a visit to see Kate and the boys during the previous autumn, I had taken a moment to sit in Iris's room. Kate had told me about the notes. Reading them while sitting on Iris's bed had been unbearable. I was mad with grief, crying bitterly into Iris's pillow before organising myself and heading back downstairs.

Each new school term was especially painful. Iris had been impeccable in her preparation for everything: the next school day, the coming term and exams on the horizon. In the days preceding the start of term, I became quieter and more withdrawn; the sudden appearance of flocks of teenagers on street corners, tube trains and in the parks was a brutal reminder of what I had lost. It seemed as if girls Iris's age appeared everywhere dressed just as she did: their hair dyed blonde; the same hoop earrings, crop tops and Ellesse or Adidas tracksuit bottoms; the ubiquitous white socks and ugly Nike slider flip flops. I took to turning my head away, trying not to see them. The run-up to Christmas 2019 brought sadness that came in waves that were hard to conceal in their acuteness, interspersed with the usual festivities in which I participated theatrically for the benefit of the younger ones. In the days before 3rd February, which would have been Iris's 16th birthday, it took all my willpower just to get out of bed each morning. On the birthday itself, I took the overground train in the early afternoon to Barnes station, where Kate collected me and drove us to Richmond Park's Roehampton Gate. We walked among the ancient, sleeping oak pollards across a landscape that hasn't changed much over the centuries. Richmond Park, protected by Charles I and enclosed inside a great wall in 1637, had been a rough wood pasture grazed by fallow and red deer for centuries before then. That weekday afternoon, the park was deserted, presumably because of the bitter cold. The air was still, the sky above a deep blue. In the years following our divorce, Kate had become more sister than ex-wife, and the loss of Iris had brought us closer. We walked briskly and shared stories of how we were each coping, of the low moments and the better times, and of the things we missed most about our daughter.

The scale of Kate's loss is cataclysmic; her eldest child and only daughter, just 20 years younger than herself. On Mother's Days and birthdays, it is daughters who most often bring their mothers hand-drawn cards and breakfast in bed and write effusive, loving posts on Instagram; it is daughters who often rely on their own mothers to help them to raise their babies. 'I've never had such mutual understanding with any person as I had with Iris, nor will I ever again,' she had told me in a text a few weeks earlier. Their relationship had been growing ever closer as Iris blossomed into a young woman. All of that future was now erased, forever, irreversibly. After her daughter's death, Joan Didion wrote in her memoir *Blue Nights* of a fear not for what has been lost, but of 'what is *still* to be lost'.

After our walk together in the park that day, we went back to Kate's house, her dogs bundling through the door ahead of us, in time for the planned gathering at teatime for sausage rolls, beer and cake. Kate had chosen to mark the occasion by asking Iris's best friends to join our family for a little celebration. The front door was left open, and before long, teenagers began to appear, boys and girls at first sombre in their shy greetings, but before long laughing and jockeying with each other at the table as if this were any other family birthday party. The Irie clothing company had given us a gift of several boxes of Irie hoodies, that being Iris's nickname in recent years, and many of the teenagers slipped them on as we handed them out. They paid special attention to Frankie and Isaac, Iris's younger brothers, who had hung back a little at first before immersing themselves in the banter. I recognised some of the girls from distant summer weekends at Cannwood, another lifetime it seemed, while others I had glimpsed at the reception following the funeral. A trickle of teenagers came and went through the backyard, heading out to leave a card or some flowers at Iris's magic London plane tree on the common behind the house.

Some of her closest girlfriends had a word in Kate's ear before kicking off their trainers at the bottom of the stairs and tiptoeing up in their socks to Iris's room on the top floor. Three-and-a-half-year-old Eliza, seeing them go, demanded that she and I follow them. She too wanted to visit the bedroom of her mythical big sister, and so up we went, Eliza full of determination, taking on one step at a time before me. I followed behind as she chattered about guardian angels and Hello Kitty and all the other little Iris-related snippets that she had gathered from bedtime stories and family photo albums since her sister had died. I felt the weight of a heavy rock inside my belly, pulling my head forward and down, my chest and shoulders concave. The whole thing was almost too much. Holding my right wrist with my left hand, I applied a gentle, comforting pressure to my abdomen as we climbed the stairs.

We surprised the three girls as we entered, each one lost in their thoughts in a different part of the room by the time we appeared. One sat on Iris's bed; another looked at the stacked hoodies and t-shirts on the upper shelves of an open cupboard, while the third was leafing reverently through the assorted schoolbooks, notes and folders on the tidy white desk by the open window. This was not Eliza's first visit to

Iris's room, and she made a beeline for the bed at the centre of the room and for the Hello Kitty under the pillow. Two ribbons that Kate had haphazardly sewn onto the back of the soft toy were well-sucked and a little stiff at the ends. Iris had grown up with Kitty's predecessor, Teddy, permanently at hand, always one of the two ribbons at the back pressed between thumb, forefinger and nostrils, the other in the mouth, even as she slept. Newly married, before Iris turned one, Kate and I had arrived at a Paris hotel room to find Teddy waiting in the cot, a gift from the hotel. In 2012, the year of our divorce, Teddy had been irretrievably lost. It had been an enormous relief that the Kitty, suitably beribboned, had so easily filled the void. The toy still smelled of Iris, an intensely familiar scent blended with the coconut and vanilla-scented shampoos and cosmetics she had taken to using as a teenager. Her black bomber jacket hung on the inside of the bedroom door. Quietly I unhooked it and buried my face momentarily in the lining on the inside. The smell of the jacket was unmistakable, as if she had taken it off that very afternoon. There was something in the pocket: mint Tic Tacs. I dropped one out and ate it. The girls filed out wordlessly before us. Smiling, I swallowed hard and, breathing deliberately, I placed the Kitty back under the pillow and made my way back downstairs, carrying Eliza on my left arm.

In the run-up to these occasions, the dread seemed to build in the background, waxing and waning but always present and growing, like smoke seeping through every crack until it becomes overwhelming. A period of crying, inevitable, would deliver a recovery of sorts. I tried breathing exercises as a way of clearing the smoke and settling my fear. In boarding school, a cliched poster hung on my wall depicting a Rastafarian sitting low on a seat in front of a colourful mural, head tilted back, eyes closed, exhaling a great cloud of blueish smoke. A caption emblazoned across the lower half of the poster read, 'Breathe in the good shit; Breathe out the bad shit.' Whilst he may have had a different message in mind, sometimes as a teenager I thought of those words, and would pause to take deep inhalations of fresh air, several times in a row, filling my lungs absolutely, and visualising the anxiety leaving my body with each exhalation that followed. Somehow, it worked. Focusing on each breath absorbed all capacity for thinking about anything else.

Suspending conscious thought in a practice sometimes described as meditation has been a mainstay of spiritual custom in one way or another throughout time. The earliest records of meditation are found in the ancient Hindu texts known as the *Vedas*, and today, secular scientists report overwhelming evidence of the mental and physical health benefits of regular meditation. The truth is that I wasn't very good at it; my mind quickly reverted to form, grabbing back control at the slightest distraction, without me even noticing, resuming its drift from one topic to the next. Even so, I began to understand the point without ever taking up the practice in any regular kind of way. Our waking thoughts are often focused on the past and the future, places in which we tend to find negativity in the form of regret, say, or fear, whereas thoughts rooted in the present, relegated to a small fraction of our day, are more likely to be positive. Mindful breathing is a good way to focus attention on what Terence McKenna described as 'the felt moment of immediate experience'. McKenna argued that this, the present moment we are experiencing right now through our senses, is the only reality on which we can count utterly. Following Iris's death, by softly fixing on what I was feeling in the present moment, the cold hardness of the stone I was sitting on in Iris's circle, the weight of my hands resting on my knees, the gentle breeze against the skin of my face, to the exclusion of all else, I found a flicker of truth and serenity that, very briefly, freed me from anxiety.

We're taught from childhood that our most important emotions and decisions emanate not from the head but from the heart or the gut. The psychologist and philosopher Carl Gustav Jung spent time in the 1920s with the Pueblo Indian people of North America, from whom he learned some of the fundamental differences between the psychology of Europeans and that of the indigenous communities of America. In his autobiographical work *Memories, Dreams, Reflections*, Jung wrote that one tribal elder had looked him straight in the eye and said of the European people surging all around the shrinking Pueblo reservation: 'Their eyes have a staring expression; they are always seeking something. What are they seeking? The whites always want something; they are always uneasy and restless. We do not know what they want. We do not understand them. We think they are mad.'

Jung asked the elder 'why he thought the whites were all mad'.

'They say that they think with their heads,' he replied.

'Why of course. What do you think with?' Jung asked.

'We think here,' the elder said, 'indicating his heart'.

I made an initial pact with myself to attempt regular meditation but failed to stick to it, only remembering to make an effort when the sadness and fear became overwhelming. Nevertheless, I began to recognise within myself a deeper personality I had not knowingly encountered before, an inner self somehow distinct from my mind, whose constant chatter narrates the passing of each day. Seasoned meditators call this other self *the witness*, training this part of us silently to observe our conscious thoughts as they materialise and allow them to drift by like clouds. Jung said, 'Every civilised human being, whatever his conscious development, is still an archaic man at the deeper levels of his psyche.' Without ever really succeeding in my attempts to meditate properly, I became fascinated by the idea that this inner self is a vital part of me, the place from which love upwells. If something of us survives death, this must be it. Often when I tried to meditate properly, I found myself jumping the gun and straining to conceive of how a direct connection with Iris might manifest, which was probably the kind of conscious and stressful thought process that the whole exercise was designed to diminish.

During the week of the first anniversary of the accident, Cannwood was more alive than ever, calling all of us irresistibly to be outside during every waking moment. Field boundaries were blurred as hedges grew fat, the ends of branches weighed down with wilting blossom now metamorphosing into hard bundles of green berries. In the margins of the hedges, suckers of blackthorn, hawthorn, dog rose and occasional willow were now bursting through long grass. Docks, nettles, delicate pink and white foxgloves, oxeye daisies and brightly flowering purple thistles in large clusters were scattered across ground otherwise carpeted with yellow creeping and meadow buttercups, the same fields that just a year earlier had been shorn ankle high. Small birds – linnets, long-tailed tits, goldfinches and yellowhammers – tittered and chattered as they busied themselves ferrying caterpillars and other small insects from the herbage back to nests concealed amid the hedgerow thorns. The whole vivid mantle was alive, an orchestra of flying insects and grasshoppers chirruping and humming, leaping outward in clouds before each footstep. A pair of kestrels chose to make their home in a particularly grand stag-headed field oak and spent their days hovering, their eyes peeled, above a territory teeming with voles, mice and other small mammals. At dusk, their place of dominance was assumed by a pair of barn owls, glimpsable in the blue-blackness of the night, sitting motionless on a wooden stake or gliding ghost-like along the contours of the changing landscape.

For me, gazing at all of this was a better way of meditating than sitting with my eyes shut in the traditional way. I loved observing minute changes in the landscape, bathing in the resurgent life all around me, fascinated, my senses on high alert, all other thoughts excluded. In his seminal book *The Nature Principle,* the author Richard Louv, famous for diagnosing a global epidemic of what he called 'nature deficit disorder', wrote:

> *Could a literal sense of spirit exist on the far edge of our senses, out where the flat earth stops and all that is beyond and within begins? Might this particular sense be activated by the other senses, when they're working at full throttle – which so often occurs when we are in nature?*

I found beauty, too, in the words of the philosopher Ralph Waldo Emerson, a leader of the transcendentalist movement of mid-nineteenth-century America, notorious for challenging views of God as separate from the world. Waldo, who went by his middle name, wrote of an 'over-soul', an eternal spirit that runs through all things, intricately connected, coming to understand Nature as a single, complete, living, conscious entity. It was in the presence of the awesome spirit described by Waldo that I found solace, hope, even joy.

For the actual anniversary of Iris's death, Kate booked a coach to transport 40 or 50 of her friends from London to Cannwood for a celebration around the stone circle. We arranged a local pizza van and made a bar to serve drinks. The weather had been a worry, so Chris, Garry, Nick and I put up a makeshift awning using six posts and a large blue tarpaulin. Kate slung coloured flowers made of paper around each stone, much as she had decorated the great Plane tree on Barnes Common a year earlier.

A welcome distraction from my dreadful sense of foreboding came in the form of a raffle prize I had won at a charity dinner the previous summer: a chance to go fishing with chef Mark Hix off the Jurassic coast of Dorset and to cook and eat with him whatever we might catch at his legendary Oyster and Fish House in Lyme Regis. I agreed a date at short notice with Mark, the day before the anniversary. There was room for three on his small boat, and I chose to take Frankie with me, Isaac never having been particularly keen on boats. It was a relief to leave Cannwood. Jemima was just stirring as I dressed to go. I kissed her, and Frankie and I left early, before anyone else was up.

From the car window, the grinding loss of wildlife that has occurred across the south-west of England was not at all obvious. As we glided through Somerset's great green checkerboard in the early-morning sun, I thought about how some people describe landscape like this 'green concrete': lush, beautiful in its way, but monocultural and somewhat lifeless. Nearly two hours later, after various games of 'I spy' interspersed with comfortable periods of silence as Frankie munched his way through a giant packet of Haribo, we arrived in Lyme Regis. We parked the car in a bay on the opposite side of the road from the dozens of small fishing and pleasure boats that filled the harbour, bobbing in neat columns on the oily water. I called Mark from my mobile phone before spotting him waving at us with both arms from the quay beside his boat at the far end of the harbour. Waving back, we walked briskly the way we had come, up some steep steps and along the footway at the top of the wall towards a lighthouse on the far corner. Gangs of herring gulls loitered on the taller masts and along the thick stone balustrade beside us, the grey and white adults standing aloof, looking into the breeze while brown-speckled juveniles just as big as their parents hopped restlessly around them, eyeing us with what seemed like amused interest.

In the water below, I spied a fat grey mullet coasting sluggishly along the harbour wall behind the boats, perhaps waiting for some excrement to appear from the side of one of the boats. Some people eat grey mullet, but I've always considered them sea rats, disturbingly at ease living among people and their boats, eating their detritus. I have never quite forgotten the experience of accidentally eating one at a lunch in the chairman's dining room at one of London's remaining family-owned banks. I had felt nauseous after being informed that the slippery fish we had just eaten, along with a delicate little potato salad, had been a grey mullet.

It was high tide, and little waves lapped around the lower steps and over the floating jetty as we made our way down to Mark's berth, where his creamy-white fishing boat was tethered. Barefoot in the back of his boat with tousled grey hair, a blue and white striped t-shirt and grubby shorts, he greeted us effusively. Never having known much about boats, I stood lamely by as he untied and hauled in ropes at each end, fired up the engine and guided the little vessel out towards the mouth of the harbour. 'We'll head to a sandbank over there. That's where we'll catch something,' he said, gesticulating loosely towards the horizon. 'Coffee?' Slowing the boat on the glassy water beyond the harbour wall, he poured us each a black coffee in three dented tin mugs before pressing on. On the floor of the boat was a blue bucket containing some dead squid. Sitting beside me, Frankie poked about in it with a large knife, lost in his thoughts. The sea is a place of forgetting, and for a while, with sun, wind and flecks of seawater on our faces, I forgot.

When the children were little, Kate and I took them on several occasions to stay in a tiny rental cottage outside the fishing town of Brixham in Devon. For Frankie, the highlight had been going out to fish for mackerel with a retired fisherman named Dennis, whom we had met on the quayside during our first visit. The diesel fumes had been suffocating on his crusty old boat, the engine noise deafening, but we always came back with a bucketful of mackerel, beautiful creatures dazzlingly striped in hues of green and blue. We cooked them each time on an open barbecue behind the cottage. Once we saw a large, circular sunfish floating on its side near the surface, as sunfish do; on another occasion, a common seal, its head craning from the swell to peer at us like an inquisitive Labrador. On another trip, in choppy conditions, we were amazed to see two common dolphins. The children squealed with excitement before they disappeared down and out of sight. Apart from herring gulls and the occasional tern, seabirds were a rarity, as they were now off Lyme Regis.

Dennis had described, without emotion, how different it had been when he was a child when there were great flocks of seabirds, whose eggs the children gathered from nests on the steep escarpment encircling the town. Dennis remembered seasonal shoals of mackerel so huge that fishermen had only to drop their baskets into the water before hauling them back out laden with fish. Dennis may have been 70 or 75 when he took us out fishing, yet by the 1950s, when he had been a boy, British waters were already savagely overfished. Imagine, I remember asking him, how things might have been above and beneath the water when his own grandfather had been a boy.

George Monbiot, author of the seminal rewilding book *Feral*, regularly recalls a passage from the diaries of Oliver Goldsmith (no relation of mine), which recounts the abundance of wildlife in British waters in the late 1700s. Describing his awe on coming close to several huge basking sharks off the coast of Scotland and calling for the establishment of genuinely protected areas covering a third of British waters from which all commercial fishing be excluded, Monbiot writes:

> We saw perhaps a dozen [basking sharks], of which one stood out: a monster twice the length of the boat that looked almost as broad as a whale. The largest basking shark ever measured was forty feet long, but the combination of hunting, bycatch and boat strikes nowadays makes it less likely that they will live long enough to reach that size. The beast we saw was probably about as big as they now get. The same feral ecstasy — a primal thrill mingled with an ancient recognition — returned every time. I would like to live in a world where such experiences are common. This is not an impossible dream. In the late eighteenth century, Oliver Goldsmith described the arrival of herring, as seen from the British shore. The fish, he recorded, were 'divided into distinct columns of five or six miles in length and three or four broad; while the water before them curls up, as if forced out of its bed … the whole water seems alive, and is seen so black with them to a great distance that the number seems inexhaustible.' The herring were followed by massive cod, spurdog, tope and smooth hound, longfin and bluefin tuna, blue, porbeagle, thresher, mako and occasional great white sharks. Moving in behind, within sight of the shore, were pods of fin whales and sperm whales. This astonishing congregation of life has all but gone, largely through overfishing. But marine ecosystems recover very quickly when they have the chance. The crucial policy is to decide that large areas should no longer be commercially exploited.

After cruising for about an hour, Mark slowed and cut the engine before clambering around the side of the boat to drop the little anchor about a mile from the shore. The sun burned hot through the haze. Looking back towards the harbour, I could just make out the white- and pastel-coloured buildings of Lyme Regis, a distant smudge clustered around the harbour and up the hill. A handful of other small boats had similarly stopped at our sandbank, accompanied by a smattering of floating gulls rocking on the swell. Every now and then, a snippet of conversation was carried to us from across the water.

Muttering some instructions, Mark handed Frankie a large cork square, around which was wrapped over and over a length of catgut line, a rough lead weight dangling from the end. He took a second from a box under the steering wheel, and then the two of them unfurled enough line each to reveal three hooks fixed roughly a foot apart along the line. Mark reached into the bucket and fished out one of the limp wet squids that Frankie had been prodding. This was our bait. Mark set about expertly slicing it up, skewering a piece onto each hook. Then we dropped a line into the water on either side of the boat and watched as the phosphorescent whiteness of the six pieces of bait spiralled down into the inky depths. The two lead weights finally found the seafloor, at which point Mark and Frankie rewound their lines a few feet. I imagined what creatures might lurk down there in the darkness. We sat back and waited, the two of them holding their lines one-handed, allowing the bait to rise and fall with the swell. Nothing.

Presently, they hauled their lines back in to check the squid was still in position on the hooks, allowing the line to accumulate loosely in two adjacent heaps on the wet plastic floor. The position of each dripping piece of squid was adjusted, and the lines were cast out again. Still nothing took the bait. After half an hour, we decided to move to another spot where the procedure was repeated, and this time almost immediately, there was a tug, first at Mark's line and then at Frankie's. Breathlessly, deadly serious, they brought in their lines as fast as their hands could work. Out came two small dogfish, one suspended on each line. They were the 'lesser-spotted' variety, Mark told us, adding that there were loads in the area, and 'good in curries'. Sinewy little sharks with pale, rough skin, they wriggled frantically as Mark extracted the hooks from their mouths one after the other. As he bashed their heads once hard against the side of the boat, they stilled, petrified, their spotted backs arched and quivering, before he slipped them into the blue bucket on top of the bait.

Dogfish, also known as rockfish, or small-spotted catshark, are abundant off Britain's south coast, probably because they are not targeted by commercial fishing boats and because they eat almost anything. We caught five before calling it a day. As he hauled in the anchor from the bow, I asked Mark if Frankie and I might swim before heading back to the harbour, and so we did, in our boxer shorts, leaping one-footed from the same side of the boat. Exhilarated, I curled forward in the water and plunged head-first down as deep as I dared go into the cold, briny water, Frankie in pursuit. Surfacing, we splashed about and swam a couple of circuits of the boat, joyful to be in the sea, perhaps a little wary of what might come up from below to bite us, before clambering back on board and pulling our clothes back onto our wet bodies.

The boat chugged back towards Lyme Regis while Mark and I exchanged stories of hope from the waters around Britain. The English Channel and North Sea have a perpetually murky turbidity to them, but it wasn't always this way. Vast oyster beds once carpeted the shallow water in a halo that encircled the British Isles, holding the seabed in place, each oyster filtering as much as 50 gallons of seawater a day. In some areas, the brilliantly green fronds of seagrass that grew in great underwater meadows had the same effect as oysters, cleaning the water and providing habitat for young fish and wildlife of all kinds. We now know that seagrass meadows rank among the most important climate solution nature has to offer, absorbing carbon from the atmosphere many times faster, even, than tropical rainforests. Britain's shallow seas were once blue, until the advent of industrial dredging for shellfish and bottom trawling, which involves dragging heavy fishing equipment along the seafloor over and over again to catch the fish, rather like flattening an entire woodland to catch a few rabbits. Local efforts to seed new oyster beds are beginning to spring up around Britain, all of them on a shoestring budget cobbled together by local communities. *Seawilding*, they call it. Or *re-oystering*. Tiny newly hatched oysters are plugged onto used oyster shells collected from restaurants and carefully laid in a mosaic across the sea floor, and miraculously it works. In some parts of coastal Britain, seagrass meadows, too, are being replanted. As more and more people understand the magic and the immense ecological and economic value of these delicate, lost ecosystems, there is a mounting backlash against the idiocy of bottom trawling and growing public pressure to protect the seabed near the shore.

Mark was right: the little sharks tasted good, diced and curried, and Frankie and I headed back well fed, following the one-way system out of Lyme Regis and out into the open country, back towards Cannwood. I awoke early the following day and went out to the stone circle, coffee in hand, to help with the mowing of a wide circle and the lighting of a big fire in the firepit at its centre.

First to arrive in the early afternoon were the four Dreamers children. Monica welled up as she told me she and her siblings had avoided that field until the stone circle had appeared, and now they came all the time to hang out here and talk about Iris. I managed to hold myself together, breathing slowly and deliberately, passing each of them a can of beer. Then came family, Kate's and my oldest friends, and before long, in rolled the bus, stopping at the top of the lane, and out they filed, boys and girls that had adored my Iris, each in their own way, dozens of relationships about which I knew nothing, but which had been central to the last years of her life. Beers, music on a large speaker by one of the stones, pizzas – it was all a strangely happy blur. The teenagers made their way to and from the pond, tumbled into the water, swimming and shouting, Isaac at the centre of it all, and to my astonishment, it was fun. Iris would have loved it, every second, and somehow, I didn't suffer.

14

Healing

If you could get rid of yourself just once, the secret of
secrets would open to you. The face of the unknown,
hidden beyond the universe would appear on the mirror
of your perception.

RUMI

Now my own suspicion is that the universe is not
only queerer than we suppose, but queerer than
we can suppose.

J. B. S. HALDANE,
Possible Worlds and Other Essays

My grief had taken me to many places in the year following my
daughter's death. In my search for understanding, I had spoken
to leaders of different faiths, participated in various spiritual
practices, and found solace in the natural world around me.

Not long after I visited the spiritualistic medium in the
autumn following Iris's death, several people suggested to me,
cautiously as they commiserated, that I consider a psychedelic
experience as a way of coming to terms with my loss. Some
referred to the healing potential of psychedelic experiences,

while others hinted at grander rewards still and the possibility of first-hand connection with the dead. One wrote:

> I am not claiming to understand how you feel, as I haven't experienced your tragic loss or anything that approaches it, so all I am able to do is try to imagine what you are going through ... I never had the pleasure of meeting Iris, but now that she has gone, it is you, not her, that is suffering, and suffering greatly. Please know that it is with the intention of reducing that suffering that this letter is written ... I want to stress that I am in no way trying to trivialise your situation; your heart has been broken, and this is just a suggestion as to how you may be able to mend it. It is not entirely without risk, and you may easily reject my idea out of hand. Most people probably would, and I, for one, certainly wouldn't blame you if you did ... I have read your moving social media posts, and I see that several people have suggested that some form of acquired religious or spiritual view of existence may help your situation ... From the point of view of Eastern religion, those lucky enough to have escaped the prison of their own thoughts cannot easily help others do so, and even those who desire nothing more than such an escape are unable to achieve it without some sort of divine providence that may or may not occur, depending on who knows what? Even those who meditate or pray for many hours a day for years are often not granted the peace and freedom they crave, and for many, although they can intuitively sense that there exists behind a veil a blissful and universal truth that will set their troubled minds free, they are unable, for whatever reason, to break through that veil and have their own experience of it, which is an essential step towards liberation.

A lengthy discourse on the writer's understanding of the Hindu concept of non-duality comes next before he goes on:

> I apologise for the length of this letter, but I felt it necessary to give an idea of the concept of non-duality to move on to my suggestion for a radical and instant process of inner transformation that is not, shall I say, mainstream … I have not had a psychedelic experience myself, but I know several who have, and I have read a good deal on the subject. It seems to me that the experience may not be much different from the awakening described by Ramana. It is common for those who have tried it to report that they felt as if they had died and come back to life, but with a radically different and improved outlook … The whole thing here is that I believe this may help with your suffering and mental anguish as it is the only 'medicine' capable of giving rise to a non-dual state of mind in which one is no longer aware of existing as an individual entity separate from God and the universe. The experience may provide an insight into the notion that there is no death, no injustice, no resentment, and all perceived grievances forgiven and forgotten as if they only occurred in a dream. I believe this is what Jesus meant when he said, 'Except a man be born again, he cannot see the kingdom of God.'

Reading this letter reminded me of my one previous psychedelic experience, an experience I had sworn never to repeat. Aged 19, in my first year of adulthood, I had travelled to a village deep in the Ecuadorian forest with some friends. Once we were there, my friend told us, we would have a chance to drink *ayahuasca*, a psychoactive brew derived from a particular vine and used as a ceremonial, spiritual medicine among indigenous peoples across the Amazon basin. My heart sank. As a teenager, I wasn't drawn to drugs, even though they were all around me, not because of any kind of morality but from fear. Having dabbled unsuccessfully here and there, I was afraid of them. Drugs didn't fit for me, somehow. I smoked marijuana, and that was it.

In the preceding weeks, blocking from my mind the terrifying prospect that loomed, I had made no effort whatsoever to find out anything about ayahuasca, or as it is sometimes known, ayawaska. *Aya*, meaning spirit, soul, corpse or dead body; *waska*, meaning rope, woody vine or liana in the Quechua languages of the western Amazon basin, translating to vine of the soul, liana of the dead, spirit vine. Ayahuasca has played a central role in the sacramental lives of societies across the Amazon basin for millennia. I knew very little of the significance of certain compounds with psychedelic properties – found in plants, fungi and even the poison on the skin of a desert-living amphibian – to the spiritual lives of indigenous societies the world over. I didn't know that indigenous peoples have looked to shamanic holy men in their midst for guidance on almost every aspect of their individual and communal lives, nor that these shamans derive their perceived foresight, wisdom and healing capabilities from journeys undertaken into the expanse of their own consciousness using psychedelic compounds, journeys in realms outside of the bounds of space and time, it is said, from which they return with new ideas and imaginings that have informed the most fundamental choices made by their kin. The first westerners who consumed ayahuasca with the tribes they encountered in the Amazon reported having mystical or religious experiences and spiritual revelations about their purpose on Earth and the nature of the universe. However, before long, predictably, the practice was denounced as the 'work of the devil' by Christian missionaries, and it would be several centuries until westerners would again come into contact with ayahuasca.

Despite my thoughts of excuses – a tummy upset, perhaps – upon arrival in the jungle, I joined my friends in the ayahuasca ritual. Our Quechua guide took on a reverential air, placing a woven palm hat bedecked with feathers on his head and lighting up a clump of incense in a half coconut shell on the floor. He began circling a steaming pot, which had simmered, suspended over a small open fire, since the morning. Soon he began chanting in his native language, quietly at first, pausing here and there to rattle a kind of a broom noisily into the darkness. His wife sat by calmly on a small rush mat, observant, while the younger children dashed about unseen, whooping, oblivious to the goings on at the centre of their little world in the jungle. We were offered no instruction on what we might expect or ought to do. Concluding the ritual, the father stooped to ladle a small measure of the viscous brew into a battered metal beaker for himself, which he knocked back in one, before calling over his son, to whom he held out a fresh measure. The teenage boy, fidgeting, looking at his bare feet, stepped forward, took the beaker from his father's hand and drank before retreating to sit on the smooth earth by his mother's feet. One by one, we followed. Nauseous with fear, I took my turn. Ayahuasca tastes foul. Warm and sweetly rooty, earthy, poisonous, the taste remained with me for months and years afterwards. I swallowed it in one go and returned to my spot by the fire. I managed to resist the urge to retch, but one of the group was sick immediately, off to one side through the gaps in his fingers, before our guide ushered him back to the centre to take a second cup straight away.

Back in our places, our guide directed us to the four hammocks slung between the stilts behind. There were hushed whispers between us as we clambered in, nervous giggles in anticipation of what was to come. I rested my head back in clasped hands, the soles of my feet pressed together, and I tuned into the nightly cacophony, the tree canopy whispering gently above. Occasional sighs and grunts from either side reminded me that I wasn't alone in the jungle. After a time, our guide began to play a simple oboe-like instrument softly, the notes blending seamlessly with the sounds of nature all around, coalescing like running water, accumulating in small pools of sound and overflowing to form a stream, multi-braided, burbling, gurgling, gathering pace and volume, eddying variously around the standout calls of a particularly raucous frog or the cries of the children still tearing about the encampment. I began to imagine myself a fallen branch clinging to the bank, the water rushing all around me, pulling at me, until soon I found myself carried along feet first, plunging downwards, flotsam now, powerless, the music assuming a new gravitas, absolutely in control of me. Around the periphery of my vision, quivering apparitions encroached upon the blackness, swirling, numinous forms at first faintly coloured but growing in confidence, dancing in tune with the music as I sailed downstream and becoming more distinct and more vivid with every breath I took. The forms began to take shape, brightly coloured patterns filling the space around me, fractal, geometric shapes, endlessly changing, folding out of themselves, growing ever larger before splitting amoeba-like, crowding me, filling all space in a great, mathematical vortex towards which I careened headlong.

Amid the mayhem, I became aware of a growing nausea. An insistent, laboured, dry retching broke through the dreamlike cloak that enveloped me, and I emerged from my reverie back into the damp darkness of the camp. Propping myself up on a shaky elbow to peer out of the right side of my hammock, ribbons of light and colour streaking across my field of vision,

I made out my nearest neighbour suspended from his, feet and legs still inside, chest heaving on the ground beneath, and face turned sideways grimacing, eyes closed. His form and everything else around shook violently, and so I saw him in double or triple, my hammock now rocking lengthways as a wave of nausea overtook me. I managed to free myself fully before the first round of vomiting, on all-fours now, the mud surface yawing, pitching and rolling beneath me. Soon I was on my face, vomiting again. I was lucid enough to understand that we had been poisoned, wondering if perhaps we were on the brink of death. With the passing of each wave of nausea, I felt relief and remained quite still, face down, so as not to invite a new one. I didn't care that my hair was wet with my own vomit. All around me, the jungle croaked and spoke and danced, and beneath me, the ground seemed at once rock hard and soft as putty, my arms delving down deep to fondle its entrails. Periodically I came round to find our guide standing over each of us in turn, shaking his broom inches away from our faces pancaked against the earth.

Flicking my head minutely, holding my eyes open, breathing deeply, I tried vainly to resist the gravity of this great force as it dragged me back down into the watery, brightly shimmering dreamworld. Only an overpowering urge to vomit brought me back each time. As the hours passed and the storm began to melt away, I found myself shivering lightly while an intense heat grew within my thorax, my liver, I assumed. I willed it to keep going. Slowly, at the first hint of dawn, the rest of us began to stir. I rolled onto my back, then onto my other side, before finally breaking into a crawl and up into my warm hammock where I slept, for real this time, deeply until mid morning.

Washing ourselves in the river, still weak and shaking a little, we babbled our relief to be alive, that it was over, laughing, incredulous that there had once been a suggestion of a second night of it. Never, ever again, I vowed to myself. It didn't occur to me that I might have missed an opportunity for spiritual enlightenment. I was just relieved to have survived the ordeal and perhaps a little happy to have such a story to tell later. Our experience that night lacked any meaningful preparation or ritual, even though indigenous communities have always tied psychedelic use to longstanding, elaborate ceremonies. The Algonquin tribes of North America used psychedelic mushrooms in puberty ceremonies during which young men leave behind their boyhood; the Celts of Britain and Ireland used them in military planning; some Amazonian tribes use ayahuasca to communicate with the non-human world; the Pygmy people of the Congo Basin consume a plant named *iboga* to convene in celebration with their departed ancestors.

The catalytic role that psychedelic compounds may have played in the evolution of the human brain, of human consciousness, imagination, spirituality and even in the emergence of monotheistic religions is almost totally overlooked. The ritual consumption of psychedelic plants and fungi stretching back to our cave-dwelling ancestors is thought to have survived to antiquity. Archaeochemical evidence discovered in Israel points to the consumption of beer infused with psychedelic fungi 13,000 years ago. Ten millennia later, some 2,000 years before the birth of Jesus, the great thinkers of Ancient Greece routinely travelled to their spiritual capital of Eleusis to participate in wild ceremonies known as the Eleusinian Mysteries, during which they consumed a potent psychedelic brew, the so-called holy wine of Dionysus, which was said to bring initiates to the brink of death. In the process, it was said, they became one with the god. The ruins of the Roman city of Pompei, entombed following the eruption of Mount Vesuvius two millennia later in the year 79 AD, have yielded evidence of wine infused with hallucinogenic herbs and fungi. Some scholars argue that the earliest Christians may have experienced a direct connection with God through the consumption of hallucinogenic wine, even suggesting that the practice may have given rise to the Eucharist, the ceremonial drinking of wine that symbolises the blood of Christ.

Upon reading that letter, with a surge of adrenalin I made the decision to take ayahuasca again. I began reading in earnest, lying awake in bed, Jemima asleep beside me, my face illuminated by the blueish, sleep-inhibiting light of my iPad. I saw that new studies were cropping up at institutes and universities all over the world, aimed at exploring the potential for psychedelics of various kinds to heal all kinds of mental disorders, from post-traumatic stress, addictions and complicated grief to depression and even end-of-life terror in terminally ill cancer patients. In the 1950s and 60s, at the time when British psychiatrist Humphry Osmond first coined the term 'psychedelic' – from the Ancient Greek words *psyche* (soul) and *deloun* (to make visible, to reveal) – there was a great deal of excitement in the field of psychiatry about the therapeutic potential of psychedelics. But Nixon's war on drugs brought an end to that line of research for what would be nearly half a century. I found an article by one lead researcher in the field, Dr Paul Liknaitzky at Australia's Monash University, who wrote that participants in his trials 'felt at one with the universe, if you like, finding themselves existing beyond space and time and thought, and these are often called mystical experiences. It's a little like what astronauts report from looking at the Earth from outer space, this enormous perspective on life that allows people no longer to fear death, or to fear anything, because they've got a new and wildly different perspective on things.' Some go further still, arguing passionately that by re-enchanting the non-human world and redefining our whole relationship with Nature, psychedelic experience may help us to find the answers to the greatest challenges we face. It had to be worth trying.

I set about researching how to go about participating in an ayahuasca retreat. I learned that ayahuasca is typically undertaken during two consecutive nights in a small group supervised by a guide, sometimes of South American origin but not always, and a small coterie of assistants who tend to the initiates, sing and play music and perform various kinds of energy 'work' during what they describe as *the circle*. Eventually, I found an experienced guide, let's call her Lita, and we convened online for a two-way interview. I found Lita warm, kind, motherly, entirely comfortable in herself and with the air of a person accustomed to overseeing the situation. I told her I was afraid at the prospect of participating in one of her retreats but sufficiently intrigued to commit to doing it. I asked her straight up if there was any realistic chance of dying during an ayahuasca retreat or of emerging damaged in some way. Reassured by her answer, I explained why I had reached out to her, that I was grieving the sudden loss a year earlier of my teenage daughter Iris, and that I had spent the time since searching for some kind of understanding. Gently, poetically, in the manner of yoga teachers, energy healers and tarot readers, Lita gave me an introduction that presumably she gives to everyone she meets 'who has received the call to *sit with grandmother*, ayahuasca, the mother of the *teacher plants*'. Lita told me that all sorts of factors could affect the ayahuasca experience, boiling them down into two categories: your physical state and your spiritual state when you take the medicine; although, of course, the two are 'mutually dependent and absolutely intertwined.'

'You have to remember that your body is not just the physical vessel in which you navigate reality; it's also connected to an unseen energetic system, receiving and giving out energy; part of all of life, absorbing, filtering, capable of becoming clogged, blocked, maybe even saturated by everything that goes into it.' So in the run-up to the ceremony, I was under strict instructions to ensure my body was as clean as possible. Apart from anything, this kind of detox would lessen the vomiting, or 'purging' as she put it, on the first night. My stomach turned at the idea. For a week, I was to follow a light and healthy diet; no animal products at all until the day of the ceremony itself, at which point I could have boiled eggs alongside a meal otherwise comprised of raw food only; until then, no white bread or sugar, no spicy food, no fermented food such as pickles, anchovies or cheese, no alcohol, caffeine or other stimulants. Oh, and no sex, whatsoever. Just vegetables, lots of them, legumes, beans, peas, grains, rice, barley and fresh fruits and juices. Lita then turned to my state of mind. 'Ayahuasca is a guiding force that stands apart from any particular system of belief and works to help us expand our boundaries and open our mind and senses to the *unknown* and *unseen*.' The key, she explained, is to bring the right mindset to the circle. I must approach this ceremony with a humble heart, a clear intention, and an open mind. What did I want from this? To find Iris? I'm not sure I knew.

One of my cousins, Tristan, a little older than me, and no stranger to loss and grief himself, agreed to participate in the ceremony as well. As we set off that midsummer morning, it occurred to me that it must be 20 years since that previous ayahuasca experience, perhaps to the very day. We had each packed a bag containing a water flask, a change of underwear, a clean shirt and a simple white, loose-fitting get-up, in my case cricket whites, with my name emblazoned across the back of the shirt; on top of all this, a white pillow rolled tightly inside a matching duvet and stuffed into the bag. I don't remember speaking much as we travelled. We daydreamed as we ate our prescribed vegetable soup sitting side by side at four o'clock, and few words were exchanged with Lita, who greeted us at the door with a warm smile and a firm, prolonged hug before leading us through to a large, simply decorated room. On three sides, sash windows as tall as the room were open from the bottom up, allowing in a soft, warm breeze; the early evening sun poured in from the other side. Two large tropical fig trees grew upwards to the ceiling from the back two corners, reaching out with sagging limbs towards the centre of the room. On the back wall between two windows, the carved wooden heads of a pair of Indian cows hung above a limestone fireplace, a circular mirror between them, their doleful eyes staring glassily at us across the room.

A pony-tailed, olive-skinned man in a colourful woollen jacket knelt on the wooden floor, arranging an assortment of objects on and around a low table; an altar of sorts, the decrepit wing of a long-dead eagle, candles of various shapes and sizes, incense, an assortment of trinkets in bronze and wood, all laid out neatly in an oval pattern, the tallest objects at the centre. Between the altar and the fireplace at the back of the room were a row of floor cushions, two on either side of a floor seat, purple with a supportive back, Lita's throne. She had always sat cross-legged throughout her ceremonies, but recently she had discovered the floor chair, which had been a tremendous blessing for her lower back, she told me. The young man bounced to his feet and hugged first Tristan, then me. 'Hey, I'm J. M., beautiful to meet you,' he said, fixing me with sparkling eyes, a hand on each of my shoulders, and sighing knowingly, then returning back to his decorating. We were the first participants to arrive. Lita directed us to take a sunbed mattress each from a stack in the corner, choose a spot (next to each other by one of the windows) and lay out our things; then to change into our whites in a hallway bathroom together, which we did while laughing nervously at the absurdity of the situation. Lita had invited us to make ourselves at home in her kitchen, and was genuinely disappointed to walk in on me scoffing a fat slice of sourdough toast slathered with butter and Marmite, an excellent way to line my rumbling stomach, I had thought, but it was far too late in the day to be eating anything, and this was a yeast confection entirely incompatible with ayahuasca.

The others appeared in ones and twos, and we congregated in the kitchen, twelve of us in total, seven initiates, four assistants comprising J. M. and three women in their twenties and thirties, and at last, Lita, imperious now in a flowing, floor-length white robe and feathery headpiece. Making a point of spending a few moments with each of us, she frequently interrupted herself to instruct the assistants softly as they busied themselves here and there in preparation. Standing, the rest of us chatted quietly until, on the stroke of ten, Lita ushered us from the kitchen, through the spartan hallway and back into the anointed room. We found our places and sat in a semi-circle facing the altar, some cross-legged, some hugging knees to chest. I was glad for the wall behind my back. Lita reminded us that once the 'circle was open', we may not speak at all; we were not to proclaim loudly some revelation or other that may come our way, nor even to whisper to each other; if we needed something, or to leave the room to visit the bathroom, we were to signal for one of her assistants to come over to us. They'd be appearing by our side periodically during the ceremony, she told us, to check in and to perform some energy healing on us. Heart pounding, hands and feet cold, I held onto the reassurance offered by Lita's natural authority and the discipline with which she marshalled us. J. M. lit the candles and incense. It was time.

Rising to open the circle, Lita began chanting softly, or was she praying? Not unlike a Catholic bishop limbering up to deliver the Eucharistic sacraments, trailing incense behind her in a gentle pirouette and moving seamlessly between the English and the Spanish, she invoked Madre Aya to be gentle with us and to guide us in fulfilling the intent that we had each brought with us. The assistants were reverent in their observation of these goings on, sitting meditatively across the altar from us, eyes closed, only J.M. standing busy around Lita, dabbing a small cymbal and smiling as he attended dreamily to her whispered commands. I can't say that I or any of the other participants were fully invested in the *meaning* of this ritual and its incantations. In different circumstances, I might have struggled not to giggle, but not this time; we were respectful. We knew we should not take this lightly, and the ritual injected a necessary seriousness into the proceedings. Lowering herself into her seat and stirring a pot that had seemingly appeared out of nowhere and now simmered on a camp stove in front of her, she called us one by one to sit cross-legged before her. A waft of incense was directed into my face, a blessing of sorts, and then my drink was handed to me in a small beaker, the sickly-sweet rooty taste familiar to me still, cloying in the back of my mouth even after I had swallowed it down. Then back to my little mattress, legs straight out in front under my duvet, my back resting against the ample pillow propped against the wall.

With each of us in our place, Lita subtly animated a laptop tucked on the floor to her left. I found myself back in the Ecuadorian rainforest, enveloped by the soft chirping of frogs, intermittent at first, distant, in tandem with the gurgling of water and a range of odd, comforting sounds of the forest that I couldn't quite place. I didn't look around at anyone else, instead resting my eyes on the flickering light of the candle on the wall and the ceiling above my head. The light outside was by now faded to a deep purple. Every now and then, a sigh, the rustling of a duvet or the sound of someone taking a sip of water before placing the flask back on the wooden floor reminded me of the presence of the others in the room. One of Lita's girls crept along the row, carefully placing a small white plastic bucket beside each of us. My stomach turned a little. J. M. began to produce a low, slow, pleasant rhythm using what seemed to me a kind of didgeridoo, and the shadows on the large, shiny leaves of the fig tree nearest me took on a strange sharpness, dancing in unison. I had not expected the brew to take effect so quickly, as my imagination drifted strangely, unpredictably, my awareness turning to a sense of being pulled downwards, not towards sleep, but rather some kind of lucid dream-state. In the dying embers of rational thought, stifled by the vividness of the dream that now consumed me, I understood that the plant I had consumed was seeping through every part of my body, poisoning me. Still, the allure of the dreaming was such that the discomfort was a small price to pay, an inconvenience. Shifting my position, I realised I should lie flat, sliding forward and repositioning my pillow beneath my head.

I was in an echoey place now. Giant brightly coloured amoebas drifted above and all around me, cloud-like, making soft clockwork sounds as hair-like cilia propelled them on their way. I heard myself. 'Iris, are you *here*? Can you believe it? I've come to the ends of the world to find you,' My voice reverberated through that strange world. I felt no fear and heard no reply. The texture of the dreaming grew steadily richer; I was in a magical, twinkling forest now, life buzzing all around me, all things at once familiar and yet indefinable, shapeshifting, everything intimately connected to everything else and to me. I noticed a pair of eyes peering shyly through the trees, the eyes of some amorphous being or perhaps the eyes of the whole; I couldn't tell. Yet all there was of *me* was a state of expansive awareness, outside of time.

Waves of knowing began to wash through me, relentlessly, overwhelmingly, as the mysterious eyes flitted, hiding, playful, octopus-like, impossible for me to fix; answers to questions I had not asked, knowledge that already existed within me, somewhere deep down and brought bubbling to the surface now in overpowering upwellings of affirmation. I knew that I would not meet Iris here dreaming, perhaps because I wasn't ready or because things just aren't as straightforward as that. I was overcome with the understanding that one way or another, all will be well; a great benevolence envelopes us, comprising all things imagined and real. I understood that Nature had beckoned me all my life, Waldo's 'great apparition which shines so peacefully all around us'. I understood now with a breath-taking, piercing clarity my love of the birds in the garden of my childhood, my fascination with their concealed clutches of cerulean eggs, and my urge to swim deep underwater before emerging, blinking and breathless into the brightness of the sun. I knew that there is God, that God is everything, and everything is God. I understood now why I had found solace on the banks and in the water of the pond that summer. God's love had held me close when I most needed it; it kept me afloat during the saddest days of my life.

I became dimly aware of a muttering, my own, over and over, "'I understand, I understand, I understand.' Finding myself back in the room, my face wet with tears, I lifted myself shakily onto one elbow. In the half-light, the room throbbed, everything within it vibrating before my eyes, colours merging into colours, shapes into shapes, Lita swaying gently between her musicians, smiling, eyes closed. Alongside me, the half-dead lay on their backs. I felt I must be skimming the brink of death. I wondered if this was the worst of it, if the effects of the medicine might soon begin to fade. A wave of nausea overtook me, and I vomited cleanly into the bucket. Managing a sip of water, spilling a little down my shirt, I lay back down flat, one hand on my heart, the other on my belly. Never in my life had I heard such beautiful music, such angelic voices. Sinking gently back into the warmth of the dreaming, I wondered how much time had passed. Hours or minutes, I had no idea.

I dreamed of the elderly, devoted Brewham vicar and his congregation of dignified old ladies attending church each Sunday in their smartest hats; I dreamed of Tibetan monks sitting in silent meditation in remote mountain caves for days on end; of the Sufi dervishes of the Mevlevi whirling in remembrance of God; of the enlightened indigenous people of the Amazon dancing night-long about a fire in the forest clearing; I dreamed of my brother-in-law Imran, so in love with Nature, so certain of his ordained purpose in the world; of my dead uncle Teddy, founder editor of *The Ecologist*, with the beard and eyes of a prophet of the Old Testament, his life devoted to rousing people from the stupor in which they go about destroying Nature, mocked for doing so, *Jimmy's eccentric older brother*. They knew. They all knew. My own father came to know. How had I missed it? Deep down, I had also known. I saw with wonder the innumerable ways in which people seek to bring themselves closer to this God, a vast and beautiful ever-evolving tapestry of rites. I returned to the blind men of the Indian parable, each one feeling a different part of the same elephant, eventually coming to blows over their wildly differing interpretations of what they felt, unaware that each of them, in their own way, was right.

Finding my voice within the dreaming, I began to ache for the awfulness of what we do to each other and to Nature, wondering why the divine consciousness does not see to it that we stop. Where is its rage? Infinitely powerful, all-knowing, but child-like somehow, I perceived innocent disappointment coupled with peaceful optimism; all is well. I saw that great swathes of people had lost touch with the divine; they sense the disconnection, they feel the void, searching with increasing fervour in the wrong places, not knowing that God is right here before our very eyes. An awesome bliss came over me; I glimpsed what it must be to feel close to God. Ayahuasca seems to be some kind of a cheat in the video game that is life on Earth, a shortcut, a key to a hidden door, and by consuming its magical compounds, my eyes were opened. The Amazonians have known the secret for millennia. I understood now why I am so agonised by the wanton killing of Nature. I knew with the highest conviction that for as long as I should live, I must devote myself to what my uncle Teddy had said 'should be the overriding human enterprise, maintaining the critical order of the biosphere', putting right what we have broken, finding harmony with Nature.

Barely perceptibly, the dreaming began to dissipate in the way that the first stirrings of dawn are felt before they are seen. The experience took on a tranquillity beneath high cirrus clouds washed pink and caressed by the cool breeze of the first light. Again, I grew dimly aware of the room. I heard the music with human ears now and was stirred anew by the deep, melodious voice of J. M., who sang in a language I couldn't place. I scanned my exhausted, recovering body. My face was streaked with tears, my body burning hot, wet with sweat, so I wriggled out of my cricket trousers and slid my bare legs out of the sides of the duvet. With unsteady hands, I took a sip of water and still the room swayed, but softly now. I noticed that some of the others were sitting up, eyes closed. I heard weeping. As my ability to recall the feeling receded, I lay dumbfounded, vowing to myself over and over that I would not allow myself later to unpick or rationalise the revelation I had experienced, which to me was as meaningful as any told in the Bible.

I caught J. M.'s eye as he looked over the room from his cross-legged position, and he grinned broadly at the sight of my bare legs and white boxer shorts. Smiling back, I beckoned him over apologetically and whispered, 'Could I trouble you for a piece of paper and a pen?'

'What paper, where?' he whispered back.

'Any paper, maybe an old envelope from the kitchen?'

Returning beaming, he handed me a large piece of white card and a chewed ballpoint pen. Half propping myself up on the wall behind, I began to scribble against one knee. One by one, the others returned to the room and sat upright, until presently Lita rose to stand, performed a short ritual with the incense, waving about a noisy brush of the kind I had seen in Ecuador two decades earlier, and that was it. The circle was closed. Low voices, hushed giggles, nothing much said; we knew there'd be time for talking the next day. The assistants brought in some warm soup with bowls and spoons. I pulled on my cricket trousers and made my way, blinking, unsteady on my feet, into the brightness of the hallway bathroom, switching on my phone as I peed. It was four o'clock in the morning. I typed out a message; 'Hi, my love. I'm fine. It's no joke this thing. I hope I can find the words to describe it to you tomorrow. Going to bed now. I love you.' Then back we all went to our mattresses to sleep a little.

I remembered the words of Terence McKenna, who suggested that these mysterious compounds send us to a 'parallel dimension' where we may encounter 'higher dimensional entities' or 'spirits of the Earth'. McKenna said that if you can trust your own perceptions, you enter an 'ecology of souls; doorways into the Gaian mind'. McKenna died in the belief that 'the planet has a kind of intelligence and is able to open a channel of communication with an individual human being,' and that psychedelic plants and fungi are the facilitators of this communication. He said, 'The universe is a puzzle, it's a problem to be solved, it's a conundrum, it's not what it appears to be, there are doors, there are locks and keys, there are levels, and if you get it right, somehow it will give way to something extremely unexpected.'

I lay in the darkness, grasping to recall how it had felt. My thoughts turned to a single moment at the age of 13; a Latin class during which the master, a rotund, dignified, white-haired man named Mr Faulkner, announced towards the end that now he would be reading us a passage from *The Wind in Willows* in which the author, Kenneth Grahame, reveals to us his own spirituality, in a chapter entitled 'The Piper at the Gates of Dawn'. The key protagonists, Ratty and Mole, have spent the night searching the river for their friend, the Otter's lost pup, Portly. At the break of dawn, they catch a faint, distant, exquisite music, which rouses in Ratty a 'longing in me that is pain and nothing seems worthwhile but just to hear that sound once more and go on listening to it for ever'. The irresistible sound lulls them into a trance, summoning them. 'Such music I never dreamed of, and the call in it is stronger even than the music is sweet!' says Ratty. '"Row on, Mole, row! For the music and the call must be for us". Rapt, transported, trembling, he was possessed in all his senses by this new divine thing that caught up his helpless soul and swung and dandled it, a powerless but happy infant in a strong sustaining grasp.' Spellbound, they find themselves drawn towards a small island in the river. 'On either side of them, as they glided onwards, the rich meadow-grass seemed that morning of a freshness and a greenness unsurpassable. Never had they noticed the roses so vivid, the willow-herb so riotous, the meadowsweet so odorous and pervading. Then the murmur of the approaching weir began to hold the air, and they felt a consciousness that they were nearing the end, whatever it might be, that surely awaited their expedition.' Fastening the boat and clambering onto the little island, they push through the herbage into a little clearing set round with 'Nature's own orchard trees, crab apple, wild cherry and sloe. "This is the place of my song-dream, the place the music played to me,"' whispers the entranced Ratty. 'Here, in this holy place, here if anywhere, surely we shall find Him!' Awestruck, the small animals come face to face with the Friend and Helper, a Pan-like figure, a wise and gentle God of Nature, standing imperious yet kind in the clearing, the fat little otter pup curled up sleeping in the grass at his hooves. 'Are you afraid?' whispers the Mole. '"Afraid?" murmured the Rat, his eyes shining with unutterable love. "Afraid! Of Him? O, never, never! And yet – and yet – O, Mole, I am afraid!" Then the two animals, crouching to the earth, bowed their heads and did worship.' The rising sun momentarily dazzles them and 'as they stared blankly, in dumb misery deepening as they slowly realised all they had seen and all they had lost', a little breeze dances up from the surface of the water and blows lightly in their faces, bringing oblivion, 'the last best gift that the kindly demi-god is careful to bestow on those to whom he has revealed himself in their helping: the gift of forgetfulness.'

I lay on my mat like the Mole, standing there blinking in the clearing, '"as one awakened suddenly from a beautiful dream, who struggles to recall it, and can recapture nothing but a dim sense of the beauty of it, the beauty!" Till that too fades away in its turn, and the dreamer bitterly accepts the hard, cold waking and all its penalties.'

I awoke with a start, disorientated. I found my cousin Tristan awake next to me, and silently we rose and left the room together, making our way into Lita's spotless, deserted kitchen. We made tea and went out of a side door into the back garden to sit on a lichen-encrusted bench beneath a lopsided apple tree. The garden gave way to a pretty, rough woodland fringed at a ramshackle barbed-wire fence with bramble, meadowsweet and willowherb. The uncut lawn, dry that summer, lay strewn with white clover and daisies. A warm, blustering wind tugged huge white clouds across the sky above, billowing upwards as they travelled. A soft rain began to fall, balmy on our faces, and then the sun was on us again. For a while, we sat quietly, appreciative of the feeling of being alive. A small number of house sparrows formed a chattering group by a fresh puddle near the house, taking turns to bathe, lowering their breasts in the shallow water and flapping their wings vigorously to shower water over themselves.

In time others joined us, bleary-eyed, the assistants, and eventually Lita carrying two large rugs. We gathered in a circle, the 12 of us, peeling and eating tangerines as we listened, and took turns to share our stories. We did our best to find the words, each story different from the previous one, some introspective, some revelatory, each profound and important. In the sharing and the laughing and the tears and the eccentricity, a bond grew between us. As we made our way back to the house, I approached Lita and told her quietly that I felt afraid to go through this a second time, and that perhaps once might be enough for me. Lita cast a bemused look sideways at me, having explained during our first meeting the importance of undertaking two sessions across consecutive nights. I knew there was no wriggling out of the second circle.

We convened at the kitchen table for a new, much thicker vegetable soup, almost a stew, delicious, with a great jug of freshly pressed juice of apple, carrot and ginger. Then we rested some more; I found solitude on a sofa in a study at the back of the house. At the setting of the sun, we were back in our places. It was as if the previous 12 hours had been an illusion. It occurred to me that the atmosphere was different this time; I wasn't the only participant visibly apprehensive as the moment approached.

The circle was opened, Lita drank from her own ceremonial cup, then I from mine, seated cross-legged before her, and then the waiting, the shadows dancing, the low rumbles and the gurgles and the soft popping sounds. My mind wandered as I began to feel the tug from beneath, sharper this time, rougher, more abrupt, dragging me down the chute. I started to panic. I knew better than to admit that I didn't want to go through with it this time; there was no choice now – this had only just begun and would last hours. There would be no enduring this, and there was no resisting it, I told myself, even as I fought to remain consciously present in the room. I can't do this again, please no. Somehow noticing my discomfort, even though I was lying supine and motionless on my mat, J. M. crossed the room and knelt by my side, taking my hand in his.

'Are you okay? he whispered.

'I'm afraid,' I heard myself say.

'Don't be afraid. Surrender to it, don't try to fight it. Breathe. Breathe.'

So we did, together.

'I'll stay with you.'

Reassured, I clasped his hand tightly to my chest with both of mine. I closed my eyes to focus on my breathing. I tried counting the breaths, but I struggled to hold onto the thread, bouncing fitfully between the terrible dreaming that summoned me with a growing force and the increasingly incomprehensible reality of the room. I must endure. At some stage, I was sick, J. M. gently holding my forehead over the white bucket. After a time, I noticed J. M. shifting his position next to me and testing my grip, making to leave, so I held his hand tighter still.

'Please stay.'

'I'll stay. Breathe. Surrender,' he whispered.

All of a sudden, my awareness alighted on the sweet music, the wistful voices of the angels tumbling like the water of a stream all around me, tugging at me as I clung to the riverbank until finally, comfortable now, releasing J. M.'s hand and closing my eyes, I succumbed and allowed myself to be swept away.

I saw Iris, not the visitation from the other place I had sheepishly anticipated in the run-up to this experiment; instead, I saw with startling clarity the nature of the girl I had known so well and the relationship that had existed between us while she was alive. Since the accident, all thoughts of Iris had been clouded with shock, anger, sadness, fear, grief. Now, for the first time since losing her, I saw once again my Iris as she had been. I was led amid a beautiful collage of dreaming, which transported me to the centre of the pure love that existed between us. I saw our little unspoken jokes, a momentary look exchanged across the table, a particular expression I knew so well, that infectious giggle; I saw a brave little ginger-haired girl buttoned up in her school uniform, casting us a little sideways smile as we waved her off for her first day at big school; I saw her way of dissecting and piecing back together an idea with a brilliance that was far beyond her years; her ability to wind me up and my often-unreasonable reaction; our shared awe in the presence of Nature's magic. I saw a tiny baby gazing with sky-blue eyes up at a 23-year-old me, awestruck, smitten; I saw her temper, her strength, her compassion, her profound goodness. As she shone before me, I was overwhelmed by waves of perfect, joyous remembering. My body heaved and shook as tears sheeted down my face.

Most of all, I felt so lucky to have known this girl for the time that I did. I yearned to reach out and grab her, to hold her tightly to me now, but there was no way of doing so. This was a game of hide and seek. I realised it had always been this way, stretching back through the time we were alive together, and forever, it seemed. Iris had never been mine; she had never belonged to anyone. She had always been evasive, somehow, difficult to grab. With the essence of her all around me now, like the glow-worms that flicker in patterns suspended at midnight over the brook at Cannwood, one by one, I saw with perfect clarity each of the souls with whom I share my life. I saw good, competent, brave Frankie, so profoundly called to Nature from the very beginning; and his younger brother Isaac, kind to his core, sensitive, understanding; both boys so in need of my love and attention as they grow into young men. I saw my two little ones, Eliza and Arlo, the characteristics of their emerging selves already apparent, radiating love and nourished constantly by ours as they go about busily learning the world and themselves each day. Waves of reassurance engulfed me. You do your best. You're doing okay.

One after another, I saw each of them, my brothers and sisters, nieces and nephews, my closest friends; I saw their goodness and their foibles, and I saw each one doing their best to be good. I saw that each one of us is fallible. Like the puppies tumbling over each other in the stable yard at Cannwood, who jump up and bite our lower legs and growl and tussle with each other, we are all susceptible to getting it wrong, to lashing out. We're imperfect animals infused with the love and goodness of a benevolent, tolerant God. I saw Jemima, a warrior, so beautiful inside and out, so good, so strong, so talented; I saw her gathering and weaving together Nature's bounty, fruits and salads and vegetables and nuts, an artist with food; I understood her extraordinary gift. I was awash with gratitude to have this woman alongside me. I ached with pride and love for each of these; for my mother, an old lady now, riven by the scars of loss and pain, shining with love and humour still; for wise, brave Kate, who walks alongside me always. Engulfed by wave after wave of love and gratitude, I thanked God for these people, for my tribe.

Gradually I began to notice a fading of the dreaming. I was in a rugged place, a vast land dotted with great smooth and rounded rocks. Twisted, gnarly trees grew along contours that snaked across the barren land, the ground beneath covered with the long grasses and thistles of late summer, dry and spent now. I saw myself, an old man, hunched forward a little, following a winding track that stretched into the distance. The sky was streaked with clouds stained the colour of peaches. Even though I walked alone, I had the sense that I had travelled alongside these people across the aeons. I began to rise, bubble-like, from the dreamlike state, emerging to find Lita smiling kindly at me from across the room. She beckoned me over, and I sat cross-legged before her. I began to cry. Lita leaned forward and pulled me into a hug, and I sobbed against the softness of her shoulder as we rocked gently back and forward. Returning to my mattress, drained and unsteady, I grasped under my mattress for the paper, leaned back against the wall and the pen and began to scribble.

At the rising of the sun, I crept out with Tristan to walk the field and woodland edges until our feet ached and our stomachs growled. We made our way back along a single-lane country road to join the others as they ate fresh fruit and began to share stories. The first to slip away, a taxi awaiting me outside, I went alone to gather my things, pausing to take out the battered piece of card from beneath the mattress. On one side of the card, I saw hearts overlaying hearts overlaying hearts, each with a name scrawled within them; at the centre, in the largest of the hearts, Iris. I turned the card over to find an intense morass of barely legible ramblings about ducks and their green eggs, beavers.

'They knew, they all knew,' I had written.

At the centre of the page, in large letters, I had scrawled *God is an Octopus.*

Epilogue

Iris, you would have turned 19 today, 3rd February 2023. Just yesterday, I bumped into a polite school leaver who had known you as he made his way alongside the park to the London School of Economics. As I walked on, my mind swam in the longing for what might have been for you. I don't cry like I used to. In a way, I've come to love the weight of our loss, which I carry around with me always. It's smooth now, no less heavy than before, but rounded at the edges and warm. And my pain seems diffused by the strange twinkling of a feeling that you are close by, even if I cannot see you. Not so long after you died, someone sent me a photograph of the medieval painting *Paradise* by Giovanni di Paolo. The painting depicts recently departed souls in an exquisite garden, rapturously reunited with their loved ones gone before. I remember returning to it again and again, wishing it to be true, clinging to that hope. I don't think things are quite as simple as is portrayed in that beautiful scene, although at the time, the notion gave me blissful relief during the madness of my grief. I do believe, though, with every fibre of my being, that we will be together again, but in a way that is simply incomprehensible to us now. The words 'I am you and you are me' echoed around and around one particular fever dream. We are part of a grand mystery that is beyond our ability to understand. None of these things meant anything to me before I lost you, my love, and now I feel it in a way that is impossible for me to explain or prove because the feeling of your closeness is so unlike everything that I perceive with my senses. At the funeral, I dumbly recited the poem '[i carry your heart with me (i carry it in]', by e. e. cummings, and it's true. That's where I find you. Love is the frequency of our ongoing connection, pure love. Sometimes the feeling is overwhelming.

Nevertheless, I miss you so much. I ache for this never to have happened; I ache for Kate's loss, for the boys and the other children, who worship you. You were so special. And so I count my blessings.

Cannwood has become a paradise. A pair of beavers settled two years ago on the wilder of our two ponds along the stream. Their huge shield-shaped lodge built of sticks is plastered with dried clay, hanging over the edge of the island onto the water. The bonsai oak directly above it has so far escaped their toothy attention, while a younger oak on the island of the other, newer swimming pond now lies felled and half submerged. The beavers have bred during each of the last two years, and the growing family has extended a string of small, perfectly engineered dams in both directions along the length of the stream, which now has the appearance of a series of small Japanese rice terraces. As well as flooding a low area on our neighbours' side, the beavers have taken a particular liking to the aspen and black poplar of the young woodland, digging little canals outwards on one side to reach them. By their felling, they have created a mosaic of sunlit clearings in the woodland that are awash with shallow water in the winter and with the colours of an English water meadow in the spring and summer. Last July, along the length of the valley, as we remembered the third anniversary of your accident, marsh marigold, wild garlic, common mallow, purple loosestrife and wild irises jostled while being tended to by small clouds of butterflies, bees and other pollinating insects. Our first longhorns arrived a year ago, five majestic cows from Knepp since joined by three new calves who are growing up having known only Cannwood, free to roam where they want, sleep where they want and eat what they want. Several devoted specialists visit us periodically to survey birds, bats, butterflies, moths and wildflowers. So far, the omens are good. You would be pleased, my love, even if by now you would hardly recognise the place of your childhood as the field shapes dissolve inexorably into the scattered scrub of the emerging woodland pasture. Several more neighbours have chosen to adopt our approach or similar, and an inkblot of wildness is expanding outwards from your great, timeless stone circle.

Last September, we gathered to celebrate the first winners of the Iris Prize; three young environmentalists who are changing their world and ours: Sam Bencheghib, whose growing initiative is keeping plastic waste away from the oceans of Indonesia; Steve Misati, icon of an extraordinary youth-led mangrove restoration movement in Kenya; and Maria Kameta, who is rolling out an affordable, clean alternative to wood fuel for countless rural households across Malawi. It's a Nobel Prize of sorts, but for young people working to restore nature, which is growing into the overriding task of our epoch. You would have loved it. And for us, we feel such joy helping these brilliant young people fulfil their aspirations in the way that you may have done, my love, had you been given the chance. I'm doing my best to fulfil mine. I plot and advocate endlessly for the restoration of beavers and other native species to our landscapes here in Britain, as well as in a growing list of European countries; I've joined the assorted ranks of writers, thinkers, campaigners and conservationists who are fighting for a return to a former vibrancy and abundance of nature in Britain, and I'm relentless in my efforts among them. At times, I like to imagine that you and I work together on these things, that you are my invisible collaborator, somewhere across a chasm, bringing me luck where I need it and colouring the sky pink and amber when I sit alone at the stone circle to think of you.

Author Acknowledgements

With gratitude to Isabel Oakeshott, who encouraged me to write this book, gave me the confidence to press ahead with it and played the role of guide and editor as I wrote it; and to Julie Bailey and the wonderful team at Bloomsbury for their kindness and creativity in the way that they have brought my book to publication. And with love and thanks to Iris's mother, Kate, my lifelong friend and inspiration; and to my wife Jemima, my eternal love.

About the Author

Ben Goldsmith is a British environmentalist and financier. Ben is a leading light in the rewilding movement in Britain and Europe, as well as a pioneer of green investment. Ben and his wife, Jemima, are rewilding their farm in Somerset, and Ben has helped to establish a number of environmental initiatives, including the Environmental Funders' Network, the Conservative Environment Network, Rewilding Britain, Beaver Trust, and the Conservation Collective, a global network of locally focused environmental foundations.

Ben was a Director at DEFRA for five years, successfully advocating for a series of ground-breaking environmental restoration policies during his tenure, including the new Environmental Land Management scheme, the Nature for Climate Fund and the Species Reintroductions task force.

The Iris Project was established by Ben Goldsmith and Kate Rothschild in partnership with the Global Greengrants Fund in loving memory of their daughter, Iris Goldsmith, a young environmentalist who loved the natural world.

Permissions

Ben Goldsmith and Bloomsbury Publishing would like to thank the below for providing permissions to reproduce copyright material within this book. While every effort has been made to trace and acknowledge all copyright holders, we would like to apologise for any errors or omissions, and invite readers to inform us so that corrections can be made in any future editions of the book.

The extract from 'The Late Fragment' by Raymond Carver on page 1 first appeared in *A New Path to the Waterfall* © the Estate of Raymond Carver 1989. It is reproduced by kind permission of Grove Atlantic.

The extract from '[i carry your heart with me (i carry it in]' by E. E. Cummings on page 19 first appeared in *COMPLETE POEMS: 1904-1962* © E. E. Cummings 1952. It is reproduced by kind permission of Liveright Publishing Corporation, a division of W.W. Norton & Company.

The extract from *The Peace of Wild Things* by Wendell Berry on page 36 is © Wendell Berry 2018. It is reproduced by kind permission of Penguin Random House.

The extract from *Medium Raw* by Anthony Bourdain on page 52 is © Anthony Bourdain 2010. It is reproduced by kind permission of Bloomsbury Publishing Plc.

The extract from *Lord of the Rings* by J. R. R. Tolkien on page 58 is © J. R. R. Tolkien 1954. It is reproduced by kind permission of HarperCollins Publishers Ltd.

The extract from *Memories, Dreams, Reflections* by C. G. Jung on page 88, translated by Richard and Clara Winston, edited by Aniela Jaffe is © C. G. Yung 1961. It is reproduced in the UK by kind permission of HarperCollins Publishers Ltd.

The extracts from *Memories, Dreams, Reflections* by C. G. Jung on pages 88, 195 and 196, translated by Richard and Clara Winston, edited by Aniela Jaffe, are translation copyright © 1961, 1962, 1963 and renewed 1989, 1990, 1991 by Penguin Random House LLC. For territories outside the UK, they are reproduced by kind permission of Pantheon Books, an imprint of the Knopf Doubleday Publishing Group, a division of Penguin Random House LLC.

The extract from 'Three New Cases of the Reincarnation Type in Sri Lanka With Written Records Made Before Verifications' by Ian Stevenson and Godwin

Index